TYING AND FISHING DEER HAIR FLIES

TYING AND FISHING DEER HAIR FLIES

50 Patterns for Trout, Bass, and Other Species

TIM JACOBS

STACKPOLE BOOKS
Guilford, Connecticut

Published by Stackpole Books
An imprint of The Rowman & Littlefield Publishing Group, Inc.
4501 Forbes Blvd., Ste. 200
Lanham, MD 20706
www.rowman.com

Distributed by NATIONAL BOOK NETWORK
800-462-6420

British Library Cataloguing in Publication Information available

Library of Congress Cataloging-in-Publication Data available

ISBN 978-0-8117-1733-5 (paperback)
ISBN 978-0-8117-6769-9 (e-book)

™ The paper used in this publication meets the minimum requirements of American National Standard for Information Sciences—Permanence of Paper for Printed Library Materials, ANSI/NISO Z39.48-1992.

Printed in the United States of America

CONTENTS

ACKNOWLEDGMENTS

In the course of 30 years of fly fishing and fly tying, you meet a lot of people who influence your thinking and understanding of this sport. There really are too many to count. However, a few in particular need to be mentioned.

I want to thank Rick Takahashi and Jerry Hubka for inviting me to contribute to their book *Modern Terrestrials* (2014). The article titled "Hunting Trout" that I wrote was included in the "Tips from the Masters" section of the book. That is really what opened the door for this book to happen. I want to especially thank Rick for writing the preface to this book. His very generous words are much appreciated.

I would like to thank all of my pro sponsors as well, in particular Phil Trimm, Colette Mayers, and Dr. Tom Whiting of Whiting Farms. They have been steadfast supporters over the years. The quality of materials that I am provided with is overwhelming at times and much appreciated. Additionally I would like to thank Donald Barnes and all of the staff at Regal Engineering. Even though I have tied on Regal vises for over 20 years, I have only been a part of their pro staff for the last few years. I appreciate their outstanding products and support.

Even though this is not necessarily associated with fly tying, I would be remiss in not thanking Van Rollo and Eric Johnson of Mountain Sports. Van has been the Sage Manufacturing rep for over 30 years, and my association with Sage dates almost as long as that. Van and Eric's support has been steadfast over the years, and I have a real enthusiasm for the rods Sage builds.

Two very special friends that I especially want to mention are Pat and Carol Oglesby. Their names are familiar to everyone who works in Trout Unlimited and the Federation of Fly Fishers, and they have been recognized repeatedly by both organizations for their contribution to conservation and the sport of fly fishing. Pat in particular was a close friend and trusted mentor. He seemed to have a special insight into all things fly fishing as well as life in general. Pat passed away this past December, and his friendship will be greatly missed.

I want to thank my family, both in Michigan and here in Colorado, for their love and support. I especially want to recognize my two daughters, Alyssa and Kelsey, as they have given my life the most meaning. Watching them grow into adulthood has been a special joy. They always keep me laughing.

Finally and most importantly I want to thank my wife, Susan. We met in Yellowstone National Park while I was on a fishing trip, so she knew from the beginning that I was a fly fisherman. She has been patient, indulgent, and most of all supportive of this avocation of mine. All that is good in my life has flowed from meeting and marrying her.

PREFACE

Those of us who enjoy sitting down at the vise and tying our own flies reap the personal satisfaction of catching fish with the flies we've tied. Those of us who sit down at the vise to create deer hair bass bugs requiring the stacking of deer hair, the spinning of deer hair, selecting colorful feathers, and precise trimming require skills that are not easily acquired. Learning how to handle deer hair and sculpt aesthetically pleasing patterns requires spending hours upon hours at the vise perfecting these skills until it becomes second nature; there are no shortcuts to learning to tie deer hair flies.

Some of our most famous bass bug deer hair tiers such as Tim England, Dave Whitlock, Billy Munn, Joe Messinger, and Chris Helm have led the way by creating patterns not only visually pleasing, but highly efficient as fish catchers. These fly designers have taken the responsibility of passing on to others the fine art of crafting a deer hair fly. One such individual who has taken up the commitment, put in the time, and been willing to push past failure is Tim Jacobs.

Tim is a natural-born educator who has taken his expertise from the classroom to the tying arena; he is a celebrated demonstration fly tier featured at many of the top fly-fishing and fly-tying venues. Showing others how to handle deer hair—how to stack various colors on top of each other and deftly contour the hair into a beautiful piece of art—has given him the opportunity to share his gift through words and photographs.

Tim's fly-tying world does not revolve around tying bass bugs exclusively, but tying all manners and styles of flies, ranging from midges to pike flies. You will enjoy, as I have, watching and learning how he approaches his fly tying. I'm pleased to count Tim as a friend and always look forward to sitting down and tying flies with him, mostly watching this craftsman create magic.

Rick Takahashi

INTRODUCTION

"Perhaps nothing had so broad an effect on American fly tying, in fact, as the use of [deer] hair."

PAUL SCHULLERY, *AMERICAN FLY FISHING: A HISTORY*

Fly fishing captivated me from the very beginning. The art of tying flies, scientific inquiry into the nature of fish habitats, the vast body of literature, and the poetic athleticism of casting a fly line all combine to make it like no other pursuit. Additionally I have found few circles of friends as inviting as the fraternity of angling friendships I have acquired over the years.

Much of our fly-fishing and fly-tying heritage was handed down to us from Great Britain. However, up through the 19th century, deer hair was not prominently used in British fly patterns. While flies imitating baitfish existed during the 19th century in the British Isles, most fly patterns were feather wing streamers. In England, wild game was scarcer than in North America and deer hunting was primarily a privilege of the upper class. Consequently deer hair as a source of material for fly tying was not as readily available as it was in North America. In addition, most of the focus for British fly fishermen was on trout and salmon, whereas in North America largemouth bass and other native warmwater fish were the inspiration for many of the uses of deer hair in fly tying.

One of the first documented uses of deer hair was from James Henshall in his *Book of Black Bass* (1881). He described the Native Americans' use of deer hair "bobs" for fishing for largemouth bass in the Southeast. Bucktail became a staple of the streamer patterns that were developed in Maine during the late 19th century. Don Gapen's Muddler Minnow and Joe Messinger's Bucktail Frog are both early examples of flaring deer hair to create spun deer hair heads. Like baseball and jazz, deer hair flies are uniquely American.

My Personal Journey

Even though it was the middle of summer, the windows were utterly dark when my grandfather would wake me up to go fishing. The smell of eggs, bacon, and black coffee would greet me as I walked out into the kitchen of our small lakeshore cottage in northern Michigan. After breakfast we would head out into the early summer morning. Sometimes we would troll but often we would cast to the shoreline using his wooden bass plugs. The bass in the shallows would often take our plugs in a rush that would be explosive. My grandfather passed away when I was 14; however, he ignited the fishing spark that still resides within me more than five decades later.

During my college years, I was working a summer job in Saginaw, Michigan, when I first noticed fly fishing. I bought a copy of *Fly Fisherman* magazine to read on my lunch break. As I was reading the magazine, one of the other summer college employees came walking past and pulled up to a stop. Asking if I was a fly fisherman, I told him that I was just beginning to get interested. As any fly fisherman would do, he immediately sat down to discuss the sport. That began a great friendship that continues to this day and was the first of what would be many friendships that developed through fly fishing.

My early efforts, as with many new to fly fishing, were focused on trout. I used our cottage as a jumping-off point for fishing the Pere Marquette River, the Manistee River, and most often the Au Sable River Valley. It was several years before my attention was turned back to warmwater fishing.

One summer day, casting from our dock, I was fishing a small trout fly and would occasionally hook one of the panfish that were around the shallow water. I hooked a fish in the deeper water and immediately knew it felt bigger than the small panfish that I had caught up to that point. I reeled up my extra line and played the fish from the reel. When it got near the dock, it suddenly took off for deep water, running about 15 yards of line off the reel. Finally I landed it—a 14-inch largemouth bass. On the small trout rod I had been casting, it was a thrill. This event was a flashback to my early fishing experiences with my grandfather, and I began to take a more serious look at warmwater fishing.

During the mid-1980s as I started to explore fly fishing for bass, I began to notice that deer hair was an essential material in many warmwater patterns. At the time not much was in print to guide my efforts; however, two items appeared that changed both my fishing and my fly tying. The first was an article in *Fly Rod & Reel* magazine in 1985 profiling Colorado fly tier Tim England. While he was not the first to use spun deer hair to create fly patterns, his flies were like no others at the time. This article, along with the photos, sparked a desire in me to learn to tie spun deer hair bass bugs. Tim's patterns to this day serve as a standard I strive to emulate. The second item was L.L. Bean's *Fly Fishing for Bass Handbook* written by Dave Whitlock. Dave's book was a constant summer companion as I began to explore the warmwater fly-fishing opportunities that were right outside my door. Fishing from our cottage proved the perfect place to experiment with both fly patterns and warmwater fly-fishing tactics.

About This Book

While I enjoy tying with many materials, working with deer hair has been a constant source of enjoyment and satisfaction to me over the years. The main focus of this book is tying flared or spun deer hair flies; however, I have included chapters on other tying techniques using deer hair as well as bucktail. Fly patterns for both trout and warmwater fish are included, with chapters organized around technique or fly patterns.

Rarely as a fly tier does an idea for a pattern spring forth as a completely original idea. Instead patterns come as variations of other fly patterns or from conversations with other fly tiers. In naming fly patterns, I have attempted to stay faithful to the traditional name where applicable, even if the pattern varies slightly from the original recipe. While I admire some tiers who give very creative names to their flies, I attempt to give pattern names that are descriptive of the fly or materials that are used to tie it.

A fly tier can be likened to a mosaic mural. When you step back you see the tier, but viewed up close you see the individual influences of many other tiers. I am certainly a mosaic of those many tiers that I have encountered over the years. Whether seeing them in person, in print, or by video, they have had a great influence on me. I am grateful to all of those fly tiers. While we all share many "tiles" in common, the mosaic that is each of us as a fly tier is unique.

Many thousands of flies have come off my vise over the years. Some I have considered functional works of art, while others I have wondered what in the world I was thinking. In this book I will present my way of tying, using the materials and tools that have worked for me and sometimes presenting alternative techniques to accomplish the same task. That said, I in no way want to represent the techniques, tools, materials, and fly patterns as *the* way of accomplishing the task. Take the ideas and adapt them to work for you. The fish are always the final arbiter of the quality and effectiveness of a fly. To my way of thinking, that's as it should be.

"For isn't fishing a happy form of play in which speculation and dispute and diversity are every bit as important as surety?"—Nick Lyons, *The Quotable Fisherman*

CHAPTER 1

Tools and Materials

"Dressing such confections of fur, feathers and steel is beautiful, and our worktables are littered with gorgeous scraps of tragopan and golden pheasant and blue chattered and Coq de Leon."

ERNEST SCHWIEBERT, 2005

Quality tools and materials are essential to tying quality flies. Fly tiers today have more and better tools and materials than we have ever had. I will describe the ones that I use, but there are a lot of quality options. Find what works best for you.

With so many great materials to choose from, it can sometimes be bewildering as to what to use. Many materials are very similar. I know in my own tying that when I see a pattern I want to tie, I will often not have the exact brand of something listed in the recipe but will have a similar material that I can substitute. Additional new materials are being introduced at an amazing pace, so no list of materials will stay current for long. Instead of focusing on a particular material, look instead at the function that material performs in the fly and choose one that will perform that same function.

Tools

VISES

The fly-tying vise is an essential tool for tying flies. I started tying on inexpensive vises and was often frustrated with their performance. I replaced one brand of vise several times. It was a collet-style vise where the hook was tightened in the jaws of the vise by using a lever at the back to draw the jaws into the collet and tighten on the hook. This style of vise worked well for tying small trout flies, but as soon as I started to tie large bass bugs, the collet would crack under the pressure and needed to be replaced. Today's collet-style vises are made much better and don't suffer these problems; however, as a result of the failure of these vises, I began to tie on a Regal vise. I have a Regal vise with a traditional head that I've tied on for almost 30 years without any problems.

Today I use three different Regal vise heads: the midge head, the traditional head, and the big game head. The heads are simple to change and can be used on either a pedestal or a C-clamp base. What I like about the Regal is that you simply depress the lever to

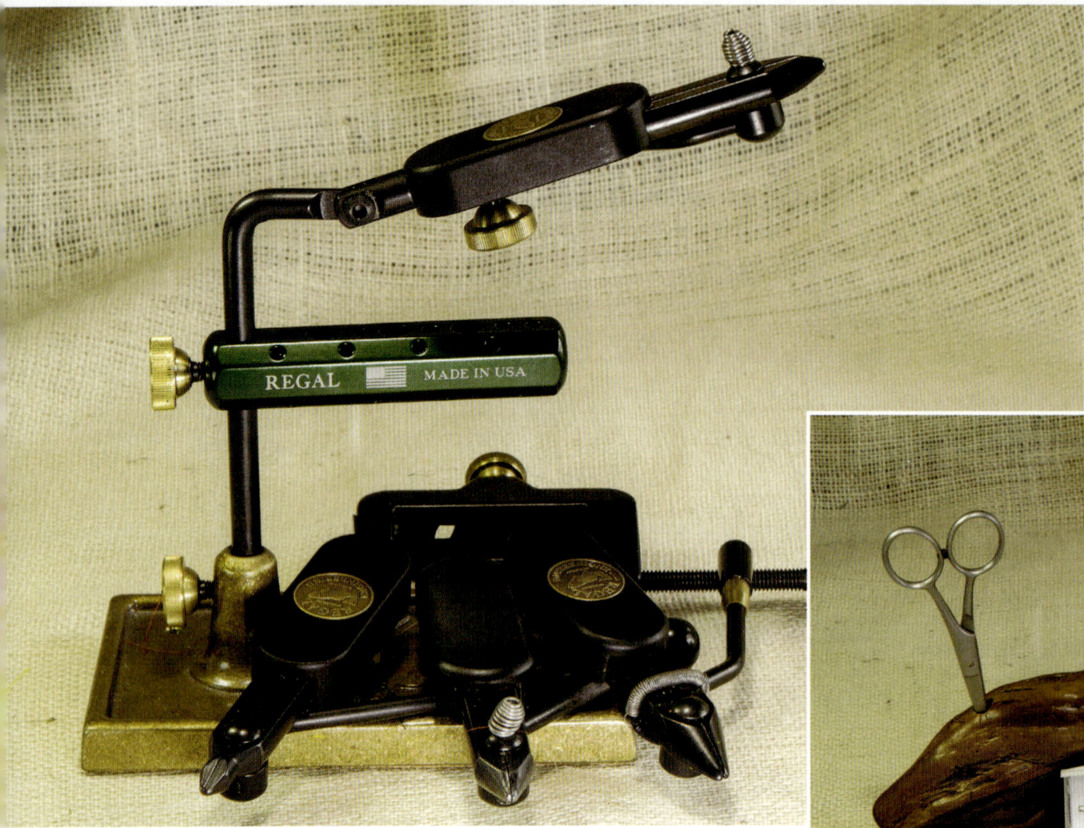

Left: Regal traditional head vise on a bronze traditional base with a tool bar. Vise heads on base, from left to right: midge head, my old traditional head, big game head. A C-clamp is in the background.

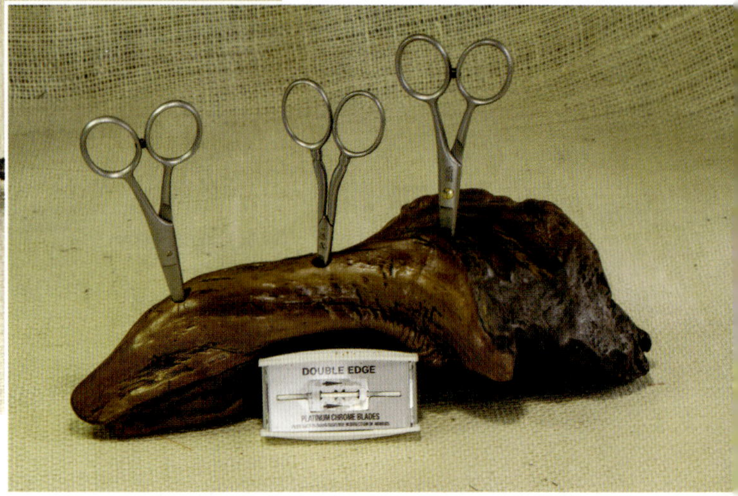

Above: Germany Solingen scissors, from left to right: curved blade hair scissors, trout shears, straight blade hair scissors. Also pictured are double-edge razor blades.

insert the hook into the vise. There is no need to adjust anything. The three different heads allow me to customize to the size of fly or hook that I am tying. I only use the pedestal in circumstances where I physically can't use the C-clamp. For the smaller flies in this book, a pedestal will work. For the larger flies, especially when you are flaring or spinning deer hair, use a C-clamp, as it more securely attaches the vise to the tying table.

SCISSORS AND RAZOR BLADES

I use Germany Solingen scissors for most of my fly tying. Chris Helm introduced me to these, and they are the best scissors I have ever used. I use the Solingen German Trout Shear for all of my smaller trout flies. For the larger spun deer hair flies, I use the Solingen German Hair scissor in both the straight and curved blade. By fly-tying standards, these are expensive scissors. I am very careful to only use them for the intended purpose and use older scissors to cut abrasive materials. I have also used Dr. Slick and Anvil scissors with good success. They are more reasonably priced.

If you are only interested in tying "fishing" flies with deer hair, you can probably just trim them with scissors. However, if you want deer hair bodies that are smoother with a more artistic trim, you need to use a razor blade. I use double-edge razor blades. Some tiers I know will break the blade in half to create two single-edge razor blades, as they consider it safer. I have become accustomed to just holding the blade on the end, so I keep the blade as it comes out of the package. Also, I often find that a part of the blade will become dull and not work the way I want it to, so by keeping the blade together, I can flip it over to access the opposite edge rather than having to put down one blade to pick up its other half.

While it goes without saying, remember to work slowly and carefully with the razor blade. One of the first times I tied flies in public, I got to the trimming portion of the demo and promptly nicked my finger with the razor blade. Needless to say, the demo quickly came to an end. Since that time I have also carried a few first-aid supplies with me, but am glad to report that I haven't needed them. Remember, be aware of the blade and work slowly!

BOBBINS

Chris Helm also introduced me to Rite bobbins in 2012. I first began using them for just my GSP threads, but it wasn't long before I began using them for my other fly-tying threads as well. Bill Merg, a German engineer, designed them and introduced them to the market in the early 1990s. Today Lyle Graff and his son, who now own Merco Products, manufacture these bobbins in southwestern Montana.

What I like about Rite bobbins is the ability to adjust the thread tension much like you would adjust the drag on a fly reel. This feature gives me a lot of thread control when spinning and flaring deer hair. They have also proved to be durable with all of my tying threads, especially GSP.

WHIP-FINISH AND HALF-HITCH TOOLS

The ability to tie a whip-finish knot by hand will be an important skill with some of the fly patterns in this book. With a little practice, it is not too difficult a skill to acquire. However, I do use the Matarelli whip-finish tool to do whip-finish knots on my thread heads. Using a whip-finish tool aids in accurate placement of the thread and has the ability to smoothly draw the knot tight.

A half-hitch tool is essential when using GSP threads and tying stacked deer hair heads or bodies.

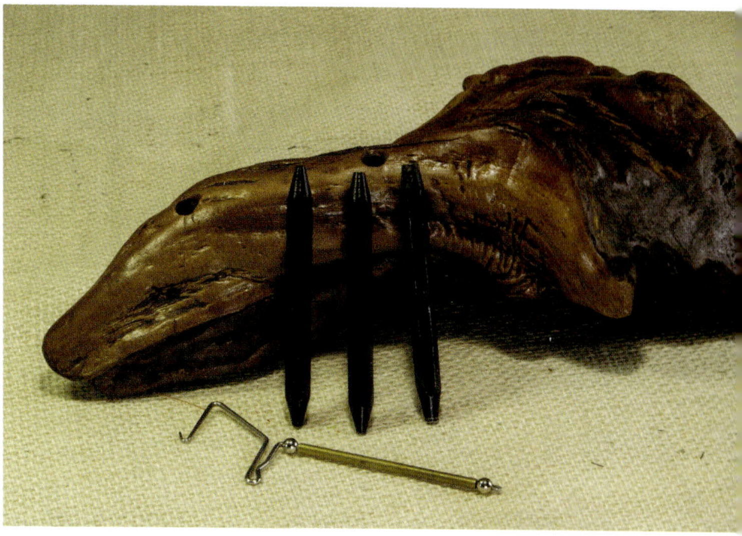

Set of three half-hitch tools, along with a Matarelli whip-finish tool.

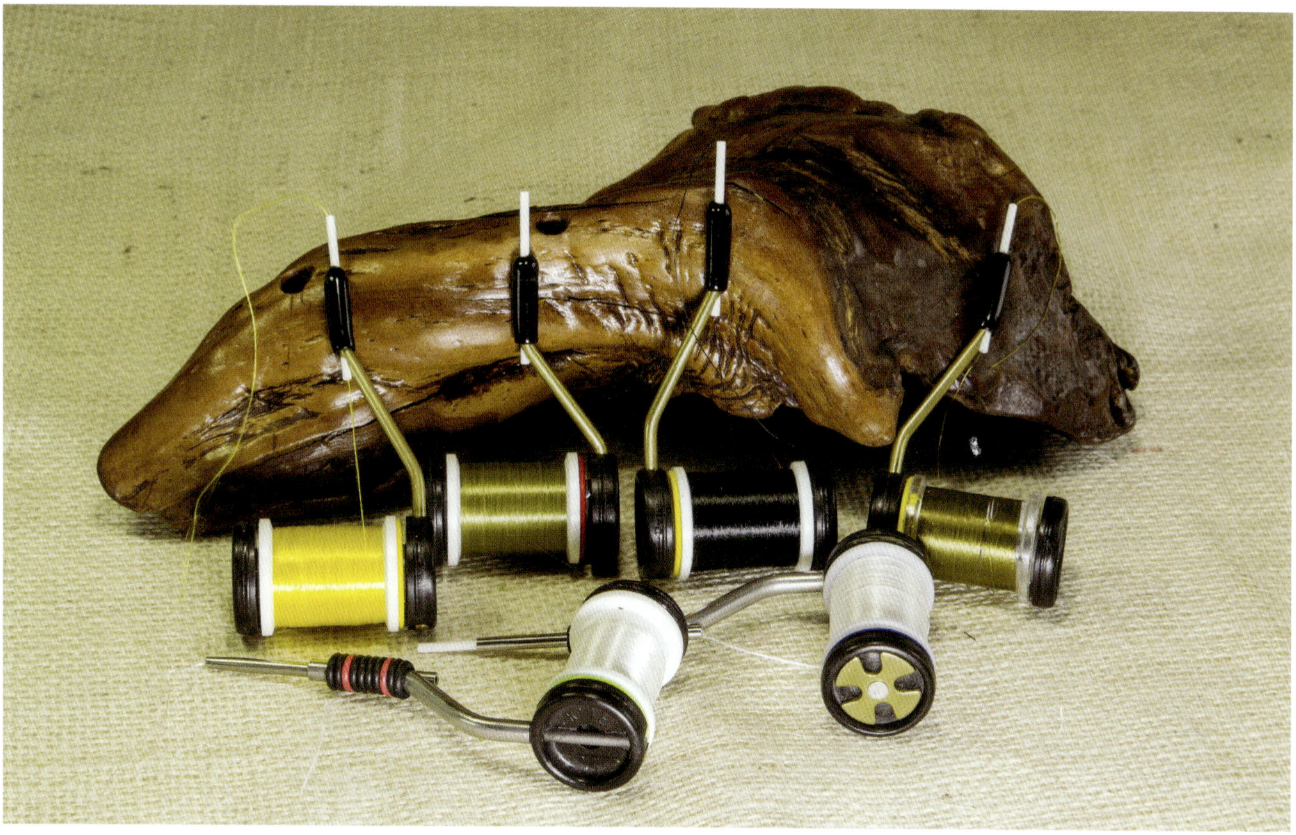

Rite bobbins. Top row, left to right: Standard bobbin with UTC 140 (Yellow), Shorty bobbin with UTC 70 (Olive), two Standard bobbins with UTC 140 (Black and Olive). Bottom row, left to right: Half-Hitch bobbin with GSP 130, CerMag bobbin with GSP 100.

Tying a half hitch after each stack of hair aids in compressing the hair with a hair-packing tool. The knot provides the tool with a point to put pressure on the stack of hair to aid in compressing it back along the hook shank. When using GSP thread for a deer hair head or body, to finish the fly I will wet the thread with some Zap-A-Gap glue and make a few wraps of thread behind the eye of the hook. I then use the half-hitch tool to place a few knots on top of the glued thread before trimming it.

HAIR STACKERS

Any time the tips of the deer hair are used to create a collar on a fly, a hair stacker is required to align the tips. You will need a variety of sizes. I use a set of three Edgin hair stackers that are marketed by Umpqua Feather Merchants. These stackers are made out of brass and have a nice weight to them. I use all three sizes. The small one is used when stacking deer hair wings on hair-wing dun patterns. The medium size is used for larger deer hair collars like those on a hopper pattern. The large size is suitable when larger amounts of hair are used for bigger hopper or Muddler fly patterns.

One of my favorite hair stackers is the PEAK Magnum Hex Stacker. This large hair stacker easily handles the substantial amount of hair that is used for larger deer hair bodies.

HAIR-PACKING TOOLS

A hair-packing tool is one of the essential tools needed when tying with deer hair. There is a variety of hair packing tools on the market. One of the tool designs to avoid is the pen cap or cylindrical style of packing tool. If the tool is large enough to fit over the eye of the hook then it will not contact the hair at the base of the hook shank. This will just bend the hair back, as opposed to actually moving the base of the hair back along the hook shank.

The tool I have been using for a number of years is the Brassie Hair Packer designed by Chris Helm. Its open plier-like action means you can pack the hair with the tool pushing right along the hook shank. If

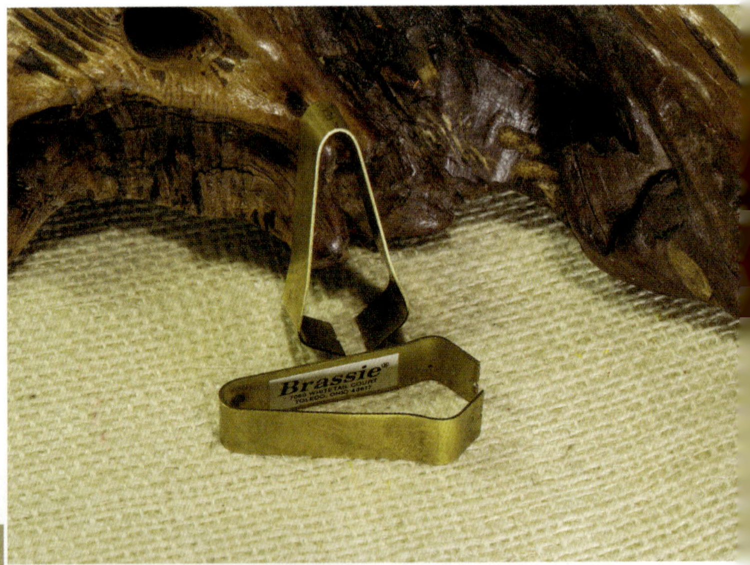

Above: Brassie hair-packing tools.

Left: Hair stackers, from left to right: Edgin brass hair stackers in medium, small, and large sizes; PEAK Magnum Hex Stacker.

each stack of hair is finished with a couple of half-hitch knots, this tool will be pushing the knots rather than the hair. If the thread/knots are compressed back on the hook shank, the hair will be much more efficiently compressed.

One of the complaints with this tool is that if too much pressure is applied, the brass will bend. I have occasionally bent this tool as well, but it is easily bent back and it's happened infrequently enough that it has not caused a serious problem. There are similarly designed tools that are larger and made with stronger materials, so if the Brassie seems too fragile, one of these packer tools is always an option.

There are limits to how much pressure can be applied when compressing a stack of hair. I have on occasion bent the hook or pushed the tail back, neither of which is desirable. Also remember that when thinking about hair density on a deer hair body, stacking hair is more important in creating that density than compressing or packing hair.

COMBS

Combs are another essential tool when working with deer hair and other materials like Icelandic sheep. I have a working selection of combs that serve different purposes. One of my favorites is simply an eyebrow comb from the makeup department of some big-box store like Target. These eyebrow combs have a small comb on one end and a brush on the other. The brush works well for cleaning the underfur out of small bunches of Compara-dun hair for hair-wing duns or other small dry flies, and the comb works well for cleaning the underfur out from larger bunches of hair.

I also have several fly-tying combs. I have two sizes of Griffin combs. The larger one is good for combing out Icelandic sheep, and the smaller one is good for large bunches of deer hair. The advantage of the Griffin combs is that they are static-free. I have used simple plastic combs in the past but they will build up static electricity, causing the hair to stick to them.

Top row: Eyebrow comb/brush, Wasatch fur comb. Below: Griffin fly-tying combs.

HACKLE PLIERS, FILE, DUBBING NEEDLE, TWEEZERS, PLIERS, HACKLE GAUGE, BOBBIN THREADER, AND HEMOSTATS

Hackle pliers are used for wrapping hackle collars on bass bugs as well as wrapping dry fly hackle. While it is possible to wrap the larger hackles by hand, using a set of hackle pliers allows more precise placement of the hackle. They are especially useful when wrapping smaller dry fly hackle. I have used Griffin Teardrop Hackle Pliers for a number of years.

I use a small file to rough up the tie-in area for the tailing materials for bass bugs. By using a file to create a small amount of "tooth" on the hook shank and then using some Zap-A-Gap glue before wrapping the thread, the tailing materials will be securely attached to the hook shank. This will help the tail stay in place as the deer hair stacks are compressed against the tail materials.

A dubbing needle, or bodkin, is simply a needle attached to a handle. It is useful for numerous tasks such as picking out folded-over hair in a deer hair head and clearing out nozzles on glue bottles.

Having a pair of pointed fine-tipped tweezers like Dr. Slick Bishop Tweezers is also essential when working with deer hair. Once the fly is tied, you can adjust the stacks of hair so the spots or rings of color line up before you begin trimming the body. You can also use the tweezers to comb through the hair to find any hair that has been inadvertently folded over after being caught under the thread. If you pull out any folded hair before you begin to trim the body, it is usually not noticeable in the finished fly.

I always begin every fly by compressing the barb to make the fly barbless. A barbless hook will hook fish quicker without the resistance of the barb having to penetrate the fish's mouth. It also allows for a quicker

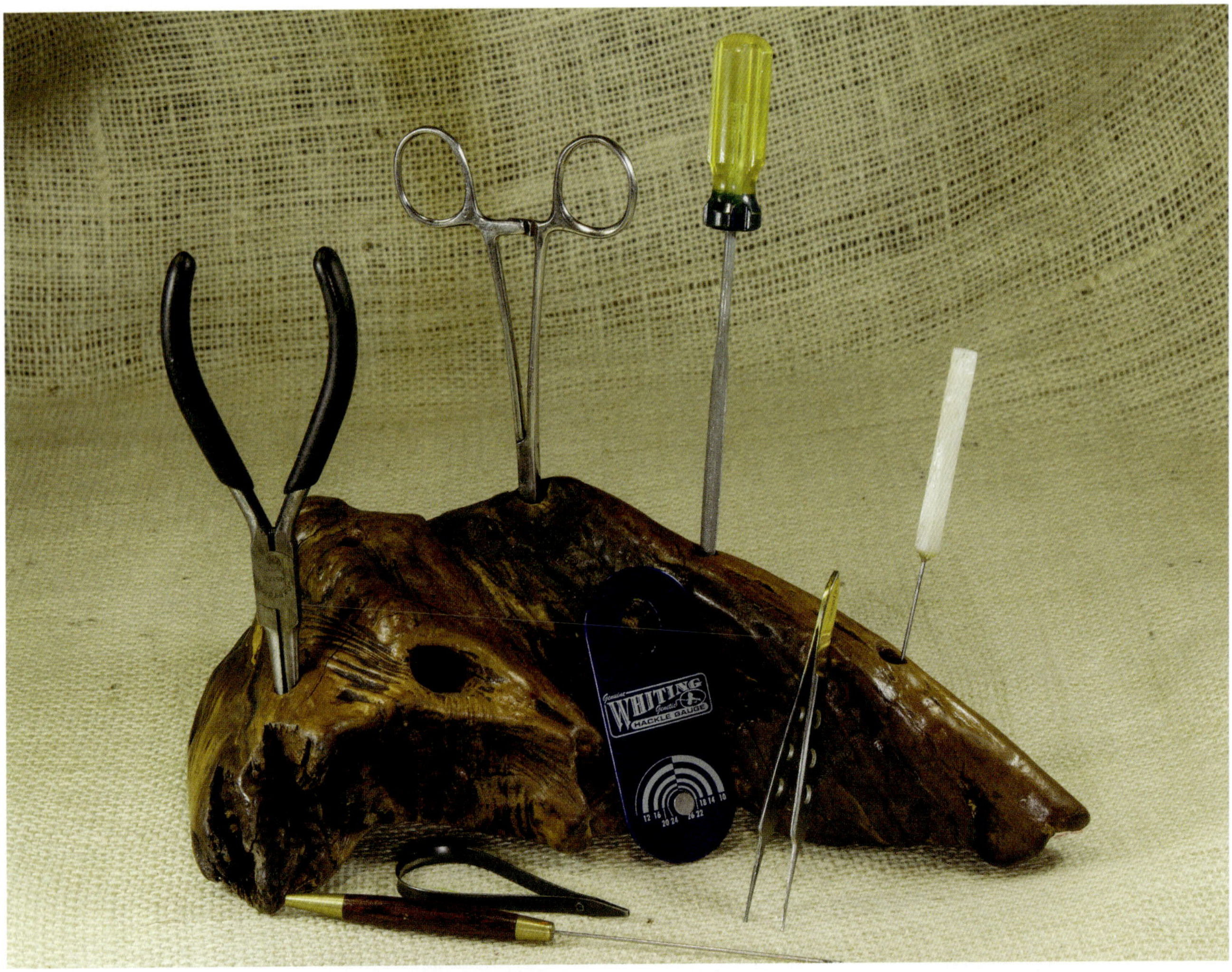

Top row, left to right: Needle-nose pliers, hemostats, file, Griffin bodkin. Bottom row, left to right: Rainy's E-Z Bobbin Threader, Griffin Teardrop Hackle Pliers, Whiting Hackle Gauge, Dr. Slick Bishop Tweezers.

Left: DIY eye tool, DIY glue applicator/bodkin.

Above: Hot Point tool with spare tip.

release of the fish and, should the need arise, the fisherman. A smooth-jawed pair of fine needle-nose pliers works best for this job. The pliers need to have a fine-enough point to crush the barb on small hooks as well as larger hooks.

A hackle gauge is used to measure barbule length. I use a Whiting Farms gauge. A hackle gauge is not really needed for measuring barbule length for deer hair bass bugs, but it is helpful for gauging barbule length for dry flies.

A bobbin threader is used to pull thread through the tube of a bobbin. I currently use Rainy's E-Z Bobbin Threader. Rather than using wire, this tool has a small-diameter stainless shaft with a small hook at the end. The hook catches the thread and pulls it through the bobbin tube.

If you want to create really smooth deer hair bodies on bass bugs, one trick is to steam the body before the final trimming. A pair of hemostats can be used to hold the deer hair body in the steam from a teakettle.

EYE TOOL AND GLUE APPLICATOR/BODKIN

Take-out bamboo chopsticks from Asian restaurants are especially useful in crafting custom tools such as pointed glue applicators. The most useful tool is a custom eye tool to apply glue into a trimmed eye socket in a deer hair body or head. Carve the chopstick into a small paddle at one end, and put a few grooves in the other end to serve as a handle. If you have a Dremel rotary tool, use a small round cutting ball to carve a small cup in the handle end of the tool. Use this cupped end to help seat the eye in the glued eye socket of a bass bug.

HOT POINT TOOL

While you can use a curved pair of scissors to create eye sockets in deer hair bass bug bodies, a much more precise socket can be created with a Hot Point tool. With this tool you can burn precise eye sockets much more easily than with scissors. The tip of the tool does not need to be red hot to do the job. Only depress the button enough to activate the tip to the point where it will singe the hair. If you just press and hold the button, the tip will get hot enough to catch the hair on fire! After singeing the hair, brush out the ash left behind with the tips of your scissors or pointed tweezers. The only downside to using this tool is the smell of burning hair.

Materials

HOOKS

The hook is the foundation of the fly and should be chosen primarily for how it functions with the fly being tied. Occasionally I will use a nickel-plated hook on some of my brighter patterns, utilizing the flash the hook itself provides as part of the fly's appearance. Normally I choose a bronzed steel hook. I don't use stainless steel hooks, as I am concerned about how long they will take to degrade in a freshwater environment if lost. Other considerations when choosing hooks are cost and availability. The hooks used for the patterns in this book are included in the fly's recipe.

THREADS

There is such a huge selection of threads to choose from when you walk into most fly shops that the prospect of choosing a thread can be daunting. Prior to 1988 threads were designated using the "aught" system with thread designations like 3/0 or 6/0. The higher the aught number, the thinner the thread. Then in 1988 Tom Schmucker of Wapsi Fly began using the denier system of measuring thread. The denier weight is the weight in grams of 9,000 meters of the thread. Wapsi began labeling their thread with the denier weight as opposed to the aught designation. With this system, the smaller the denier number meant that the thread diameter was thinner as long as you were comparing threads of the same material. This caused confusion when trying to compare different threads from different companies.

Numerous articles have been written about the sizing and tying properties of different threads. While there are a number of equivalent threads that can be used for the flies in this book, I have used just two different types and only a few sizes. For most of the flies, I have used Wapsi Ultra Thread waxed nylon thread. Since the smallest flies here are about a size 16, the smallest waxed nylon thread is the UTC 70. UTC 140 waxed nylon thread is used for most of the medium to larger flies.

Various bass bug hooks, dry fly hooks, and streamer hooks.

Wapsi UTC 140, UTC 70, and GSP threads.

For all of the flared or spun deer hair work, I have used Wapsi GSP thread. This is a gel-spun thread that has excellent properties for spinning and flaring deer hair. Gel-spun threads have a greater strength for a given size compared to waxed nylon and are soft enough to not readily cut through the hair. For the smaller deer hair heads, I use the smaller deniers like a GSP 75 or GSP 100. For most deer hair work, I use GSP 130, which is strong enough for all but the largest heads, where GSP 200 can be used.

When comparing waxed nylon thread to gel-spun thread, one of the most notable characteristics is that gel-spun thread is very slippery. When starting a waxed nylon thread on a hook shank, it only takes a few wraps back over itself to adhere. If the same is done with gel-spun thread, it will quickly slide off the hook shank. For that reason, Zap-A-Gap glue is used to both start the gel-spun thread and tie it off.

HAIR

The primary sources for hair for the fly tier is whitetail deer, mule deer, and elk. While other sources of hair exist, the hair from any of these three ungulates satisfies most fly-tying needs. The northern woodland whitetail deer is probably the most common source for a variety of tying needs. The deer harvested in southern Michigan, northern Ohio, Indiana, and Illinois produce some of the best hair.

Early season hair, or **Comparadun hair,** is harvested around the first of October and is about 1 inch long. This hair is best for tying Compara-duns, Elk Hair Caddis, and small spun deer hair heads on patterns like small Letort Hoppers or Muddlers. When selecting a piece for tying hair-wing duns, look for hair that has short, even tips and little or no taper, as this hair should have the ability to flare close to the tips.

Often labeled as **general purpose hair** or **Humpy hair,** midseason hair is generally harvested around the end of October. This hair is usually about 1½ inches long. Look for even tips, as most patterns tied with this hair make use of the tips to create hair collars. Like early season hair, if there is little or no taper to the hair, it will probably flare close to the tips. This hair is most often used for Muddler Minnows, spun deer hair head hoppers like the Dave's Hopper, bullet-head hoppers, Humpies, and other folded hair patterns.

Nature's Spirit Comparadun deer hair.

Nature's Spirit All Purpose and Humpy deer hair.

Left: Nature's Spirit dyed spinning deer hair.

Late season hair is generally harvested around the end of November. This hair is usually about 2 inches long and is labeled as **spinning hair.** When buying a piece of this hair, look at the individual shafts. The hair should have a crinkled appearance. What you are seeing is the cellular structure of the hair. Compressing these air cells with thread is what causes the hair to flare. Another indicator that you have a good piece of hair for spinning or flaring is to squeeze it with your hand. It should have a sponge-like feel to it. Again, you are feeling the compression of the air cells in the individual shafts of hair. This longer hair is used for all but the largest spun deer hair heads.

White deer belly hair is a specialty hair that only occurs on whitetail deer. There is only a small amount of it on each hide. This is an excellent hair for hair-wing dun patterns. This hair typically flares easily and has even tips. It creates a wing that is easy to see and is a favorite of Midwestern fly tiers for tying hair-wing dun patterns that are fished in low-light conditions.

Cow elk spinning hair is probably the longest and largest of the hair options for tiers. This hair is generally up to 4 inches long. It is usually a darker gray than whitetail deer. When dyed it is generally darker than the same color of whitetail hair. I usually reserve this hair for the largest of hair heads on flies for pike and muskie.

Whitetail Fly Tieing Supplies white deer belly hair.

Nature's Spirit cow elk spinning hair.

BUCKTAIL

Bucktail is an essential component of most baitfish fly patterns. Just as deer body hair differs from hide to hide, some bucktails have hair that is wavy and others have hair that is relatively straight. Most bucktails have hair that range from 3 to 4 inches.

When tying with bucktail, remember that normally the underside bottom third of the tail will have the longer coarse hair. This hair will also retain some of the body hair's flaring characteristics. The hair in the upper two-thirds of the tail will tend to be shorter and will not flare as much as the lower hair when thread pressure is applied.

Various colors of Nature's Spirit select northern bucktail.

FEATHERS

A wide variety of feathers are available to fly tiers today. Where possible I like to use natural materials, so many of my bass bugs will use several types of feathers. Being a Whiting Farms Pro Team fly tier gives me access to the many products offered by them. All of the feathers used in the patterns in this book are Whiting products.

Today dry fly hackle comes in many varieties and colors, both natural and dyed. For most tiers the dry fly cape is probably the best buy, as it contains a wider range of sizes than does the saddle. If you are a commercial tier and tying hundreds of the same fly, the saddles with their extremely long feathers and similar size range are probably going to serve your purpose.

Whiting dry fly hackle, left to right: white dyed dark olive, barred medium ginger, brown, natural dun.

Hebert Miner dry fly hackle, left to right: light ginger, dun grizzly, medium ginger, dun badger.

However, not being a commercial tier, I like the capes better since they provide a broader range of sizes. Feathers on capes are also getting longer. It not unusual to get two or three patterns hackled with one feather.

When looking for feathers for tails on a bass bug, I like a feather that has a good web. Feathers that have little web will tend to become very slim when they get wet and then the tail doesn't balance well with the deer hair body. The best feather that I have used is the Whiting black laced hen. The saddles from this bird have shorter, more rounded feathers that don't work as well; however, the capes have exceptional feathers that serve this purpose. The cape feathers tend to be longer and are heavily webbed. Additionally, the black fringe around the edge of the feather is a nice accent. These capes naturally are white with a black fringe, so they can be dyed into a variety of colors.

Whiting black laced hen capes, left to right: white dyed red, white dyed yellow, white dyed olive.

Other products that I use to create hackle collars on many of the bass bugs are Whiting American rooster capes and saddles or Coq de Leon capes. The American capes and saddles in natural grizzly or dyed grizzly provide attractive collars. The Coq de Leon capes have finely spotted barbules and look great when used in a hackle collar as well.

Whiting Bird Fur is another unique feather that I make generous use of in most of the bass bugs (see "Whiting Bird Fur" sidebar in chapter 8). This feather adds texture and movement to a fly pattern and is available in a wide variety of natural colors as well as dyed colors.

Schlappen feathers, from the tail of the chicken, were not used very often in fly tying in the past. However, with the large flies being tied today for muskie and pike, this feather is now considered a valuable tying material. Schlappen feathers come in

Whiting American hackle, left to right: grizzly saddle, grizzly dyed olive cape, grizzly dyed yellow saddle.

Whiting Coq de Leon capes, left to right: badger dyed burnt orange, badger dyed copper olive, badger dyed olive, dark pardo.

Whiting Bird Fur, left to right: grizzly dyed olive, white dyed yellow, white dyed red, white dyed burnt orange, natural white.

Whiting schlappen, left to right: grizzly dyed olive, grizzly dyed orange, grizzly dyed yellow, grizzly dyed burnt orange, grizzly dyed chartreuse.

Various types of leg material.

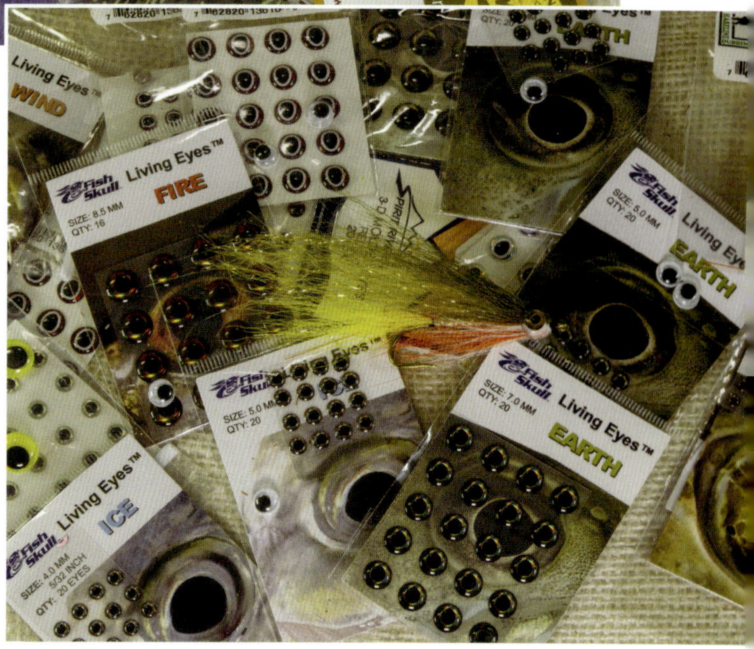

Various types of eyes.

a variety of natural colors as well as "dyed on white" and "dyed on grizzly." When creating long fly patterns, these feathers are a key component of many of the flies being tied today.

LEGS

Rubber legs add a lot of movement to both surface and diving bass bugs. The two primary sources for legs in most of my patterns are Hareline's Grizzly Barred Rubber Legs and Montana Fly Company's Speckled Centipede Legs. Both of these rubber leg materials have accent color bars or specks along with the main color. With the wide variety of colors offered, it is easy to find a legging material that works with any color scheme. Additionally, several colors can be used on one fly to complement the color scheme of the body and tail.

EYES

On topwater, waking, or diving deer hair flies, I am not sure you even need eyes, but they sure make the pattern come to life. For deer hair heads, I primarily use eyes from Hareline. I particularly like the Oval Pupil 3D eyes, which really pop some color and life into a lot of fly patterns. Hareline's regular 3D domed eyes look good on a fly pattern as well. For deer hair bodies, it's better to have eyes with some type of a reflective base. Eyes without bases will not stand out as well when applied to deer hair. Doll eyes are relatively inexpensive, look good, and provide some additional flotation to the pattern.

For almost all of my bucktail patterns, I use Flymen's Fish-Skull Living Eyes in conjunction with their Fish-Mask. The four Living Eyes colors—earth, wind, fire, and ice—match most baitfish eyes. When used in conjunction with a Fish-Mask, they have a great realistic look.

Yak hair and Icelandic sheep are two natural materials that I use quite often. Yak hair is translucent and is available in many dyed colors. Additionally, when it is wet it retains some stiffness so doesn't tend to foul around the bend of the hook when being cast. Icelandic sheep is another good natural streamer hair. It has a soft texture,

FLASH

It's quite easy to over-flash a fly pattern. If a fly is intended to be fished in stained or muddy water, more flash material should be used, but for clear-water fishing situations, a small amount of flash will work better than tying a fly that is too bright.

For that reason my favorite flash material is Hareline's Ice Wing Fiber or some other similar fine flash material. When a little of it is included in a pattern, it provides some sparkle to the fly. A good test of how much flash is correct for clear-water flies is to look at the fly in the water. If it is lit up by the sun, it should just sparkle and you should not really see any actual flash material. Most fish are attracted to flash, but I have seen fish inspect but not eat flies in clear water that have too much flash.

Holographic Flashabou is another material that adds a lot of attractiveness to a fly pattern. Used sparingly it looks good in clear water and can really add to the fish seeing the fly in stained or muddy water. Krystal Flash is also excellent for providing a discreet amount of sparkle to a fly. It comes in either regular size or a midge size that has a smaller diameter than the regular size.

This is only a small sample of the flash materials that are available. It seems that new types of flash material appear every year. Be creative but sparing in your use of flash.

Various types of flash material.

STREAMER HAIR

Streamer hair is an essential material for larger warmwater fly patterns. Synthetic or natural hair can often be used interchangeably. It is hard to get the size in muskie or pike flies without using some type of streamer hair as part of the pattern.

Sides: Hareline Icelandic sheep. Center: Spirit River yak streamer hair.

Center: Wapsi Supreme Hair. Sides: Puglisi Fiber synthetic streamer hair.

Left to right: Sally Hansen Hard as Nails, Zap-A-Gap, Dave's Flexament, Fly-Rite Fly-Tite Fly Tying Cement with applicator bottle. Bottom: Amazing GOOP All Purpose Contact Adhesive.

which gives it great movement in the water. Icelandic sheep should be tied using a core material of some stiffer synthetic material, since it does have a tendency to foul around the hook shank when being fished (see "Working with Icelandic Sheep" sidebar in chapter 8).

Wapsi Supreme Hair is a stiff synthetic streamer hair that is commonly used in saltwater patterns. I primarily use the material as a starting point in constructing longer tails, especially those that use Icelandic sheep. This material helps prevent the softer materials that are tied around it from fouling on the hook as the fly is being cast.

Puglisi Fiber is a synthetic streamer hair material that can often be used interchangeably with Icelandic sheep or yak hair. It comes in a wide range of colors. It is a good choice when tying muskie or pike flies, as it is very durable.

As with flash material, this is a category of fly-tying materials where new materials are introduced at a rapid pace. This is only a small sample of what is available.

GLUES AND EPOXIES

Different types of adhesives or glues play an important role in constructing quality deer hair flies. Understanding this role helps in selecting the correct glue for the desired purpose.

Zap-A-Gap is a superglue (cyanoacrylate) that is critical for many tying situations. Cyanoacrylate glues have some variations in their formulations, but Zap-A-Gap is the brand that is most often used in fly tying. When these glues are deprived of oxygen, such as being trapped between two surfaces, they quickly cure. This is why Zap-A-Gap is such a good adhesive to use in conjunction with gel-spun thread. When gel-spun thread is wrapped through a thin layer of Zap-A-Gap applied to the hook shank, the thread forms a tight bond with the hook. A small amount of Zap-A-Gap is also necessary for adhering some materials like Icelandic sheep to the fly. Pacer Technology produces Zap-A-Gap glues and in addition to their Medium CA glue,

Loon Outdoors UV Clear Fly Finish, left to right: flow, thin, thick.

which is used for most applications, they also produce a Thin CA. This thinner Zap-A-Gap glue penetrates quickly and is especially useful for materials like Icelandic sheep or some synthetic streamer hair. Zap-A-Gap is also marketed as being waterproof.

Dave's Flexament and GOOP are two adhesives that are important to have. Both of these are flexible when cured. If they are not identical formulas, then they are really close. I thin my Dave's Flexament with Toluene paint thinner; however, you can buy a thinner that is designed specifically for the product. Toluene is a toxic substance, so handle it with care. I store my can in the garage, and whenever I am adding it to my tying bottle, I do it outdoors so as not to expose myself to the fumes. That said, I keep my Dave's Flexament thinned to about the consistency of water.

Toluene is also a thinner for GOOP. I use these two adhesives in conjunction with each other to add eyes to my deer hair bass bugs. I put a few drops of Dave's Flexament in the eye socket and then add a small dab of GOOP. The thinner Flexament will interact with the GOOP, drawing it down into the hair of the eye socket, then when the eye is seated in the glued socket, a more durable bond is created.

When tying a hackle collar on a bass bug tail, add some Dave's Flexament just before wrapping the hackle, then wrap the hackle collar over the glued area and tie off the tail. This adds to the durability of the tail.

The Fly-Rite Company sells Fly-Tite, a flexible tying cement that is nontoxic. Ethyl alcohol is used as a solvent or thinner. This tying cement works well with a thin-nozzle applicator bottle. It is an excellent cement to use at the base of stacks of hair in bass bugs to increase their durability.

While I will use Zap-A-Gap and a few half-hitch knots when tying off gel-spun thread, I like to come back and add a waxed nylon thread head over the gel-spun to finish the fly. I then coat this thread head with Sally Hansen Hard as Nails nail polish. This penetrates the thread head, making a secure finish for the fly. Use a feather to clear out the eye itself since Hard as Nails, as its name implies, cures hard. If it's covering the eye of the hook, it can be difficult to clear out, and even if you do clear it out, it can leave sharp edges that can abrade tippet material when fishing.

There was a time when tiers who wanted to do an epoxy head on a fly pattern had to mix and apply the epoxy to the head, then quickly place the fly on a rotating wheel to cure. UV epoxies have changed all of that. These epoxies are incredibly easy to use and cure almost instantly when exposed to a UV light source. Loon Outdoors makes a product called UV Clear Fly Finish. Flow is the thinnest resin; thin resin is next in viscosity, followed by thick resin. These UV epoxies have made creating epoxy heads easy. When used in conjunction with the Fish-Skull Fish-Masks made by the Flymen Fishing Company, great-looking streamer heads become even easier.

CHAPTER 2

Hair-Wing Duns

On one hot float in August . . . we stopped in at Gates Lodge . . .
"They stopped rising to our dry flies," I said to Rusty. "Should we fish nymphs?"
Rusty's eyebrows lifted. "Just fish closer to the wood."
"No nymphs?"
He stared at me.
"Just hit the wood," he said slowly.
JOSH GREENBERG, *RIVERS OF SAND*

Fishing to rising trout is at the heart of fly fishing. It has a long and storied tradition and is considered one of the true art forms of the sport. Fishing with light, small fly rods, long leaders, fine tippets, and delicately dressed flies are at the center of many anglers' lives. While there are many ways to approach trout fishing, few compare to matching the hatch for rising trout.

When fished among a hatch of naturals, it's easy to see why hair-wing dun flies are so effective. At times it is hard to distinguish the fly from the hatching mayflies around it. When there is a very sparse hatch or no hatch at all, these flies are great searching patterns as well. Deer hair for the wing and, as with the Robert's Drake, deer hair for the body makes for a fly pattern that floats well and is durable. Whether tied as a no-hackle, parachute-style fly, thorax, or standard hackled fly, these patterns deserve a place in the trout angler's fly box.

Robert's Drake

Formed by the confluence of Kolke Creek and Bradford Creek, Michigan's Au Sable River flows south for a short distance. Turning at the town of Grayling, it flows east for about 100 miles and eventually drains into Lake Huron. Not far downstream from Grayling, the Mainstream of the Au Sable is joined by the North Branch and South Branch. Both of these tributaries are noted rivers along with the Mainstream.

Winding through the glacial moraines of northern Michigan, snowmelt and rainfall get filtered through the sand and gravel substrates to return to the river in the form of its many streamside springs. This is one of the most stable river systems in the world. Here crystal-clear water flows across amber gravel and sand bottoms. The banks are lined with cedar trees that eventually become the renowned sweepers that are an iconic feature here. On the higher banks are the towering eastern white pine trees that are reminiscent of the primeval forests that once flourished and were the focus of the lumber industry of the late 19th century. Here also in the jack pine forest is the nesting ground for the endangered Kirkland warbler. And, of course, this is the river system that was once home to the now-extinct Michigan grayling. There is a unique beauty to this river valley.

These are also storied, historic waters for fly fishermen. Thaddeus Norris, one of America's most influential fly-fishing authors in the late 19th century, first wrote about the Au Sable River in *Scribner's Monthly* in 1879, describing the grayling fishing of the day. The story of the demise of the Michigan grayling is one of the sad undercurrents that quietly haunts this river valley to this day. The last reported grayling caught was on the East Branch in 1915. Through logging and overfishing, this unique species of grayling is now extinct.

In a cabin along the banks of the Au Sable, George Griffith, Art Neumann, and others conceived the idea that today is Trout Unlimited. Vince Marinaro devoted the last chapter of his book *In the Ring of the Rise* (1976) to the Au Sable river system and extolled its virtues as a prime trout fishery. Many other noted authors have written about this river system, including Ernest Schwiebert, Carl Richards, and Doug Swisher as well as some more modern voices. The late Rusty Gates's book *Seasons of the Au Sable* (2007) eloquently chronicles a year and its passing seasons along the banks of the river. Josh Greenberg's *Rivers of Sand* (2014) is one of the latest books to document the fly-fishing opportunities along the Au Sable as well as other Great Lakes fisheries. The Anglers of the Au Sable, a Federation of Fly Fishers affiliate, as well as Trout Unlimited chapters from around the state of Michigan are today's champions of this great river system and its surrounding ecosystem.

The Au Sable hosts an array of mayfly hatches, beginning with the always-anticipated Hendrickson hatch that arrives each year at the end of April in time for opening day. Hatching mayflies along with caddisflies and stoneflies continue throughout the summer into the fall. The mayflies range from one of the largest mayfly species, the Hex (*Hexagenia limbata*), to one of the smallest, the Trico (*Tricorythodes stygiatus*).

Unique to Michigan, the Robert's Drake is one of the most iconic fly patterns used here. Clarence Roberts, a native of northern Michigan, was a conservation officer in the Grayling area during the 1950s and 1960s. A fly tier and fisherman, he developed the Robert's Drake to imitate the numerous large mayflies present in the Au Sable. Tied as a Robert's Yellow Drake, Robert's Olive Drake, or Rusty's White Knot, this pattern is a template for many of these mayfly hatches. A white deer hair wing keeps these flies visible as the light wanes when fishing through a summer evening.

While these flies are tied to imitate certain mayfly hatches, they also work well as searching patterns. The Rusty's White Knot is one of the most commonly used summer patterns here. Additionally, I have used this pattern as a template for the Green Drake hatch in Colorado. As a template, this fly pattern can be tied to imitate most medium to large mayfly hatches.

TYING THE ROBERT'S YELLOW DRAKE

- **Hook:** #8-16 Tiemco 100 or #4-10 Tiemco 5212
- **Thread:** Yellow or hopper yellow UTC Ultra Thread 70
- **Tail:** Pheasant tail fibers
- **Body:** Nature's Spirit Humpy deer hair (Natural)
- **Wing:** White deer belly hair
- **Hackle:** Brown Whiting dry fly hackle

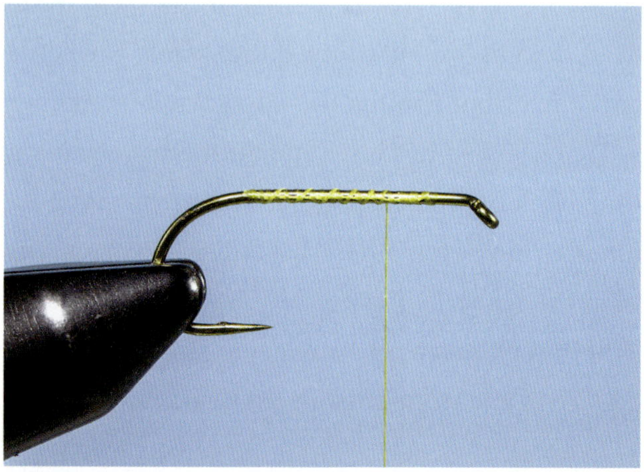

STEP 1: Wrap the hook shank with thread starting at the front. Wrap back to the tie-in point at the back of the hook and return the thread ¾ of the way to the front of the hook.

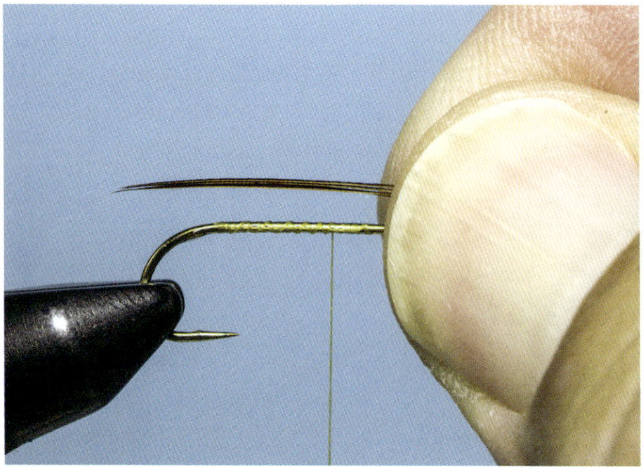

STEP 2: Select 3 or 4 pheasant tail fibers. Even the tips and measure them against the length of the hook shank. The tail should extend 1 to 1¼ times the length of the hook shank behind the tie-in point at the back of the hook.

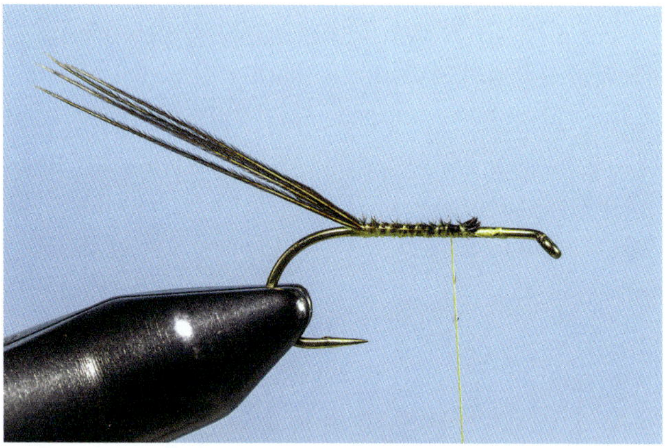

STEP 3: Using a pinch wrap, bind the fibers to the hook shank. Pull the tails slightly towards you as you wind the thread back to the tie-in point so the tail is bound to the top of the hook shank. Wrap the thread one time under the tail and pull forward to angle the tail up. Then wrap the thread half the way back up towards the eye of the hook.

STEP 4: Cut a small bunch of deer hair, comb out the underfur, and stack the hair to even the tips. Measure the tips to the back of the bend of the hook, holding the hair above the hanging thread. Grasp the hair with your other hand and cut at the length measured.

STEP 5: Keeping the hair in place, make 2 or 3 loose wraps around the butts of the hair and tighten, binding the hair to the hook shank. Continue holding the hair and begin to spiral-wrap the thread back to the tie-in point.

STEP 6: At the tie-in point of the hook, pull both the tail and hair tips up and wrap one time under the tips and tail. Pull the thread forward to set an upward angle to the tail and tips, then continue an open spiral wrap to the front of the hook shank.

STEP 7: Cut a small bunch of white deer belly hair, comb out the underfur, and stack. With the tips evened, measure the wing length to equal the body length. Switch hands, keeping the measured length, and cut the butts off.

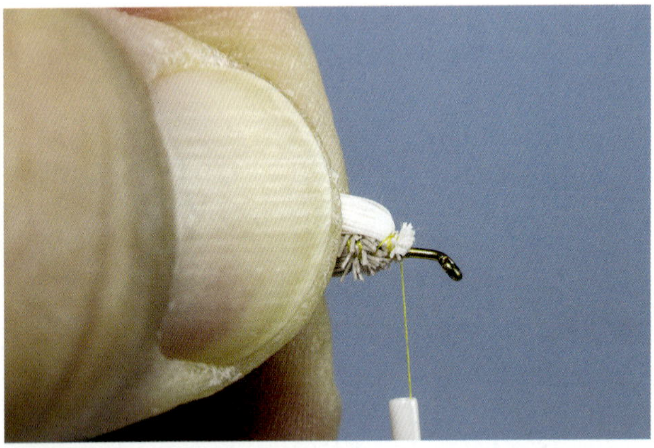

STEP 8: Set the butts of the deer hair wing just in front of the body. Make 2 or 3 loose wraps and tighten, binding the hair to the hook shank. While still holding the wing, continue wrapping through the butts of the hair to both bind the wing to the hook and cover the butts of the hair.

STEP 9: Pull the wing upright and wrap behind the wing. Continue wrapping to cover the butts of both the body and wing. Make 3 or 4 post wraps around the base of the wing. Do not do wrap too high up on the wings, as this will tend to bunch the hair together. You want a flared wing as in the photo.

STEP 10: Prepare a fly feather as shown (see "Posting a Dry Fly Wing and Wrapping a Parachute Hackle" sidebar). Attach the feather directly in front of the wing on the opposite side of the hook.

STEP 11: Make the first wrap of hackle around the back of the wing and continue wrapping so the hackle is being wrapped away from you as it goes around the front of the wing. Make 3 to 5 wraps of hackle down the wing.

(continued on page 26)

POSTING A DRY FLY WING AND WRAPPING A PARACHUTE HACKLE

While the origins of the parachute style of hackling a dry fly are somewhat obscure, Carl Richards and Doug Swisher's book *Selective Trout* (1971) popularized the parachute dun. Posting a wing on a dry fly and wrapping a dry fly hackle in the parachute style creates a fly that lands upright and presents a realistic silhouette of a mayfly dun.

Unlike posting a wing with a synthetic material, when posting a wing tied with deer hair it's important not to wrap too far up the wing. To keep the wing flared with a good profile, only do 3 or 4 wraps of thread at the base of the wing. You can post the wing by wrapping the thread either clockwise or counterclockwise around the base of the wing. When you finish posting the wing and make the next wrap around the hook shank, the thread should still be moving away from you as you cross the top of the hook.

There is more than one way to mount the feather and wrap the hackle around the wing. One is to strip the barbules off the stem of the feather and attach the bare stem to the posted wing. You then wrap the feather down the wing and tie off the feather at the bottom of the wing.

A second way is to attach the feather directly in front of the wing with the feather to the back of the wing. After making your first wrap, continue wrapping down the wing. Tie off the feather to the hook shank in front of the wing.

In both methods you should wrap the feather counterclockwise around the wing when viewed from above. In doing this the feather will always be traveling away from you as it passes around the front of the posted wing. Also, in both methods the concave side of the feather should be facing down so the barbules are oriented down. The advantage of the first method is the parachute hackle looks neater, but this tying technique is a bit more difficult. The second method is easier, but because the hackle is being overwrapped by itself, you get a few barbules that are askew. Both ways produce a fly that fishes equally well.

Attach a wing to a hook shank and stand it up with thread wraps at the front and back. To post the wing, make 3 or 4 wraps of thread at the base of the wing. Finish by wrapping the thread around the hook shank. When returning the thread to the hook shank, the wraps should be moving away from you as you travel over the top of the hook shank with the thread.

The wraps of thread that post the wing are the red thread wraps.

(continued on next page)

If posting the wing by wrapping the thread clockwise (as seen from above), the thread should be returned to the hook shank at the back of the wing. Return the thread to the hook shank by wrapping over the top of the shank with the thread moving away from you.

If posting the wing by wrapping the thread counter-clockwise (as seen from above), the thread should be returned to the hook shank at the front of the wing. Return the thread to the hook shank by wrapping over the top of the shank with the thread moving away from you.

The two methods of prepping a feather. The top feather is used in the first technique and the bottom feather is used in the second.

METHOD 1. STEP 1: For the first method, attach the feather just in front of the wing and with a few posting wraps of thread around the wing. Note that the concave side of the feather is to the back. Return the thread to the back of the wing and trim the stem of the feather.

STEP 2: Starting at the top, wrap the feather down the wing. While holding the feather, wrap the thread around the base of the wing above the tip of the feather. Trim the feather.

STEP 3: After trimming the feather, return the thread to the front of the wing, make a thread head, and use a whip-finish knot to tie off the thread.

Top view.

METHOD 2. STEP 1: For the second method, attach the feather just in front of the wing. Note that the concave side of the feather is down. Leave the thread in front of the wing.

STEP 2: After the first wrap of hackle, make each succeeding wrap below the previous wrap working down the wing with 3 or 4 wraps of hackle. Pull the wing and hackle back, pinch the feather to the hook shank, and wrap with thread. Trim the tip of the feather, make a thread head, and finish with a whip-finish knot.

STEP 3: Reposition the wing to an upright position. Side view.

Top view. ■

STEP 12: Grasp and pull back both the hackle and the wing while holding the tip of the hackle feather. Bind the tip of the feather to the hook shank with 2 or 3 wraps of thread. Cut the tips of the feather and finish the head with several wraps of thread. Clip away any stray fibers and do a whip-finish knot to complete the fly. The wing should still be flared; if not, use your fingers to flare the wing and force the wraps of hackle down to the base of the wing.

Robert's Drake (top view).

Robert's Drake (side view).

Green Drake Sparkle Dun

The Frying Pan River, which headwaters on the western slope of the Central Sawatch Range in Colorado, is one of the premier trout streams in the United States. Legend has it that the river got its name when Ute Indians attacked a trapping party. All but two of the trappers were killed, and one of the survivors was injured to the point he could not travel. Putting his injured partner in a cave above the river, the other trapper went for help. To insure he would find the cave on his return, he hung a frying pan along the side of the river.

The confluence of the Frying Pan and the Roaring Fork River is in the town of Basalt. Ruedi Reservoir sits 14 miles above Basalt and creates an outstanding tailwater fishery on the river. However, even before the reservoir was built, the Frying Pan was considered an outstanding trout river. Ernest Schwiebert mentions the Frying Pan numerous times in *Matching the Hatch* (1955) and *Trout* (1978). According to Ernie, some of the best fishing on the river lies under the reservoir. He fished these serpentine meadow sections as a young man and discovered a superb dry fly fishery.

While that water is lost to modern fly fishers, the Frying Pan of today is still an exceptional dry fly river. Beginning in April numerous species of small Blue-Winged Olive mayflies begin to hatch. As the season progresses the mayflies become lighter in color, with the Pale Morning Duns arriving at the end of June and hatching through September. In the fall the Blue-Winged Olives return to the river. With the exception of the winter months, the Frying Pan is rarely without some type of mayfly emergence each day. Of course, the preeminent hatch on the Frying Pan is the Green Drake (*Ephemerellidae Drunella)*. It will begin in early July and extend into September with warm fall weather.

One of the best fly patterns to imitate these various hatches is the Sparkle Dun.

Doug Swisher and Carl Richards published *Selective Trout* in 1971, ushering in the modern era of mayfly design. Among the many innovative mayfly patterns was the idea of a stacked deer hair wing mayfly imitation. With the publication of *Hatches* in 1975, Al Caucci and Bob Nastasi, who were also working with hair-wing dun patterns, codified this pattern and coined the name Compara-dun for one of the most successful adult mayfly designs in use today.

Craig Mathews, searching for a fly pattern to fool the selective trout during the Pale Morning Dun hatch on the Henry's Fork, modified the Compara-dun by replacing the tailing fibers with Z-Lon to change the fly pattern from an adult mayfly imitation to an emerging mayfly imitation, dubbing it the Sparkle Dun. I was introduced to this pattern at a fly-tying seminar in Steamboat Springs, Colorado, that Crag conducted in conjunction with the Yampa Valley Fly Fishers in the late 1980s. The pattern has proven successful throughout the West as well as for rivers like the Au Sable in Michigan. The Sparkle Dun has been a dependable hatching mayfly imitation for nearly three decades.

Used as a template, the Sparkle Dun can imitate most mayfly hatches. In its simplest form, it requires only three materials: early season whitetail or elk hair for the wing, dubbing of a suitable color, and Z-Lon fibers for the trailing shuck. The selection of deer hair for this fly is critical. The hair must have short, fine tips. For smaller flies, the hair must have the capacity to flare very near the tips when attached to the hook. One of the variations for this pattern is to use a goose biot for the abdomen. This gives the fly a slender and segmented look. For larger mayfly imitations, you can rib the pattern with thread to also give the pattern a segmented look.

This pattern floats well and can be fished in riffles and faster water. It also gives a good profile for slower water where trout get a good look at the fly.

TYING THE GREEN DRAKE SPARKLE DUN

- **Hook:** #8-12 Tiemco 100
- **Thread:** Olive UTC 70
- **Wing:** Dark Dun Nature's Spirit Compara-dun deer hair
- **Tail:** Dark olive Z-Lon
- **Body:** Colorado Green Drake TroutHunter dry fly dubbing
- **Rib:** Olive UTC 280

STEP 1: Wrap the hook shank with thread starting at the front and winding back to the tie-in point on the hook. Return the thread ⅔ of the way back to the eye of the hook.

STEP 2: Cut a small bunch of dark dun deer hair, comb out the underfur, and stack the bunch to even the tips. Measure out a length of hair equal to the length of the hook shank.

STEP 3: Continue holding the hair by the butts and wrap 2 or 3 loose turns of thread; tighten to flare the hair tips. Continue holding the butts of the hair and do a few additional wraps to secure the wing.

STEP 4: While still holding the butts of the hair, trim the butts close to the tie-in point.

STEP 5: Lift the wing up and check its position on the hook shank. At this point the wing can still be slid either backward or forward to adjust it to that ⅔ point on the hook shank. When the wing is in the correct position, wrap the thread up against the front of the wing, forcing it to stand up. Return the thread to the back of the wing and continue to secure the butts of the wing.

STEP 6: Secure the Z-Lon fiber for the tail just behind the wing. Holding the end of the Z-Lon and pulling it slightly toward you, wrap the thread back to the tie-in point on the hook, securing the tail to the top of the hook.

STEP 7: Cut the Z-Lon to equal the length of the body.

STEP 8: Wrap the thread a short distance back toward the wing.

STEP 9: Attach the ribbing thread at the back of the wing and wrap back to the tying thread.

STEP 10: Using the tying thread to secure the ribbing thread, wrap the tying thread back to the tie-in point. If the ribbing thread is wrapped all the way to the tie-in point, it has a tendency to slide down the hook shank. By securing the ribbing thread with the tying thread, it stays in place as you dub the body.

STEP 11: Apply a small amount of dubbing to the tying thread.

STEP 12: Wrap the dubbing forward. Each time you wrap, tighten the dubbing on the thread by twisting it counterclockwise. Create a body that tapers toward the wing.

STEP 13: Spiral-wrap the ribbing thread forward and secure it in front of the wing with a whip-finish knot. Apply dubbing to the tying thread and dub in back and front of the wing to form a thorax. Finish the fly with a small thread head and whip-finish knot. Side view.

STEP 14: Using your fingers, flare the wing to so it has a 180-degree spread side to the side. Front view.

PALE MORNING DUNS

During the summer on most western trout rivers, there are numerous small mayfly hatches that are various shades of yellow, sulphur yellow, or orange-yellow. Anglers often identify all of these mayflies as "Pale Morning Duns." The true Pale Morning Dun of the West has been identified as *Ephemerella,* with a couple of species that fall under this genus. However, the "Pale Evening Duns" of the Midwest are also identified as a genus *Ephemerella* mayfly.

A number of years ago, a friend and I took a trip to Yellowstone National Park. We arrived at the Buffalo Ford (now known as the Nez Perce Ford) section of the Yellowstone River. While putting on our waders, we talked to a couple of anglers who were walking back to their car, and they reported the "Pale Morning Duns" were hatching. When we arrived at the river, I collected a few of the hatching mayflies and they had the shrunken hind wing of a *Baetis* mayfly. Instead of it being a Pale Morning Dun, it was some species of a sulphur *Baetis*. We still fished our PMD patterns and caught fish. You don't need to identify mayflies beyond size and color to successfully catch fish. By having a range of summer mayfly patterns in the colors listed above, hook sizes ranging from #12 to #18, and various profiles, you will have the flies to be successful with these summer hatches.

The legendary Joe Brooks advocated that PMD fly patterns be tied with a muted orange-colored dubbing. His thought was that the sunlight passing through the translucent body of the dun gave the fly an orange cast. This has certainly proven true in my own fishing, as orange-colored PMD patterns have been very successful. ■

Brown Drake Biot Sparkle Dun

The Brown Drake (*Ephemera simulans*) is present in many rivers across the country and is one of the earliest large mayflies to appear. As with many large mayflies, if you see a few on the water, you can fish a Brown Drake fly pattern. This variation on the Sparkle Dun uses a goose biot for the abdomen. The biot gives the abdomen a slender, segmented look. By matching the biot and dubbing color, this pattern serves as a template for many mayfly species. The biot works especially well for smaller mayflies.

TYING THE BROWN DRAKE BIOT SPARKLE DUN

- **Hook:** #8-12 Tiemco 100
- **Thread:** Hopper yellow UTC 70
- **Wing:** Dark Dun Nature's Spirit Comparadun deer hair
- **Tail:** Amber Z-Lon
- **Abdomen:** Tannish yellow Nature's Spirit goose biots
- **Thorax:** Tannish Yellow TroutHunter dry fly dubbing

STEP 1: Wrap the hook shank with thread starting at the front and winding back to the tie-in point on the hook. Return the thread ⅔ of the way back to the eye of the hook.

STEP 2: Cut a small bunch of dark dun deer hair, comb out the underfur, and stack the bunch to even the tips. Measure out a length of hair equal to the length of the hook shank.

STEP 3: Continue holding the hair by the butts at the desired length and wrap 2 or 3 loose turns of thread; tighten to flare the hair. Continue holding the butts of the hair and do a few additional wraps to secure the wing.

STEP 4: Trim the butts of the hair close to the thread wraps and stand the wing up using wraps of thread in front of the wing. Attach the Z-Lon tail just behind the wing and wrap back to the tie-in point, securing the Z-Lon to the top of the hook shank.

STEP 5: Wrap the thread forward and back to create a smooth tapered body and return to the tie-in point.

STEP 6: Attach a goose biot by the tip at the tie-in point and wrap the thread forward to just behind the wing (see "Working with Biots" sidebar).

STEP 7: Attach your hackle pliers to the butt of the biot and make evenly spaced wraps forward covering ½ to ⅔ of the body length. Tie off the butt of the biot and trim if needed.

STEP 8: Apply a small amount of dubbing behind the wing and in front of the wing to create a thorax and whip-finish to complete the fly.

Brown Drake Biot Sparkle Dun (side view).

Brown Drake Biot Sparkle Dun (front view).

WORKING WITH BIOTS

A biot feather comes from the leading edge of the primary flight feathers of a bird. For fly-tying purposes we use biots from either a goose or a turkey. When you look at a biot, there is a ridge along one side that has a ruffled appearance (you may need magnification to see this).

Depending on how you attach the biot, you can get a smooth look by making the ridge the leading edge as you wrap the feather. This means that the smooth edge is the trailing edge and covers the ridged edge with each wrap. If you reverse the feather and make the trailing side the ridged side of the biot, you get a more-pronounced segmented look. There is no "correct" way of wrapping the biot. Either way creates a slim, segmented abdomen and it just depends on which look you prefer.

Cut the strip of biots near the center to access the longer ones. From that point on, strip the biot off rather than cut it. This gives you a longer biot, making it easier to wrap. Additionally, biots can be brittle, particularly at the tips. Soaking the biots in water will make them much tougher and less prone to breaking. Use a small bowl with a little water to soak the individual biots.

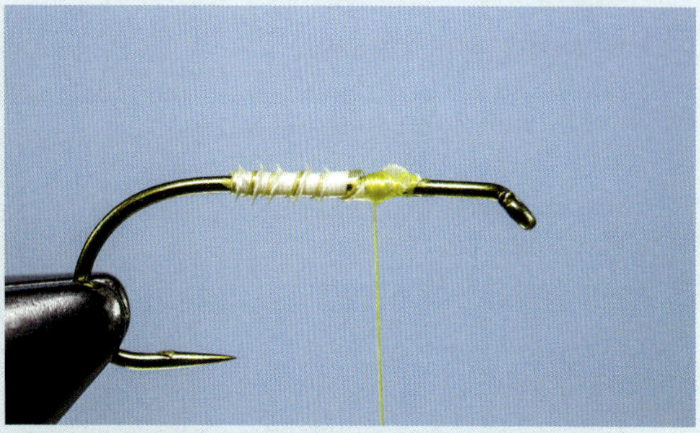

When the trailing edge is the ridged side, the body has a ribbed look.

When the trailing edge is the smooth side, the body has a smooth, segmented look. ■

Compendium of Hair-Wing Dun Fly Patterns

The following flies are variations on the Robert's Drake and Sparkle Dun fly patterns.

HI-VIS ROBERT'S DRAKE

- **Hook:** #8-16 Tiemco 100 or #4-10 Tiemco 5212
- **Thread:** Yellow or hopper yellow UTC 70
- **Tail:** Pheasant tail fibers
- **Body:** Natural Nature's Spirit Humpy deer hair
- **Wing:** White deer belly hair
- **Hackle:** Whiting High & Dry Hi-Vis; from left to right: pink, orange, chartreuse
- **Originator:** Variation of a Robert's Drake

ROBERT'S DRAKE HEX

- **Hook:** #4-6 Tiemco 5263 or Tiemco 5212
- **Thread:** Yellow or hopper yellow UTC 70
- **Tail:** Medium ginger Whiting CDL Tailing Pack
- **Body:** Yellow and olive Nature's Spirit cow elk spinning hair
- **Wing:** White deer belly hair
- **Hackle:** Brown Whiting dry fly hackle
- **Originator:** This pattern is a variation of a Hex pattern tied by Michigan fly tier Don Meyer. It is also a variation of a Robert's Drake.

ROBERT'S OLIVE DRAKE

- **Hook:** #10-16 Tiemco 100
- **Thread:** Olive UTC 70
- **Wing:** Dark Dun Nature's Spirit Comparadun deer hair
- **Hackle:** Dark dun Whiting dry fly hackle
- **Tail:** Nature's Spirit moose body hair
- **Body:** Dark Dun Nature's Spirit Compara-dun deer hair
- **Originator:** Variation of a Robert's Drake

RUSTY'S WHITE KNOT

- **Hook:** #8-12 Tiemco 100
- **Thread:** Dark brown UTC 70
- **Wing:** White deer belly hair
- **Hackle:** Dark dun Whiting dry fly hackle
- **Tail:** Nature's Spirit moose body hair
- **Body:** Mahogany deer hair
- **Originator:** Rusty Gates (variation of a Robert's Drake)

BORCHER'S PARACHUTE

- **Hook:** #10-16 Tiemco 100
- **Thread:** Black UTC 70
- **Wing:** White deer belly hair
- **Hackle:** Brown and grizzly Whiting dry fly hackle
- **Tail:** Nature's Spirit moose body hair
- **Body:** Turkey tail fibers wrapped around the hook shank
- **Originator:** Art Neumann (variation of a Borcher's Drake)

ADAMS PARACHUTE

- **Hook:** #10-16 Tiemco 100
- **Thread:** Black 6/0
- **Wing:** White deer belly hair
- **Hackle:** Brown and grizzly Whiting dry fly hackle
- **Tail:** Nature's Spirit moose body hair
- **Body:** Adams gray TroutHunter dry fly dubbing
- **Originator:** Variation of Leonard Halladay's Adams dry fly

ROBERT'S COLORADO GREEN DRAKE

- **Hook:** #8-12 Tiemco 100
- **Thread:** Olive UTC 70
- **Wing:** Dark dun deer hair
- **Hackle:** Dark dun Whiting dry fly hackle
- **Tail:** Nature's Spirit moose body hair
- **Body:** Green Drake Whitetail Fly Tieing deer hair
- **Originator:** Variation of a Robert's Drake

GREEN DRAKE BIOT SPARKLE DUN

- **Hook:** #8-12 Tiemco 100
- **Thread:** Olive UTC 70
- **Wing:** Dark dun Nature's Spirit Comparadun deer hair
- **Tail:** Dark olive Z-Lon
- **Abdomen:** Colorado Green Drake TroutHunter goose biots
- **Thorax:** Colorado Green Drake TroutHunter dry fly dubbing
- **Originator:** Variation of Craig Mathews's Sparkle Dun

MAHOGANY BIOT SPARKLE DUN

- **Hook:** #8-12 Tiemco 100
- **Thread:** Brown UTC 70
- **Wing:** White deer belly hair
- **Tail:** Dark olive Z-Lon
- **Abdomen:** Mahogany Nature's Spirit goose biots
- **Thorax:** Mahogany TroutHunter dry fly dubbing
- **Originator:** Variation of Craig Mathews's Sparkle Dun

ADAMS GRAY BIOT SPARKLE DUN

- **Hook:** #8-16 Tiemco 100
- **Thread:** Black UTC 70
- **Wing:** White deer belly hair
- **Tail:** Dark dun Z-Lon
- **Abdomen:** Muskrat gray Nature's Spirit goose biots
- **Thorax:** Adams gray TroutHunter dry fly dubbing
- **Originator:** Variation of Craig Mathews's Sparkle Dun

SULFUR BIOT SPARKLE DUN

- **Hook:** #14-18 Tiemco 100
- **Thread:** Watery olive UTC 70
- **Wing:** Bleached Nature's Spirit Comparadun hair
- **Tail:** Amber Z-Lon
- **Abdomen:** Sulphur yellow TroutHunter goose biots
- **Thorax:** Sulphur yellow TroutHunter dry fly dubbing
- **Originator:** Variation of Craig Mathews's Sparkle Dun

LIGHT CAHILL BIOT SPARKLE DUN

- **Hook:** #8-12 Tiemco 100
- **Thread:** Tan UTC 70
- **Wing:** Bleached Nature's Spirit Comparadun deer hair
- **Tail:** Amber olive Z-Lon
- **Abdomen:** Light Cahill Nature's Spirit goose biots
- **Thorax:** Light Cahill TroutHunter dry fly dubbing
- **Originator:** Variation of Craig Mathews's Sparkle Dun

BLUE-WINGED OLIVE SPARKLE DUN

- **Hook:** #14-18 Tiemco 100
- **Thread:** Olive UTC 70
- **Wing:** Dark dun Comparadundeer hair
- **Tail:** Dark olive Z-Lon
- **Body:** BWO TroutHunter dry fly dubbing
- **Originator:** Variation of Craig Mathews's Sparkle Dun

BLUE-WINGED OLIVE BIOT SPARKLE DUN

- **Hook:** #14-18 Tiemco 100
- **Thread:** Olive UTC 70
- **Wing:** Dark dun Comparadun deer hair
- **Tail:** Dark olive Z-Lon
- **Abdomen:** Blue Winged Olive Nature's Spirit goose biots
- **Thorax:** BWO TroutHunter dry fly dubbing
- **Originator:** Variation of Craig Mathews's Sparkle Dun

PALE MORNING DUN SPARKLE DUN

- **Hook:** #14-18 Tiemco 100
- **Thread:** Watery olive UTC 70
- **Wing:** Dun Nature's Spirit Comparadun deer hair
- **Tail:** Amber Z-Lon
- **Body:** Pale Morning Dun TroutHunter dry fly dubbing
- **Originator:** Variation of Craig Mathews's Sparkle Dun

PALE MORNING DUN BIOT SPARKLE DUN

- **Hook:** #14-18 Tiemco 100
- **Thread:** Watery olive UTC 70
- **Wing:** Dun Nature's Spirit Comparadun deer hair
- **Tail:** Amber Z-Lon
- **Abdomen:** Pale Morning Dun TroutHunter goose biots
- **Thorax:** Pale Morning Dun TroutHunter dry fly dubbing
- **Originator:** Variation of Craig Mathews's Sparkle Dun

ORANGE PMD SPARKLE DUN

- **Hook:** #14-18 Tiemco 100
- **Thread:** Olive Danville 6/0
- **Wing:** Dun deer hair
- **Tail:** Dark olive Z-Lon
- **Body:** Sulphur orange Hareline Micro Fine Dry Fly Dub

CHAPTER 3

Bullet Heads and Humpies

"Fishing is the chance to wash one's soul with pure air. It brings meekness and inspiration, reduces our egoism, soothes our troubles and shames our wickedness. It is discipline in the equality of men—for all men are equal before fish."

HERBERT HOOVER

As we pulled into the paved parking lot of one of the more popular attractions at Yellowstone National Park, our skepticism of the young guide's directions grew. He had told us of a "secret" place where there was an abundance of Yellowstone cutthroats that not many people fished. Pulling our gear out of the car, we prepared for the hike ahead. As we walked down the paved trail, we were conspicuous with our fishing gear among the people who were traveling down the path. There were families, older couples, and a large group of people that had unloaded from a bus, most of whom had cameras strung around their necks.

When we got to the point in the trail where it doubled back and away from the Yellowstone River, we left the trail and tourists behind us as we descended to the riverbank. Turning upstream we began walking along the edge of the river. Just as the guide had told us, there was very little trail. We encountered the bluff that blocked us from continuing upstream just where he said we would, and our confidence began to grow. By now we had left the crowds behind.

We climbed the bluff and stepped into the crescent-shaped meadow that was covered in waist-high sage. There was no evidence of any trail. The thought of grizzly bears crossed my mind as we walked across the meadow to the opposite end where we could descend to the river again. However, nothing other than the distant roar of the river disturbed the almost reverential quiet that permeated the meadow.

Getting to the far end of the meadow, we stepped out to the edge of the bluff and looked down into the river. There was an island with a side channel below us, and at the head of the island was a huge logjam. Immediately behind the logjam was a large, deep pool of clear water. The pool was filled with large Yellowstone cutthroats and the water was so clear that even from where we stood high above the river, we could clearly see the crimson splashes of color on their gill plates and flanks. The near-vertical bank dropping down to the river from the bluff made fishing there very difficult, so we continued walking upstream where the bluff gradually descended to the riverbank.

Farther upstream was a long gravel bar on our side of the river with a side channel. We stopped there and exchanged our hiking boots for wading boots. I assembled my rod and pulled out my box of Humpy dry flies. After attaching a fly to my leader, I began to cast upstream in the side channel. Almost immediately I hooked an 18-inch cutthroat. After releasing the fish, with a few more casts, I was hooked up again. These were not the selective trout of the Henry's Fork or the spring creeks in Livingston, Montana, that we had been fishing earlier in the week. Large attractor dry flies were all that was called for, and the box of Humpies that I brought were really all the flies that were needed.

It's hard to say how many fish we caught that day. Anglers sometimes talk of 100-fish days, but with a little math you can quickly calculate that a true 100-fish day means one fish every 6 minutes for 10 hours straight. I doubt we caught 100 fish, but it felt like it.

After a time I went to the bank to get some food out of the daypack. Sitting on the bank, I marveled at the power of the river. I was reminded that just slightly over 100 years earlier Chief Joseph and the Nez Perce people were pursued across the Yellowstone River very near the spot we were fishing. It was astounding to think of them actually crossing this river.

Seven years later the landscape of my memory was dramatically altered as the Yellowstone fires of 1988 roared through this place as well as much of the rest of the park.

Trout fishing today often requires flies that imitate the prevailing hatches of insects. It's good to occasionally encounter those circumstances when we can be less precise in our imitations and rely instead on attractor patterns like the Humpy.

Humpy

While the origin of the Humpy is somewhat obscure, its early roots are probably out of California. Jack Horner, a California fly tier, tied a fly he named the Horner's Deer Fly that pulled deer hair over the top of the body. A variation of Horner's pattern and a name that still is in use today is the Goofus Bug. However, Jack Dennis—Jackson Hole, Wyoming, fly tier, guide, and fly shop owner—probably did more to develop and popularize the fly we know today as the Humpy.

This fly is best known as an attractor pattern for western trout fishing. It is also an excellent pattern for bluegill, smallmouth, and other warmwater species. It can be tied with a variety of body color and hackle combinations. The pattern can be made more durable if a very thin coat of Dave's Flexament is added to the deer hair that is pulled over the back of the body. This step will also make the fly slightly heavier. When I tie a Humpy for panfish, I will add the glue to the back, but for trout fishing I leave the back unglued, as I want a fly with better floating characteristics.

TYING THE HUMPY

- **Hook:** #8-16 Tiemco 100
- **Thread:** Yellow UTC 70 for #12-16, UTC 140 for #8-10
- **Back/wing:** Natural Nature's Spirit Humpy or All Purpose deer hair
- **Hackle:** Barred dark ginger Whiting dry fly hackle
- **Tail:** Natural Nature's Spirit moose body hair

STEP 1: Start the thread at the center of the hook shank. Wrap a thread base back to the rear tie-in point and then spiral-wrap the thread back to the center of the hook.

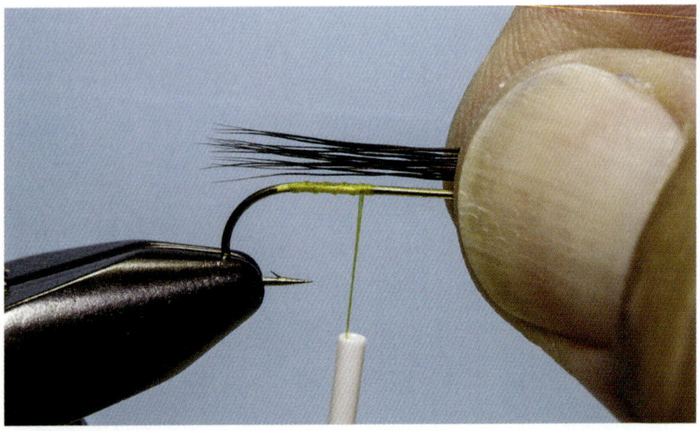

STEP 2: Cut a small bunch of moose body hair, clean out the underfur, and stack it to even the tips. Measure a length equal to the back of the eye to the back of the bend of the hook. Trim the butts of the hair at that length.

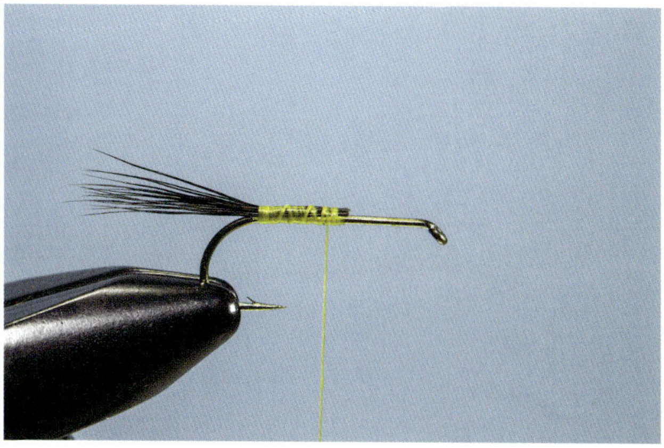

STEP 3: Attach the moose hair tail at the center of the hook. Hold the tail up and slightly toward you as you wrap back to the rear tie-in point. Make one wrap of thread under the rear of the tail and pull the thread forward to set the tail at a slight upward angle. Spiral-wrap the thread back to the center of the hook.

STEP 4: Cut a small bunch of deer hair. Clean and stack the hair to even the tips. Measure the hair so it has a length equal to 2 lengths of the hook shank or equal to a length from the back of the eye to the back of the tail. Trim the butts to equal that length.

STEP 5: Attach the butts of the hair to the center of the hook shank with 2 or 3 wraps of thread.

STEP 6: Wrap the butts of the hair back to the rear tie-in point. Completely cover the butts with the thread. Return the thread to the center of the hook shank.

STEP 7: Pull the deer hair forward and make 2 or 3 wraps to secure at the center of the hook shank.

STEP 8: Continue holding the tips of the hair as you wind a smooth thread body to the center of the front half of the hook shank.

STEP 9: Hold the tips of the hair upright and wrap thread in front of the tips. Wind back into the tips, forcing them to stand upright.

STEP 10: Evenly separate the tips of the hair to form the wings of the fly. Use a figure 8 wrap to keep the tips apart. Once the wings have been evenly separated, make 3 or 4 wraps of thread at the base of each wing to create a posted wing.

STEP 11: Return the thread to just in front of the body.

STEP 12: Prep an appropriately sized hackle (the barbule length should be 1½ times the length of the gape of the hook). Attach the base of the hackle feather with the concave or underside of the feather facing you with 3 or 4 wraps of thread. Continue wrapping the thread to the front of the wing. Wrap the hackle forward, making sure to keep the concave side to the front of the fly (this is wrapping a hackle dry fly style). Make an equal number of hackle wraps in front of the wings as in the back of the wings. Tie off the tip of the feather and trim. Wrap a thread head and use a whip-finish knot to complete the fly. If more hackle is desired, a second hackle feather can be attached to add to the density of barbules in the collar.

Side view.

Bullet-Head Damsel

During the 1980s I lived in Steamboat Springs, Colorado, and Steamboat Lake, north of Steamboat Springs, was noted for the prolific damselfly hatches that occurred there during the summer months. Using a float tube to access the bays on the north side of the lake, we would paddle out though the channels in the weed beds. Casting to those edges was a productive tactic using either damsel nymphs or damsel dry flies. The Bullet-Head Damsel was a favorite damsel dry fly pattern that produced on a consistent basis. This pattern is also effective on panfish during the summer on warmwater lakes. To make the fly more durable, the body can be treated with a thin coat of Dave's Flexament.

TYING THE BULLET-HEAD DAMSEL

- **Hook:** #8-10 Tiemco 100
- **Thread:** Black UTC 70
- **Wing:** White deer belly hair
- **Hackle:** Dark dun Whiting dry fly hackle
- **Body:** Blue Wapsi deer body hair

STEP 1: Wrap a thread base in the center half of the hook shank. Prep and stack a small bunch of white deer belly hair. Measure a length of hair equal to the length of the hook shank and trim the butts at that point.

STEP 2: With the tips of the hair pointing to the rear of the hook, tie in the butts of the hair. After securing the butts, pull the wing forward and make several wraps of thread against the rear of the wing, forcing it to stand upright. After the wing is upright, make 3 or 4 posting wraps at the base of the wing. Note that the wing is tied in at a point ⅓ of the hook shank length behind the eye of the hook.

STEP 3: Select an appropriately sized hackle. Prep the base of the feather and attach it right at the base of the wing. Stand the feather up against the wing so the concave side is facing away from you. Prep a small bunch of blue deer body hair. Trim the butts of the hair and attach them directly in front of the wing with the tips pointing forward. Hold the tips forward and wrap the thread toward the eye of the hook and then wrap back to the front of the wing.

STEP 4: Pull an even amount of hair back along each side of the wing to form the bullet head. Make several wraps of thread directly in front of the wing.

STEP 5: Continue making open spiral wraps of thread back to the rear tie-in point. At the rear tie-in point, make 2 or 3 wraps of thread to secure the deer hair. While continuing to hold the hair, make open spiral wraps of thread back toward the tips of the hair, creating an extended body. Just in front of the tips of the hair, make 3 or 4 wraps of thread on top of each other, then return the thread to the wing making open spiral wraps. The thread tension needs to be enough to hold the hair together but not enough to make the hair want to flare.

STEP 6: Wrap the hackle around the wing, with the first wrap going behind the wing. As you wrap around the front of the wing, the feather should be going away from you. After making 4 to 6 wraps of hackle, tie the tip of the feather off directly in front of the wing and trim.

STEP 7: Spiral-wrap the thread to the eye of the hook and make a small thread head. Use a whip-finish knot to tie off the thread and trim. Trim the tips of the hair so the length of the body is about 2½ times the length of the hook shank. Side view.

Deer Hair Ant

During the summer months, trout will often position themselves along the banks of rivers. If left undisturbed, they will actively feed along the water's edge. It is a rare trout that will not tip up and sip in a well-presented ant pattern. Ants are one of the more versatile fly patterns that anglers can use. I carry a variety of ant patterns, but this simple deer hair ant has proven its worth on many occasions. Just as with the Humpy and Bullet-Head Damsel, this pattern can be made more durable by applying a thin coat of Dave's Flexament to the deer hair.

TYING THE DEER HAIR ANT

- **Hook:** #10-16 Tiemco 100
- **Thread:** Black UTC 70
- **Body:** Black Nature's Spirit deer spinning hair

STEP 1: Wrap a thread base the length of the hook shank. Prep a bunch of black deer hair; trim the butts and tips even. If there is a lot of taper in the deer hair, take half of the hair and reverse it so each end has some of the butts and some of the tips. Attach the butts of the hair ⅔ of the way back towards the rear tie-in point. While holding the hair, bind down the butts. Continue wrapping the thread back, going slightly past the tie-in point.

STEP 2: Return the thread to the front of the butts of the hair.

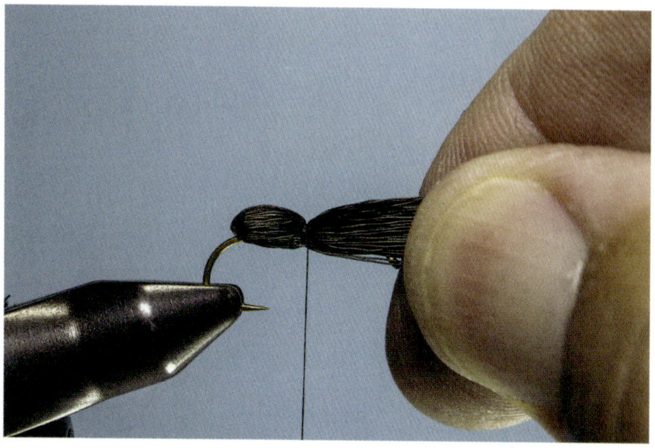

STEP 3: Pull the hair forward and bind down with 3 or 4 wraps of thread. This creates the abdomen of the ant.

STEP 4: Lift the hair up and wrap the thread ⅓ of the way towards the eye.

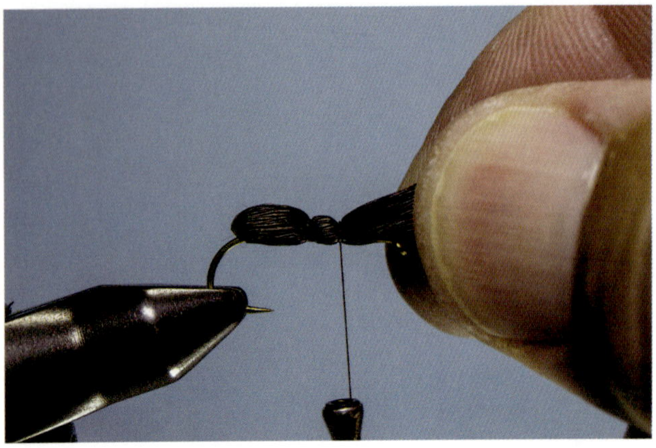

STEP 5: Pull the hair forward and make 3 or 4 wraps of thread, creating the thorax of the ant.

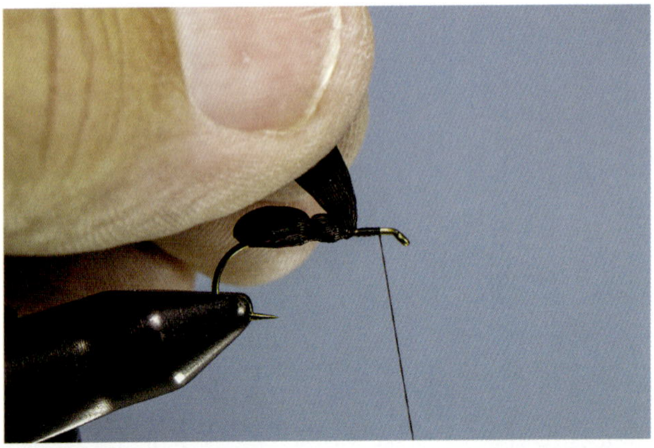

STEP 6: Lift the hair again and advance the thread to behind the eye of the hook.

STEP 7: Pull the hair forward and make 3 or 4 wraps of thread, creating the head of the ant. Then return the thread to the wraps of thread behind the head.

STEP 8: Pull 6 to 8 hairs back and bind them down with 1 wrap of thread.

STEP 9: Repeat on the near side. Use a whip-finish knot just behind the head and trim the thread. Lift up the hair in front and trim it at the same angle as the eye of the hook.

STEP 10: Pull the legs up and trim to a length equal to about 1½ the gape of the hook.

Whit Hopper

The Whit Hopper, like the Dave's Hopper, is another Dave Whitlock fly pattern. This fly was one of the first bullet-head patterns that I tied. Like the Bullet-Head Damsel, this fly also has an extended deer hair body. This pattern has good flotation and can also be used as an indicator if you want to use a bead-head nymph as a dropper.

TYING THE WHIT HOPPER

- **Hook:** #4-10 Tiemco 5263
- **Thread:** Hopper yellow UTC 140
- **Body:** Yellow Nature's Spirit cow elk spinning hair
- **Wing:** Nature's Spirit turkey quill segment over natural Nature's Spirit All Purpose deer hair
- **Legs:** Pheasant tail
- **Head:** Natural Nature's Spirit All Purpose deer hair
- **Glues:** Zap-A-Gap for securing body to hook; Dave's Flexament to seal body and head; Sally Hansen Hard as Nails for thread head

STEP 1: Apply a small amount of Zap-A-Gap glue to the rear ¾ of the hook shank and wrap a thread base. Return the thread to the front of the thread base. Leave the front ¼ of the hook shank bare (this is the area the head will be tied).

STEP 2: Cut and prep a small bunch of the yellow cow elk. Trim the butts of the hair and attach with 3 or 4 wraps of thread. Pull the hair back so it encompasses the hook shank.

STEP 3: Spiral-wrap the thread back, creating a segmented body. Extend the wraps back behind hook shank but around the hair, creating 2 additional body segments. Make 3 or 4 wraps of thread around the last segments. Spiral-wrap the thread back to the front with the thread crossing the first set of spiral wraps on the top of the body and aligning with the thread wraps on the bottom of the body.

STEP 4: Trim the butts of the hair behind the last thread wraps. The body should extend behind the rear tie-in point by a length equal to 1 to 1¼ times the gape of the hook. A small amount of thin Dave's Flexament could be added along the top of the body to seal the hair and give the body some additional strength.

STEP 5: Cut, prep, and stack a small bunch of the all-purpose deer hair. Measure a length equal to the length of the body and trim the butts.

STEP 6: Align the butts of the hair with the front of the body and attach with 3 or 4 wraps of thread.

STEP 7: Make 2 or 3 loose wraps of thread behind the tie-in point to gather in the wing.

STEP 8: Cut a segment of the turkey quill equal to the width of the hook gape. Trim the butts straight across and attach with 3 or 4 wraps of thread at the front tie-in point above the deer hair underwing.

STEP 9: Grasp the tip of the turkey quill wing segment so it folds lengthwise in half. Trim the tips with your scissors held at an angle with the tips pointing back towards the rear of the fly. The quill wing should be equal in length to the deer hair underwing.

STEP 10: Apply some Zap-A-Gap to the thread and make several wraps to secure the wing materials.

STEP 11: Prepare a knotted section of pheasant tail fibers to create a hopper leg. Attach this leg to the near side of the body at the front tie-in point with 3 or 4 wraps of thread.

STEP 12: Attach a prepared pheasant leg to the far side of the hook at the front tie-in point.

Top view of finished body, wing, and leg portion of the fly.

STEP 13: Cut, prep, and stack a bunch of the all-purpose deer hair. Measure a length equal to 3 times the length of the front ¼ of the hook shank. Trim the butts.

STEP 14: Reverse the bunch of hair so the tips are facing to the front of the fly. Align the butts of the hair with the front of the body. Attach the hair with 3 or 4 wraps of thread.

STEP 15: Pull the hair back and advance the thread forward to just behind the hook eye. Pull the hair forward and make 3 or 4 wraps of thread, securing the hair right behind the eye of the hook.

STEP 16: Trim the butts of the hair and return the thread to the original tie-in point.

STEP 17: Pull the hair back so it encompasses the hook shank and secure it with 2 or 3 wraps of thread.

STEP 18: Tighten the thread wraps so the collar flares and then make several more wraps of thread to secure the head and collar.

STEP 19: Whip-finish the thread at the back of the head and trim. Attach the thread at the eye of the hook and wrap a thread head. Use a whip-finish knot to secure the thread and trim. Apply some thinned Dave's Flexament to the thread wraps at the rear of the head and the top of the head. Finish the thread head with some Sally Hansen Hard as Nails. Side view.

Top view.

Compendium of Bullet-Head and Humpy Fly Patterns

The following flies are variations on bullet-head and Humpy fly patterns.

HI-VIS HUMPY

- **Hook:** #8-16 Tiemco 100
- **Thread:** Black UTC 70 for #12-16, UTC 140 for #8-10
- **Back/wing:** Nature's Spirit Humpy or All Purpose deer hair
- **Hackle:** Whiting High & Dry Hi-Vis; from left to right: pink, orange, chartreuse
- **Tail:** Nature's Spirit moose body hair

ROYAL HUMPY

- **Hook:** #8-16 Tiemco 100
- **Thread:** Red UTC 70 for #12-16, UTC 140 for #8-10
- **Back:** Natural Nature's Spirit Humpy or All Purpose deer hair
- **Wing:** White deer belly hair
- **Hackle:** Brown Whiting dry fly hackle
- **Tail:** Nature's Spirit moose body hair

PARACHUTE HUMPY

- **Hook:** #8-16 Tiemco 100
- **Thread:** Yellow UTC 70 for #12-16, UTC 140 for #8-10
- **Back:** Natural Nature's Spirit Humpy or All Purpose deer hair
- **Wing:** White deer belly hair
- **Hackle:** Barred dark ginger Whiting dry fly hackle
- **Tail:** Natural Nature's Spirit moose body hair

HUMPY TRUDE

- **Hook:** #8-16 Tiemco 100
- **Thread:** Yellow UTC 70 for #12-16, UTC 140 for #8-#10
- **Back/wing:** Nature's Spirit Humpy or All Purpose deer hair
- **Hackle:** Barred dark ginger Whiting dry fly hackle
- **Tail:** Nature's Spirit moose body hair

MADAM X

- **Hook:** #10-16 Tiemco 100
- **Thread:** Yellow or hopper yellow UTC 140
- **Tail/head/wing:** Natural Nature's Spirit All Purpose deer hair
- **Legs:** Speckled yellow Montana Fly Company Centipede Legs (medium)
- **Originator:** Doug Swisher

DEER HAIR BEETLE

- **Hook:** #10-16 Tiemco 100
- **Thread:** Black UTC 70
- **Back:** Black Nature's Spirit deer spinning hair
- **Body:** Peacock herl
- **Legs:** Black Hareline Round Rubber Legs (fine)

DEER HAIR INCH WORM

- **Hook:** #10-16 Tiemco 100
- **Thread:** Black UTC 70
- **Body:** Black Nature's Spirit deer spinning hair

CHAPTER 4

Bucktails

"Of all the artificial flies anglers collect, dress, trade, treasure, and use . . .
only one type hooks more and bigger fish consistently . . .
streamers and bucktails . . . the big fish flies."
JOSEPH D BATES JR., *STREAMERS AND BUCKTAILS: THE BIG FISH FLIES*

The use of bucktail in streamer fly patterns is a definitively North American concept. While it's difficult to determine the exact origins, the first use of bucktail in baitfish patterns certainly began in the Northeast, particularly Maine. Theodore Gordon, considered the father of American dry fly fishing, is best known for adapting British dry fly patterns to American rivers. However, he also popularized streamer fishing with his Bubble Puppy fly pattern.

Gordon began tying and experimenting with streamer fishing in the late 1800s, fishing not just for trout but for a variety of species including pike, striped bass, and other warmwater fish. Much like today's pike and muskie flies, the Bubble Puppy was not just a single pattern but a series of patterns that evolved over time and was customized for different fish. Many of Gordon's contemporary fly fishermen, like Edward Ringwood Hewitt and George LaBranche, focused on the imitation of aquatic insects as the source of trout food but they also fished streamer flies. Ruben Cross, another contemporary of Gordon's, was one of the first to put white bucktail under the hook shank to simulate the belly of a baitfish.

William Scripture, a lawyer from New York, was another early advocate of bucktail streamers. His early-20th-century bucktail streamers tended to be simpler, usually with a single-color wing. Scripture's bucktails certainly served as an early template for what we now consider a traditional bucktail streamer.

Quebec fly tier Charles Langevin is credited with originating one of the most recognizable bucktail patterns, the Mickey Finn, in the 1930s. This fly appeared in catalogs of the day as simply the Red and Yellow Bucktail. John Alden Knight, best known for creating the solunar tables, is credited with naming and popularizing the pattern. The Mickey Finn is one of those bucktail streamers that has survived for nearly a century and still appears to this day in many catalogs and in the fly bins of many shops.

Ray Bergman had a chapter on bucktails in his signature book *Trout* (1938). While William Scripture's bucktails were simple one-color patterns, Bergman favored color combinations. His favorites were two-color combinations, including brown and white, black and white, yellow and orange, and red and white. All of these color combinations were tied in the traditional style with a tinsel body of either gold or silver on hooks that ranged from 2X to 6X long in sizes ranging from 6 to 12. Finally, in classic Bergman style, he narrates a few tales of streamer fishing.

Joseph Bates Jr. is probably most responsible for codifying and popularizing streamer patterns, including bucktail fly patterns, with his books *Streamer Fly Tying and Fishing* (1950) and *Streamers and Bucktails* (1979). Bates chronicled the development of streamer and bucktail fly patterns from their early beginnings through the first half of the 20th century.

Present-day writers, fly tiers, and anglers have also contributed to the development of bucktail fly patterns. Bob Clouser's Deep Minnow is one of the most effective bucktail patterns in use today. As described in *Clouser's Flies* (2006), the pattern was first developed as a smallmouth fly. The Clouser Deep Minnow along with its many variations have probably accounted for more fish being caught in more types of water than any other bucktail fly tied today.

Together these authors, fly tiers, and anglers have advanced the idea of imitating the baitfish that are preyed upon by the many gamefish we pursue as fly fishers. With the availability of modern materials that those early tiers could not have imagined, we have an unprecedented ability to imitate natural prey fish as well as tie a host of attractor patterns.

Black-Nose Dace

Art Flick introduced the Black-Nose Dace bucktail streamer in 1969 with the publication of his book *New Streamside Guide to Naturals and Their Imitations* (1969). The theme of his book was the correlation of natural trout foods to the flies that imitate them. With this in mind, he developed and tied the Black-Nose Dace bucktail streamer. This fly imitated the baitfish that inhabited the Catskill rivers that he predominately fished. In the original description he advocated using polar bear and black bear hair, but conceded that bucktail was a suitable substitute. Since neither bear material is available or appropriate for use today, the pattern is tied with bucktail, which is readily available.

The fact that the Black-Nose Dace is still found in most fly catalogs today is a testament to its durability as a productive fly pattern. As tied here, the fly is modernized with the use of Hareline Ice Wing for the tail and UV epoxy for finishing the head.

TYING THE BLACK-NOSE DACE

- **Hook:** #4-10 Tiemco 9395
- **Thread:** Black UTC 140
- **Tail:** Red Hareline Ice Fur
- **Body:** Silver side of UTC Mylar Tinsel (medium) overwrapped with silver UTC French Tinsel (medium), coated with Loon UV Clear Fly Finish (thin or flow and thick), cured with a UV light)
- **Wing:** Nature's Spirit bucktail, brown over black over white

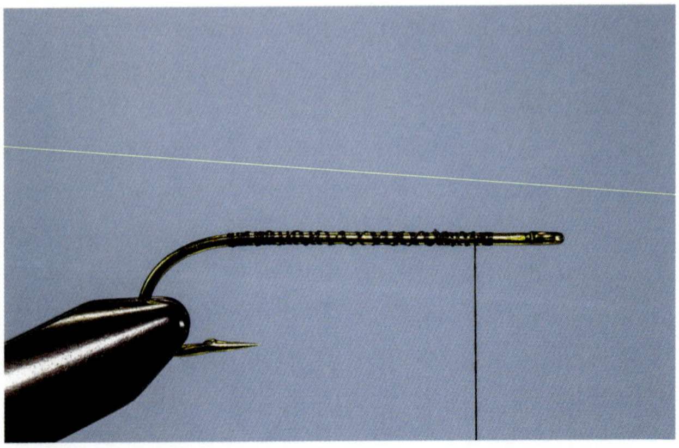

STEP 1: Start the thread one eye length behind the eye and wrap the thread back to the tie-in point of the hook. Wrap the thread back to the tie-in point at the front of the hook.

STEP 2: Cut a small amount of Ice Fur and attach at the tie-in point at the front of the hook shank. Pull the Ice Fur slightly towards you and wrap towards the back of the hook shank, attaching the Ice Fur to the top of the hook shank.

STEP 3: Return the thread to the tie-in point at the front of the hook and trim the tail even with the back of the bend in the hook.

STEP 4: Tie in the French Tinsel and attach it to the top of the hook shank. Return the thread to the tie-in point at the front of the hook shank.

STEP 5: Attach the Mylar Tinsel to the front of the hook shank. This tinsel has a gold side and a silver side. Since you want to use the silver side, attach the tinsel so the silver side is against the hook shank.

STEP 6: Pull the Mylar Tinsel up, creating a fold that exposes the silver side. While keeping some tension on the tinsel, wrap it to the back of the hook.

STEP 7: Wrap the Mylar Tinsel back to the front of the hook shank. Tie off and trim.

STEP 8: Wrap the French Tinsel, keeping an even space between each wrap. Tie off and trim.

STEP 9: Put a small coat of thin or flow Loon UV Clear Fly Finish on the body. Rotate the vise to allow the epoxy to flow evenly and cure with a UV light.

STEP 10: Cut a small bunch of white bucktail; comb out any short hairs and even the tips by using a stacker. Measure the bucktail so the majority of tips extend one hook gape behind the tail. Keeping that measurement, trade hands and trim the bucktail at that point.

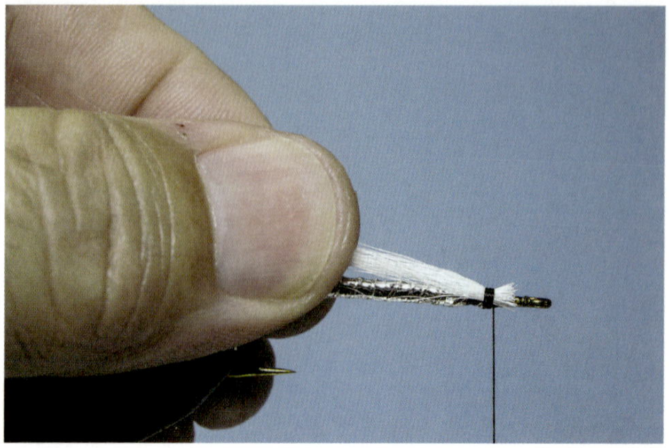

STEP 11: Attach the bucktail to the hook shank just behind the eye.

STEP 12: Brush a small amount of Zap-A-Gap on the thread and wrap the white bucktail, allowing the glue to flow into the hair. This will help to lock the hair in place, as bucktail can easily "shed" out of the fly when you begin to fish it.

STEP 13: Cut, prepare, measure, and trim a small amount of black bucktail in the same way as the white bucktail.

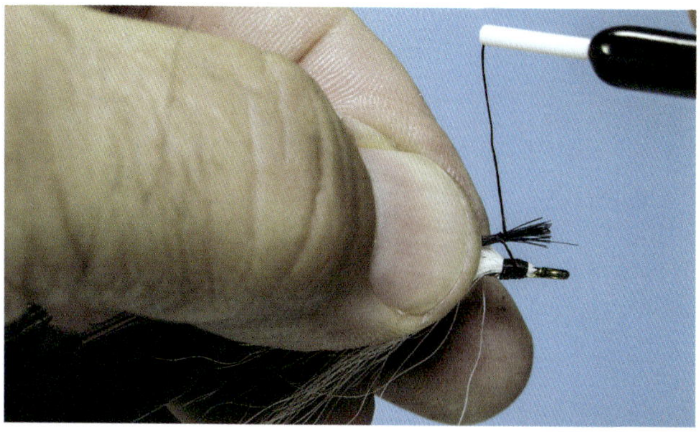

STEP 14: Make a wrap of thread around the butts of the black bucktail before pulling it down to the hook shank. This will keep the bucktail together as a bunch, making for a more-distinct black line through the fly. This is an optional step, and the bucktail could be attached to the fly in the same manner as the white bucktail.

STEP 15: Cut, prepare, measure, and trim a small amount of brown bucktail in the same way as the white bucktail. Attach it to the hook shank and brush a small amount of Zap-A-Gap on the thread. Wrap the thread, allowing the glue to flow into both the brown and black bucktail.

STEP 16: Finish the fly by wrapping a thread head. Whip-finish and trim the thread.

STEP 17: Apply a small amount of thick Loon UV Clear Fly Finish. Rotate the vise to allow the epoxy to flow evenly around the thread wraps. Be certain the eye of the hook remains free of the epoxy (clear the eye with a feather if some of the glue flows into the eye). Cure with a UV light.

Side view.

Fish-Mask Bucktail

While it is uncertain whether Joe Brooks actually created the Blonde series of bucktail flies, he is certainly credited with popularizing the pattern during the 1950s. The Blonde style of bucktail departed from the standard traditional bucktail by starting the fly with a bucktail tail. When compared to traditional bucktail flies, this created a larger profile on the same size hook. This tail can be thought of as an extension of either the belly color or the midline color of the baitfish. In the perch color that is tied here, I used yellow to extend the midline color. On other pattern colors like the juvenile bass, the tail color is an extension of the belly color.

The fly is finished with Flymen's Fish-Skull Fish-Mask. This creative head won Best of Show–Fly Tying Materials at the 2013 International Fly Tackle Dealer Show and Best Tying Material at the 2014 Outdoor Canada New Fly Fishing Gear Awards. The Fish-Mask is compatible with UV epoxies and makes creating heads quick and easy. I have tied many pike and muskie flies with the older, slower curing epoxies where you have to put the fly on a rotating wheel to cure. I really appreciate the ease with which the Fish-Mask head has allowed me to create attractive and effective heads on baitfish patterns.

TYING THE FISH-MASK BUCKTAIL (PERCH)

- **Hook:** #4 Tiemco 9395
- **Thread:** Black UTC 140
- **Tail:** Yellow Nature's Spirit bucktail
- **Body:** Gold side of UTC Mylar Tinsel (medium) overwrapped with gold UTC French Tinsel (medium), coated with Loon UV Clear Fly Finish (thin or flow, cured with a UV light)
- **Wing:** Yellow Nature's Spirit bucktail, with gold Hareline Ice Wing Fiber
- **Gills:** Minnow gills Dave Whitlock SLF Dubbing
- **Head:** Nature's Spirit bucktail (top: olive; bottom: orange over white); finished with a Flymen Fish-Skull Fish-Mask (#4) and wind Flymen Fish-Skull Living Eyes (4 mm); coated with Loon UV Clear Fly Finish (thin or flow and thick), cured with a UV light

STEP 1: Attach the thread at the front of the hook shank and wrap back to the tie-in point at the rear of the hook. Leave a space open behind the eye that is about ¼ of the hook shank long.

STEP 2: Cut a small bunch of yellow bucktail; comb out any short hairs and even the tips by using a stacker. Measure the hair so one shank length of hair extends behind the tie-in point at the back of the hook shank. Grasp the hair with your other hand at the front tie-in point and trim the butts.

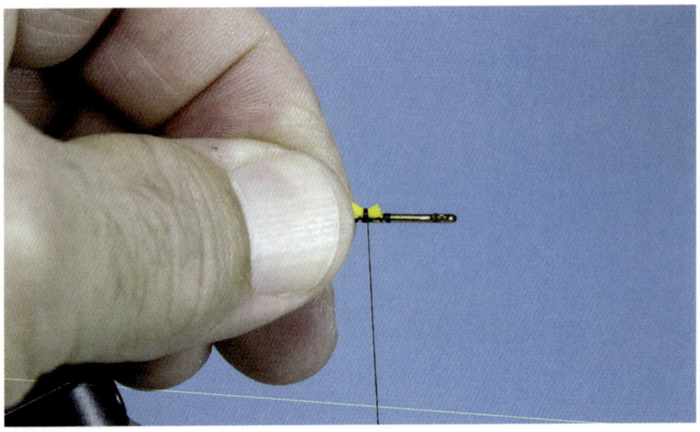

STEP 3: Tie in the butts of the bucktail. Keep tension on the hair and wrap back, keeping the hair on the top of the hook shank.

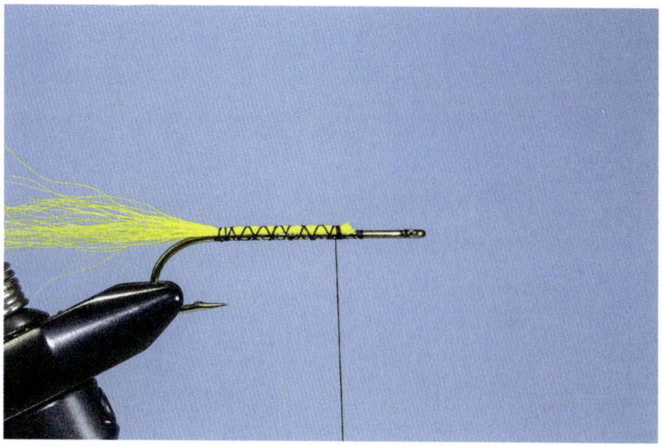

STEP 4: Wrap the thread back to the front tie-in point.

STEP 5: Attach the French Tinsel at the front tie-in point and wrap the thread to the back tie-in point, binding the tinsel to the top of the hook shank. Return the thread to the front tie-in point.

STEP 6: Attach the Mylar Tinsel to the front of the hook shank. This tinsel has a gold side and a silver side. Since you want to use the gold side, attach the tinsel so the gold side is against the hook shank. Pull the Mylar Tinsel up, creating a fold that exposes the gold side. While keeping some tension on the tinsel, wrap it to the back of the hook. Wrap the Mylar Tinsel back to the front of the hook shank; tie off and trim.

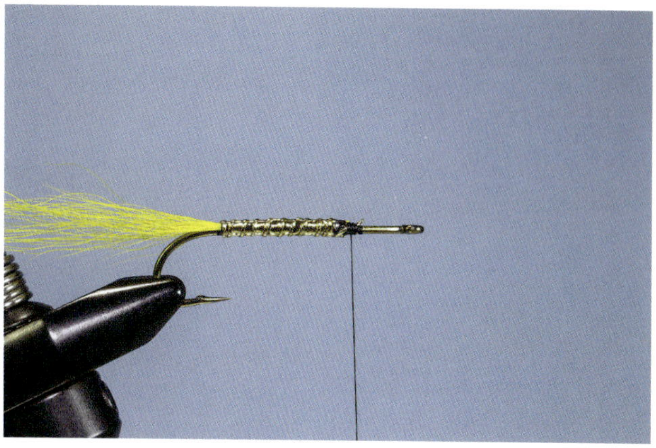

STEP 7: Wrap the French Tinsel forward, keeping an even space between each wrap; tie off and trim. Put a small coat of thin or flow Loon UV Clear Fly Finish on the body. Rotate the vise to allow the epoxy to flow evenly and cure with a UV light.

STEP 8: Cut and prepare a small amount of yellow bucktail. Measure the length equal to the back of the tail and trim.

STEP 9: Attach the yellow bucktail at the front tie-in point.

STEP 10: Apply a small amount of Zap-A-Gap to the thread. Wrap the butts of the bucktail with the thread.

STEP 11: Attach a small amount of Ice Wing Fiber at the front tie-in point.

STEP 12: Fold the Ice Wing Fiber back and tie off. Trim the material slightly longer than the bucktail wing.

STEP 13: Dub a small amount of the minnow gills SLF Dubbing over the wraps of thread at the front tie-in point.

STEP 14: Cut and prepare a small amount of white bucktail. Measure the bucktail so the majority of tips extend just behind the back tie-in point. Trade hands, grasping the hair at the measured point.

STEP 15: Trim the butts, leaving an additional length of bucktail equal to ¼ of the measured length.

STEP 16: Trade hands and reverse the hair so the butts are extending towards the back of the hook. Place the hair under the front of the hook with the butts up against the dubbing. Make a few wraps of thread to hold the hair in place.

STEP 17: Trade hands, grasping the butts of the hair. Make a few tight wraps to secure the hair to the bottom of the hook shank.

STEP 18: Side view of the secured bundle of white hair on the bottom of the hook shank.

STEP 19: Cut and prepare some olive bucktail. Measure a length equal to the length of the wing.

STEP 20: Trim the butts, leaving an additional length of bucktail equal to ¼ of the measured length.

STEP 21: Trade hands and reverse the hair so the butts are extending towards the back of the hook. Place the hair on the top of the hook with the butts up against the dubbing. Make a few wraps of thread to hold the hair in place. Treat the thread with some Zap-A-Gap and make a few wraps to secure the olive bucktail to the top of the hook shank and the white bucktail to the bottom.

STEP 22: Cut and prepare some orange bucktail. Measure a length about a hook gape shorter than the tail. Trim the same as the white and olive bucktail. Attach to the bottom of the hook shank in the same manner as the white bucktail.

STEP 23: Treat the thread with some Zap-A-Gap and make a few wraps to secure the orange bucktail. Use a whip-finish knot to finish and cut the thread. The bucktail should be separated with the olive on the top of the hook shank and the white and orange on the bottom. About an eye length of hook shank should be open behind the eye of the hook.

STEP 24: Fold the hair back, creating a bullet-shaped head. Apply a small amount of thick Loon UV Clear Fly Finish to the head.

STEP 25: Slide the Fish-Mask over the bullet head of hair. Reattach the thread at the front of the Fish-Mask and build a head of thread; whip-finish and cut the thread. Use a UV light to cure the epoxy under the Fish-Mask.

STEP 26: Apply a small amount of Zap-A-Gap to the eye socket and place a Flymen Living Eye in the socket. Rotate the vise and repeat on the opposite side.

STEP 27: Apply a small amount of thin or flow Loon UV Clear Fly Finish to the eye socket. Rotate the vise back and forth to allow the epoxy to flow around the eye, then cure with a UV light. Repeat on the opposite side.

STEP 28: Add another small coat of thin or flow Loon UV Clear Fly Finish to the eye socket and cure. Repeat on the opposite side.

STEP 29: Apply a small amount of thin or flow Loon UV Clear Fly Finish to the head thread wraps. If any epoxy gets into the eye, pull a feather through the eye to clear the glue. Use a UV light to cure the epoxy.

STEP 30: Using a permanent black marking pen, add some black bars to the top bucktail wing.

The Fish-Mask Bucktail (Perch).

BUILDING A MODERN BUCKTAIL STREAMER

While anglers have been trying to catch Great Lakes muskie on flies for a long time, the sport has developed an almost cultlike fanaticism in the last decade that mirrors the traditional tackle muskie world. I freely admit that I am a member of that cult. Fly fishing for muskie has been a highlight of my recent summers. Robert Tomes's *Muskie on the Fly* (2008) is one of the few books written about this exciting pursuit. It has been a constant summer companion and has taken on the dog-eared look of a well-traveled book.

While similar in appearance to pike, the muskie is far different in its behavior. The follow in muskie fishing, where the muskie will cruise behind your fly but not eat it, is a well-known phenomenon. Pike tend to be far more aggressive in chasing down and eating a fly. Fly fishing for either species usually requires large streamer fly patterns, which make liberal use of bucktail.

Flies that would have been considered large a decade ago are only average size today. With modern rods and lines, the ability to fish ever-larger fly patterns has become common. The key to designing large flies is to use materials in such a way as to give the appearance of a large fly, but be light enough to cast. Flies can quickly become overdressed, making them hard to cast even with the powerful rods in use today.

Traditional bucktail fly patterns have been around for many decades, some for more than a century. This has led to a codification of patterns with recognizable names like the Mickey Finn, Black-Nose Dace, and Lake Erie Shiner. With just the name alone, a very definite fly pattern comes to mind for most anglers. This is not the case, however, with the very large patterns being tied today. While there has been some attempt to name large fly patterns, the naming of recognizable patterns is in a far greater state of flux compared to traditional bucktails. An Internet search of any particular modern named muskie or pike fly brings up a host of images with no real consistent pattern.

Tying these streamer flies for muskie and pike is a creative process that uses innovative techniques and artistic materials. Most of these large patterns are created with some combination of four materials: bucktail, feathers, flash material, and some type of streamer hair (either natural or synthetic). Additionally there are some creative tying techniques that give the fly an appearance of size while still making it relatively easy to cast. ■

Yak Hair Bucktail

This pattern is a modest scaled-up version of the Fish-Mask Bucktail. The size 4 Fish-Mask Bucktail is about as large a fly as you can tie using only bucktail as the main material. The Yak Hair Bucktail is almost double the length of the Fish-Mask Bucktail and requires the addition of streamer hair. Yak hair is a natural streamer hair; it is somewhat translucent and looks great in the water. However, you could also substitute one of the many synthetic streamer hair materials that are available today.

TYING THE YAK HAIR BUCKTAIL (JUVENILE BASS)

- **Hook:** #2 Tiemco 9395
- **Thread:** Black UTC 140
- **Tail:** White Nature's Spirit bucktail
- **Body:** Gold side of UTC Mylar Tinsel (large) overwrapped with gold UTC French Tinsel (large), coated with Loon UV Clear Fly Finish (thin or flow, cured with a UV light)
- **Wing:** Black Spirit River yak streamer hair, with gold Hareline Ice Wing Fiber
- **Gills:** Minnow gills Dave Whitlock SLF Dubbing
- **Head:** Nature's Spirit bucktail (top: olive; bottom: white); finished with a Flymen Fish-Skull Fish-Mask (#5) and earth Flymen Fish-Scull Living Eyes (5 mm); coated with Loon UV Clear Fly Finish (thin or flow and thick, cured with a UV light)

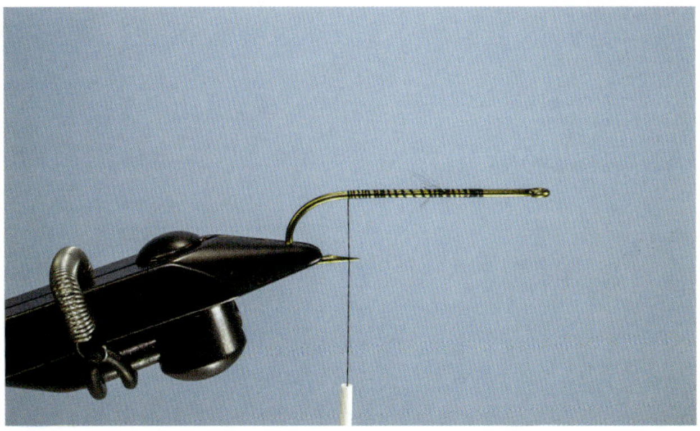

STEP 1: Attach the thread at the front of the hook shank and wrap back to the tie-in point at the rear of the hook. Leave a space open behind the eye that is about ¼ of the hook shank long.

STEP 2: Cut a small bunch of white bucktail; comb out any short hairs and even the tips by using a stacker. Measure the hair so one shank length of hair extends behind the tie-in point at the back of the hook shank. Grasp the hair with your other hand at the front tie-in point and trim the butts. Tie in the butts of the bucktail. Keep tension on the hair and wrap back, keeping the hair on the top of the hook shank. Wrap the thread back to the front tie-in point.

STEP 3: Attach the French Tinsel at the front tie-in point and wrap the thread to the back tie-in point, binding the tinsel to the top of the hook shank. Return the thread to the front tie-in point.

STEP 4: Attach the Mylar Tinsel to the front of the hook shank. This tinsel has a gold side and a silver

side. Since you want to use the gold side, attach the tinsel so the gold side is against the hook shank. Pull the Mylar Tinsel up, creating a fold that exposes the gold side. While keeping some tension on the tinsel, wrap it to the back of the hook. Wrap the Mylar Tinsel back to the front of the hook shank; tie off and trim.

STEP 5: Wrap the French Tinsel forward. Keep an even space between each wrap; tie off and trim.

STEP 6: Put a small coat of thin or flow Loon UV Clear Fly Finish on the body. Rotate the vise to allow the epoxy to flow evenly and cure with a UV light.

STEP 7: Select a small bunch of black yak streamer hair. The length should be slightly more than double the length of the hook shank and tail. Bind the hair down in the middle of the bunch at the front tie-in point.

STEP 8: Fold the hair back and bind with several wraps of thread. Trim the hair at an angle so it is slightly longer than the tail, creating a tapered wing.

STEP 9: Select a small bunch of gold Ice Wing Fiber. Attach it in the middle of the bunch similar to how you attached the yak hair.

STEP 10: Fold the Ice Wing Fiber back, working it around the yak hair, and tie down. Add a few drops of Zap-A-Gap to the thread and make a few more wraps, allowing the glue to flow into the yak hair and Ice Wing Fiber.

STEP 11: Dub some minnow gills SLF Dubbing over the glued wraps of thread. Advance the thread to the front of the hook shank and wrap a thread base. Return the thread to the center of the open portion of the hook shank.

STEP 12: Cut and prepare some white bucktail. Measure the bucktail so the majority of tips extend to about ½ the distance of the tail from the front of the hook shank.

STEP 13: Trim the butts, leaving an additional length of bucktail equal to ¼ of the measured length.

STEP 14: Place the hair under the front of the hook with the tips forward and butts up against the dubbing. Make a few wraps of thread to hold the hair in place.

STEP 15: Cut and prepare some olive bucktail. Measure a length equal to the length of the body and tail.

STEP 16: Trim the butts, leaving an additional length of bucktail equal to ¼ of the measured length.

STEP 17: Place the hair on the top of the front of the hook with the tips forward and butts up against the dubbing. Make a few wraps of thread to hold the hair in place. Treat the thread with some Zap-A-Gap and make a few wraps securing the olive bucktail to the top of the hook shank with the white bucktail at the bottom. Whip-finish and cut the thread. About an eye length of hook shank should be open behind the eye of the hook.

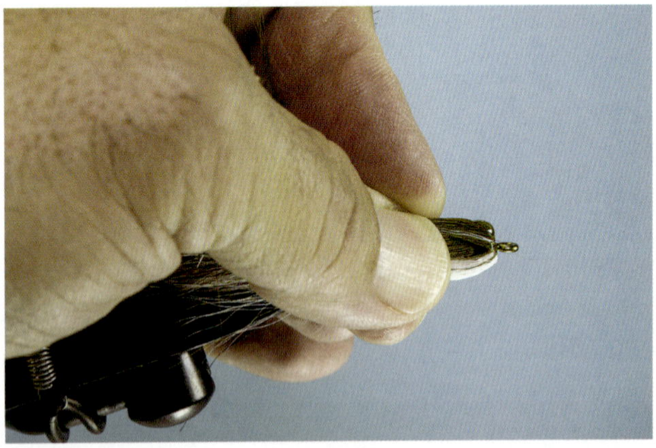

STEP 18: Fold the hair back, creating a bullet-shaped head. Apply a small amount of thick Loon UV Clear Fly Finish to the head.

STEP 19: Slide the Fish-Mask over the bullet head of hair. Reattach the thread at the front of the Fish-Mask and build a head of thread; whip-finish and cut the thread. Use a UV light to cure the epoxy under the Fish-Mask.

STEP 20: Apply a small amount of Zap-A-Gap to the eye socket and place a Flymen Living Eye in the socket. Rotate the vise and repeat on the opposite side. Apply a small amount of thin or flow Loon UV Clear Fly Finish to the eye socket. Rotate the vise back and forth to allow the epoxy to flow around the eye and cure with a UV light. Repeat on the opposite side. Add another small coat of thin or flow Loon UV Clear Fly Finish to the eye socket and cure. Repeat on the opposite side. Apply a small amount of thin or flow Loon UV Clear Fly Finish to the head thread wraps. If any epoxy gets into the eye, pull a feather through the eye, clearing the glue. Use a UV light to cure the epoxy. Use a permanent black marking pen to add some black bars to the top bucktail wing.

The Yak Hair Bucktail (Juvenile Bass).

Articulated Pike/Muskie Bucktail (Chartreuse and White)

The key to this pattern is to not overdress it. I have fished large muskie flies that were so heavy that they were a challenge to cast even with the 11-weight Sage Musky rod that I was using. Making use of body tubing, bucktail can be tied halo style or allowed to envelop the fly while being retrieved without too much material inside the halo of bucktail. This creates the illusion of a large fly without overdressing the fly pattern. Casting a 10- or 11-weight rod all day is difficult enough without adding an undue amount of weight to the end of the leader.

TYING THE ARTICULATED PIKE/MUSKIE BUCKTAIL (CHARTREUSE AND WHITE)

Tail

- **Hook:** #3/0 Daiichi 2461
- **Thread:** Black UTC 140 for tail, red for thread head
- **Tail:** White Nature's Spirit bucktail
- **Body:** Silver side of UTC Mylar Tinsel (large) overwrapped with silver UTC French Tinsel (large), coated with Loon UV Clear Fly Finish (flow, cured with a UV light); clear Flymen Fish-Skull Blane Chocklett's Body Tubing (⅛ inch)
- **Wing:** Chartreuse Spirit River yak streamer hair; fluorescent chartreuse Hareline Ice Wing Fiber; grizzly dyed chartreuse Whiting schlappen; Nature's Spirit bucktail, chartreuse over white
- **Glues:** Zap-A-Gap for starting thread at tie-in point and securing tubing and bucktail; Loon UV Clear Fly Finish (thick) for thread head

Body

- **Articulated shank:** Blane Chocklett's Articulated Big Game Shank (40 mm)
- **Thread:** Black UTC 140
- **Body:** Clear Flymen Fish-Skull Blane Chocklett's Body Tubing (¼ inch); Nature's Spirit bucktail, chartreuse over white; pearl Hareline Cactus Chenille (large)
- **Gills:** Red Hareline Ice Fur
- **Head:** Hareline Ice Wing Fiber, fluorescent chartreuse over pearl; Nature's Spirit bucktail, chartreuse over white; Flymen Fish-Skull Fish-Mask (#7); wind or fire Flymen Fish-Skull Living Eyes (7 mm)
- **Glues:** Zap-A-Gap for starting thread at tie-in point and securing tubing, bucktail, and eyes; Loon UV Clear Fly Finish (thick under the head, thin over the head)

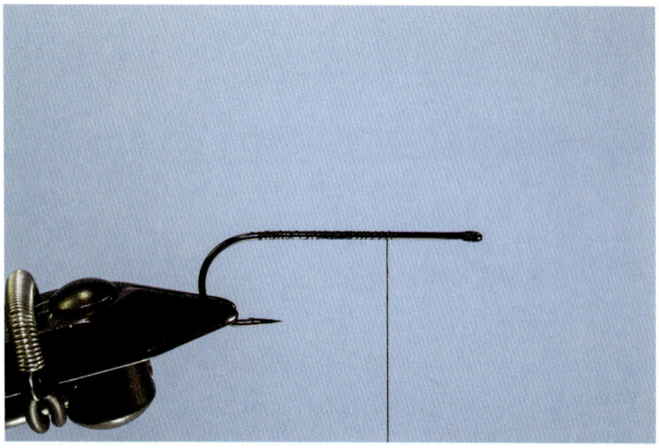

STEP 1: Attach the black thread at the rear tie-in point. Wrap forward ⅔ of the hook shank length.

STEP 2: Cut, prep, and stack a bunch of white bucktail. Measure the length of the tail so it extends 1 to 1¼ of the length of the hook shank behind the rear tie-in point. Return the thread to the front of the bucktail.

STEP 3: Create a Mylar Tinsel and French Tinsel body. Coat with the thin UV epoxy and cure with a UV light. Tie off the thread and trim.

STEP 4: Cut a piece of ⅛-inch body tubing equal to the length of the Mylar body. Slide the tubing onto the body and restart the thread. Attach the tubing to the hook shank directly in front of the Mylar body with several thread wraps and add a few drops of Zap-A-Gap.

STEP 5: Push the tubing forward, creating a cone with the open end facing forward. Make several wraps of thread and then add several drops of Zap-A-Gap to the thread wraps. Use a whip-finish knot to tie off the thread and trim.

STEP 6: Push the tubing back to create a cone shape with the open end facing the rear of the hook shank.

STEP 7: Reattach the thread. Cut a small bunch of yak hair. Pull the fibers to create a tapered end. Trim the opposite end so the bunch is 3 times the length of the hook shank. Attach the trimmed end to the hook shank directly in front of the tubing.

STEP 8: Attach a small amount of the Ice Wing Fiber over the yak hair.

STEP 9: Attach 2 schlappen feathers, one to each side of the hook shank. The feathers should extend back to a length equal to the length of the yak hair.

STEP 10: Clean and prep some white bucktail. Attach the white bucktail to the bottom of the hook shank. Repeat with chartreuse bucktail on the top of the hook shank. Apply a few drops of Zap-A-Gap and make several more wraps of thread through the glued area. Use a whip-finish knot to tie off the thread and trim.

STEP 11: Attach the red thread and create a thread head. Use a whip-finish knot to tie off the thread and trim. Apply some thick Loon UV Clear Fly Finish to the thread head. Rotate the fly to allow the resin to flow around the thread head and cure with a UV light.

STEP 12: Attach the large end of the articulated shank to the eye of the hook. Apply a thin coat of Zap-A-Gap to the shank and wrap a thread base using the black thread.

STEP 13: Cut a piece of the ¼-inch body tubing equal to the length of the shank. Attach the rear end of the tubing to the rear of the shank with several wraps of thread.

STEP 14: Push the tubing back to create a cone shape with the open end facing the rear of the shank. Make several wraps of thread over the end of the tubing and add several drops of Zap-A-Gap to the thread wraps.

STEP 15: Clean and prep some white bucktail. Attach the white bucktail to the bottom of the hook shank. Repeat with the chartreuse bucktail on the top of the hook shank. Apply a few drops of Zap-A-Gap and make several more wraps of thread through the glued area.

STEP 16: Attach the Cactus Chenille in front of the bucktail. Wrap a chenille body over the thread wraps. Trim the chenille and make several more wraps of thread.

STEP 17: Cut a small piece of the red Ice Fur. Attach it so each end extends along the side of the hook shank. Trim the Ice Fur even with the back end of the chenille body.

STEP 18: Attach some pearl Ice Wing Fiber to the bottom of the hook shank so the longer length extends to the front. Repeat with the chartreuse Ice Wing Fiber on the top of the hook shank.

STEP 19: Clean and prep some white bucktail. Attach the white bucktail to the bottom of the hook shank with the tips facing forward and the butts against the front of the chenille body. Repeat with the chartreuse bucktail on the top of the hook shank. Wrap a thread band that extends forward to just behind the eye of the shank. Apply a few drops of Zap-A-Gap and make several more wraps of thread through the glued area. Use a whip-finish knot to tie off the thread and trim.

STEP 20: Sweep the Ice Fiber and bucktail back, keeping the chartreuse on the top of the shank and the white on the bottom. Apply some thick Loon UV Clear Fly Finish to the top of the chartreuse bucktail.

STEP 21: While holding the bucktail back, slide the Fish-Mask over the eye of the shank. Hold the mask in place and restart the thread directly in front. Wrap a thread head that prevents the mask from sliding forward. Use a UV light to cure the resin under the Fish-Mask.

STEP 22: Place a small amount of Zap-A-Gap in each eye socket and place the eyes on each side. Brush a thin coat of flow Loon UV Clear Fly Finish over the head and thread wraps, then cure with a UV light. More than one coat can be applied if desired.

Side view.

Compendium of Bucktail Fly Patterns

Traditional Bucktails

SCRIPTURE SINGLE-COLOR BUCKTAIL

- **Hook:** #4-10 Tiemco 9395
- **Thread:** Black UTC 140
- **Tail:** Red Hareline Ice Fur
- **Body:** Silver or gold side of UTC Mylar Tinsel (medium) overwrapped with silver or gold UTC French Tinsel (medium), coated with Loon UV Clear Fly Finish (thin or flow, cured with a UV light)
- **Wing:** Nature's Spirit bucktail or Wapsi bucktail; top to bottom, left to right: white, black, chartreuse, olive, shad gray
- **Head:** Black thread coated with Loon UV Clear Fly Finish (thick, cured with a UV light)

MICKEY FINN

- **Hook:** #4-10 Tiemco 9394
- **Thread:** Black UTC 140
- **Body:** Silver UTC Mylar Tinsel (medium) overwrapped with silver UTC French Tinsel (medium), coated with Loon UV Clear Fly Finish (thin or flow, cured with a UV light)
- **Wing:** Nature's Spirit bucktail or Wapsi bucktail, yellow over red over yellow
- **Head:** Black thread coated with Loon UV Clear Fly Finish (thick, cured with a UV light)

ROYAL COACHMAN

- **Hook:** #4-10 Tiemco 9395
- **Thread:** Black UTC 140
- **Tail:** Golden pheasant tail fibers
- **Body:** Peacock herl, red floss
- **Wing:** White Nature's Spirit bucktail or Wapsi bucktail
- **Throat:** Variant Whiting 4 B's hen saddle
- **Head:** Black thread coated with Loon UV Clear Fly Finish (thick, cured with a UV light)

LAKE ERIE SHINER

- **Hook:** #4-10 Tiemco 9394
- **Thread:** Olive UTC 140
- **Body:** White floss overwrapped with pearl Saltwater Flashabou
- **Wing:** Nature's Spirit bucktail or Wapsi bucktail, dark olive over light olive; olive Hareline Ice Fiber
- **Throat:** Nature's Spirit bucktail or Wapsi bucktail, blue over white
- **Head:** Olive thread coated with Loon UV Clear Fly Finish (thick, cured with a UV light)
- **Originator:** Floyd Franke

BLACK GHOST BUCKTAIL

- **Hook:** #4-10 Tiemco 9395
- **Thread:** Black UTC 140
- **Tail:** Yellow Nature's Spirit bucktail or Wapsi bucktail
- **Body:** Black floss overwrapped with silver UTC French Tinsel (medium), coated with Loon UV Clear Fly Finish (thin or flow, cured with a UV light)
- **Wing:** White Nature's Spirit bucktail or Wapsi bucktail
- **Throat:** Yellow Nature's Spirit bucktail or Wapsi bucktail

Fish-Mask Bucktails

MICKEY FINN

- **Hook:** #4 Tiemco 9394
- **Thread:** Black UTC 140
- **Tail:** Red Nature's Spirit bucktail
- **Body:** Silver side of UTC Mylar Tinsel (medium) overwrapped with silver UTC French Tinsel (medium), coated with Loon UV Clear Fly Finish (thin or flow, cured with a UV light)
- **Wing:** Red Nature's Spirit bucktail, with red Hareline Ice Wing Fiber
- **Gills:** Minnow gills Dave Whitlock SLF Dubbing
- **Head:** Nature's Spirit bucktail (top: yellow; bottom: yellow); finished with a Flymen Fish-Skull Fish-Mask (#4) and fire Flymen Fish-Scull Living Eyes (4 mm); Loon UV Clear Fly Finish (thin or flow, cured with a UV light)

JUVENILE BASS

- **Hook:** #4 Tiemco 9395
- **Thread:** Black UTC 140
- **Tail:** Black Nature's Spirit bucktail
- **Body:** Gold side of UTC Mylar Tinsel (medium) overwrapped with gold UTC French Tinsel (medium), coated with Loon UV Clear Fly Finish (thin or flow, cured with a UV light)
- **Wing:** Black Nature's Spirit bucktail, with gold Hareline Ice Wing Fiber
- **Gills:** Minnow gills Dave Whitlock SLF Dubbing
- **Head:** Nature's Spirit bucktail (top: olive; bottom: white); finished with a Flymen Fish-Skull Fish-Mask (#4) and earth Flymen Fish-Scull Living Eyes (4 mm); Loon UV Clear Fly Finish (thin or flow, cured with a UV light)

SHAD

- **Hook:** #4 Tiemco 9394
- **Thread:** Black UTC 140
- **Tail:** Black Nature's Spirit bucktail
- **Body:** Silver side of UTC Mylar Tinsel (medium) overwrapped with silver UTC French Tinsel (medium), coated with Loon UV Clear Fly Finish (thin or flow, cured with a UV light)
- **Wing:** Black Nature's Spirit bucktail, with pearl Hareline Ice Wing Fiber
- **Gills:** Minnow gills Dave Whitlock SLF Dubbing
- **Head:** Nature's Spirit bucktail (top: black; bottom: white); finished with a Flymen Fish-Skull Fish-Mask (#4) and ice Flymen Fish-Skull Living Eyes (4 mm); Loon UV Clear Fly Finish (thin or flow, cured with a UV light)

RED AND WHITE

- **Hook:** #4 Tiemco 9394
- **Thread:** Black UTC 140
- **Tail:** White Nature's Spirit bucktail
- **Body:** Silver side of UTC Mylar Tinsel (medium) overwrapped with silver UTC French Tinsel (medium), coated with Loon UV Clear Fly Finish (thin or flow, cured with a UV light)
- **Wing:** Red Nature's Spirit bucktail, with red Hareline Ice Wing Fiber
- **Gills:** Minnow gills Dave Whitlock SLF Dubbing
- **Head:** Nature's Spirit bucktail (top: red; bottom: white); finished with a Flymen Fish-Skull Fish-Mask (#4) and fire Flymen Fish-Skull Living Eyes (4 mm); Loon UV Clear Fly Finish (thin or flow, cured with a UV light)

CHARTREUSE AND WHITE

- **Hook:** #4 Tiemco 9394
- **Thread:** Black UTC 140
- **Tail:** White Nature's Spirit bucktail
- **Body:** Silver side of UTC Mylar Tinsel (medium) overwrapped with silver UTC French Tinsel (medium), coated with Loon UV Clear Fly Finish (thin or flow, cured with a UV light)
- **Wing:** Chartreuse Nature's Spirit bucktail, with chartreuse Hareline Ice Wing Fiber
- **Gills:** Minnow gills Dave Whitlock SLF Dubbing
- **Head:** Nature's Spirit bucktail (top: chartreuse; bottom: white); finished with a Flymen Fish-Skull Fish-Mask (#4) and fire Flymen Fish-Skull Living Eyes (4 mm); Loon UV Clear Fly Finish (thin or flow, cured with a UV light)

FIRE TIGER

- **Hook:** #4 Tiemco 9394
- **Thread:** Black UTC 140
- **Tail:** Yellow Nature's Spirit bucktail
- **Body:** Gold side of UTC Mylar Tinsel (medium) overwrapped with gold UTC French Tinsel (medium), coated with Loon UV Clear Fly Finish (thin or flow, cured with a UV light)
- **Wing:** Yellow Nature's Spirit bucktail, with gold Hareline Ice Wing Fiber
- **Gills:** Minnow gills Dave Whitlock SLF Dubbing
- **Head:** Nature's Spirit bucktail (top: chartreuse spotted with Winsor & Newton Black Indian Ink; bottom: orange); finished with a Flymen Fish-Skull Fish-Mask (#4) and fire Flymen Fish-Skull Living Eyes (4 mm); Loon UV Clear Fly Finish (thin or flow, cured with a UV light)

LAKE ERIE SHINER

- **Hook:** #4 Tiemco 9394
- **Thread:** Black UTC 140
- **Tail:** White Nature's Spirit bucktail
- **Body:** White floss overwrapped with pearl Wapsi Saltwater Flashabou, coated with Loon UV Clear Fly Finish (thin or flow, cured with a UV light)
- **Wing:** Light olive Nature's Spirit bucktail, with pearl Hareline Ice Wing Fiber
- **Gills:** Minnow gills Dave Whitlock SLF Dubbing
- **Head:** Nature's Spirit bucktail (top: olive; bottom: blue over white); finished with a Flymen Fish-Skull Fish-Mask (#4) and ice Flymen Fish-Skull Living Eyes (4 mm); Loon UV Clear Fly Finish (thin or flow, cured with a UV light)
- **Originator:** Variation of a Floyd Franke pattern

Yak Hair Bucktails

PERCH

- **Hook:** #2 Tiemco 9395
- **Thread:** Black UTC 140
- **Tail:** Yellow Nature's Spirit bucktail
- **Body:** Gold side of UTC Mylar Tinsel (large) overwrapped with gold UTC French Tinsel (large), coated with Loon UV Clear Fly Finish (thin or flow, cured with a UV light)
- **Wing:** Yellow Spirit River yak streamer hair, with gold Hareline Ice Wing Fiber
- **Gills:** Minnow gills Dave Whitlock SLF Dubbing
- **Head:** Nature's Spirit bucktail (top: olive; bottom: white over orange); finished with a Flymen Fish-Skull Fish-Mask (#5) and wind Flymen Fish-Skull Living Eyes (5 mm); Loon UV Clear Fly Finish (thin or flow, cured with a UV light)

SHAD

- **Hook:** #2 Tiemco 9395
- **Thread:** Black UTC 140
- **Tail:** White Nature's Spirit bucktail
- **Body:** Silver side of UTC Mylar Tinsel (large) overwrapped with silver UTC French Tinsel (large), coated with Loon UV Clear Fly Finish (thin or flow, cured with a UV light)
- **Wing:** Black Spirit River yak streamer hair, with pearl Hareline Ice Wing Fiber
- **Gills:** Minnow gills Dave Whitlock SLF Dubbing
- **Head:** Nature's Spirit bucktail or Wapsi bucktail (top: shad gray; bottom: white); finished with a Flymen Fish-Skull Fish-Mask (#5) and ice Flymen Fish-Skull Living Eyes (5 mm); Loon UV Clear Fly Finish (thin or flow, cured with a UV light)

FIRE TIGER

- **Hook:** #2 Tiemco 9395
- **Thread:** Black UTC 140
- **Tail:** Yellow Nature's Spirit bucktail
- **Body:** Gold side of UTC Mylar Tinsel (large) overwrapped with gold UTC French Tinsel (large), coated with Loon UV Clear Fly Finish (thin or flow, cured with a UV light)
- **Wing:** Yellow Spirit River yak streamer hair, with gold Hareline Ice Wing Fiber
- **Gills:** Minnow gills Dave Whitlock SLF Dubbing
- **Head:** Nature's Spirit bucktail (top: chartreuse spotted with Winsor & Newton Black Indian Ink; bottom: orange); finished with a Flymen Fish-Skull Fish-Mask (#5) and fire Flymen Fish-Skull Living Eyes (5 mm); Loon UV Clear Fly Finish (thin or flow, cured with a UV light)

LAKE ERIE SHINER

- **Hook:** #2 Tiemco 9395
- **Thread:** Black UTC 140
- **Tail:** White Nature's Spirit bucktail
- **Body:** White floss overwrapped with pearl Wapsi Saltwater Flashabou, coated with Loon UV Clear Fly Finish (thin or flow, cured with a UV light)
- **Wing:** Olive Spirit River yak streamer hair, with pearl Hareline Ice Wing Fiber
- **Gills:** Minnow gills Dave Whitlock SLF Dubbing
- **Head:** Nature's Spirit bucktail (top: olive; bottom: blue over white); finished with a Flymen Fish-Skull Fish-Mask (#5) and ice Flymen Fish-Skull Living Eyes (5 mm); Loon UV Clear Fly Finish (thin or flow, cured with a UV light)
- **Originator:** Variation of a Floyd Franke pattern

Articulated Pike/Muskie Bucktails

BASS

Tail

- **Hook:** #3/0 Daiichi 2461
- **Thread:** Black UTC 140 for tail, red for thread head
- **Tail:** White Nature's Spirit bucktail
- **Body:** Gold side of UTC Mylar Tinsel (large) overwrapped with gold UTC French Tinsel (large), coated with Loon UV Clear Fly Finish (flow, cured with a UV light); black Flymen Fish-Skull Blane Chocklett's Body Tubing (⅛ inch)
- **Wing:** Black Spirit River yak streamer hair; gold Hareline Ice Wing Fiber; grizzly dyed olive Whiting schlappen; Nature's Spirit bucktail, olive over white
- **Glues:** Zap-A-Gap for starting thread at tie-in point and securing tubing and bucktail; Loon UV Clear Fly Finish (thick) for thread head

Body

- **Articulated shank:** Blane Chocklett's Articulated Big Game Shank (40 mm)
- **Thread:** Black UTC 140 for tail, red for thread head
- **Body:** Black Flymen Fish-Skull Blane Chocklett's Body Tubing (¼ inch); Nature's Spirit bucktail, olive over white; gold Hareline UV Polar Chenille
- **Gills:** Red Hareline Ice Fur
- **Head:** Pearl Hareline Ice Wing Fiber; Nature's Spirit bucktail, olive over white; Flymen Fish-Skull Fish-Mask (#7); earth Flymen Fish-Skull Living Eyes (7 mm)

- **Glues:** Zap-A-Gap for starting thread at tie-in point and securing tubing, bucktail, and eyes; Loon UV Clear Fly Finish (under the head: thick; over the head: thin)

PERCH

Tail

- **Hook:** #3/0 Daiichi 2461
- **Thread:** Black UTC 140 for tail, red for thread head
- **Tail:** Yellow Nature's Spirit bucktail
- **Body:** Gold side of UTC Mylar Tinsel (large) overwrapped with gold UTC French Tinsel (large), coated with Loon UV Clear Fly Finish (flow, cured with a UV light); yellow Flymen Fish-Skull Blane Chocklett's Body Tubing (⅛ inch)
- **Wing:** Yellow Spirit River yak streamer hair; yellow Hareline Ice Dub Shimmer Fringe; grizzly dyed yellow Whiting schlappen; Nature's Spirit bucktail, olive over orange
- **Glues:** Zap-A-Gap for starting thread at tie-in point and securing tubing and bucktail; Loon UV Clear Fly Finish (thick) for thread head

Body

- **Articulated shank:** Blane Chocklett's Articulated Big Game Shank (40 mm)
- **Thread:** Hopper yellow UTC 140,
- **Body:** Yellow Flymen Fish-Skull Blane Chocklett's Body Tubing (¼ inch); Nature's Spirit bucktail, olive over orange; yellow Hareline Polar Chenille
- **Gills:** Red Hareline Ice Fur
- **Head:** Yellow Hareline Ice Dub Shimmer Fringe; Nature's Spirit bucktail, olive over orange and white); Flymen Fish-Skull Fish-Mask (#7); wind Flymen Fish-Skull Living Eyes (7 mm)
- **Glues:** Zap-A-Gap for starting thread at tie-in point and securing tubing, bucktail, and eyes; Loon UV Clear Fly Finish (under the head: thick; over the head, thin)

CHAPTER 5

Techniques for Spinning and Flaring Deer Hair

"Skill at the riverside, or at the fly-tying table, never came, nor ever will come to us by any road than that of practice."

GEORGE M. KELSON, *THE SALMON FLY*

Flaring or spinning deer hair seems to be that one technique that challenges many fly tiers. While it does require some practice, selecting the right materials and tools is essential for success. Choosing the right hair for spinning and using the proper thread are key.

Selecting the Proper Hair

When selecting hair for any spinning or flaring purpose, look for hair that has a crinkled appearance in the individual shafts. The hair should also have a soft or sponge-like feel to it. Both of these characteristics are identifiers for the cellular structure that makes the hair buoyant and allows it to flare when compressed with thread.

For most trout patterns like Muddlers and hoppers, use hair that is labeled as **general purpose hair** or **Humpy hair.** When selecting a piece, look for hair that has even tips, as many of these fly patterns incorporate a hair collar. For larger heads, look for hair that is labeled as **spinning hair.** This is typically late season whitetail deer hair that is about 2 inches long. The spinning characteristics are more important than having even tips, although some of these larger patterns do incorporate hair collars. For the largest hair heads, use hair labeled as **spinning cow elk.** This is typically the longest hair and the individual shafts of hair are normally larger than whitetail hair. (See "Hair" in chapter 1, "Tools and Materials.")

Note the crinkled appearance of the hair. This hair will flare and spin easily.

Gel-Spun Thread

One of the main frustrations in spinning hair is having the thread break. While lighter denier nylon thread works well for flaring the hair in a hair-wing dun pattern, it is impractical to expect that same thread to work in spinning a Muddler-style head or a large bass bug head. You can use heavier denier nylon threads for hair work, but to get a thread that has sufficient strength you are adding a lot of thread bulk to the fly. Some tiers have used Kevlar threads for hair work, but I find that this is a rather sharp thread that can cut hair when pressure is applied.

The best thread for spinning hair is gel-spun thread. Gel-spun thread is much stronger than nylon thread of the same size but is softer than Kevlar thread, so it isn't as prone to cutting the hair. UTC GSP thread from Wapsi is the thread I use most often. A 75- or 100-denier is the thread of choice for Muddler or hopper heads. A 130-denier is the main thread for most spun deer hair heads. Use a 200-denier for the largest deer hair heads. For most fly patterns, step-tie the bodies (see sidebar "Step Tying Large Flies" in chapter 7) using appropriate-size nylon thread, and then complete the deer hair work with the gel-spun thread. Since most of the flies will be finished with a nylon thread head, color in the GSP threads is not important. For that reason, I only use white GSP thread.

While a waxed nylon thread will adhere to the hook shank using a jam knot with a few turns of thread, gel-spun threads are very slippery and will not behave the same way. Zap-A-Gap glue should be used to start the GSP thread and to tie it off.

Once the gel-spun thread is attached to the hook, wrap a thread base on the bare hook shank where the deer hair work will be done. At one time it was believed that you needed to have a bare hook shank in order to spin deer hair. However, this is not the case, and most deer hair tiers today use a thread base for spinning and flaring deer hair. It helps to control the hair as it is spun or flared on the hook shank. Additionally when using a hair-packing tool, the thread will facilitate the movement of the hair as it is packed. Also, if glue is used where the hair is attached to the hook shank then the thread base will help to wick the glue back, securing the hair to the hook. I use a thread base for all of my spinning or flaring hair techniques.

Wapsi UTC GSP (spooled on a Rite CerMag bobbin) used with Zap-A-Gap glue is the proper thread to spin or flare deer hair.

SELECTING THE RIGHT AMOUNT OF HAIR

A stack of hair consists of the bundles of hair flared on the bottom, top, or side of a body with the thread wrapped in the same plane.

To successfully create a spun or flared deer hair head, one consideration is how much hair to use in each bundle. As a general rule, cutting off a bunch of hair that is about the diameter of a lead pencil is often used as a guide. While this works most of the time, it isn't an absolute rule.

For all but the smallest bass bugs, I like to get three stacks of hair on the body. When using a Tiemco 8089 bass stinger hook or an equivalent in a size 10, if three stacks of hair are going to be used, each bunch of hair selected for the stack must be smaller than the diameter of a pencil. Additionally for smaller bass bugs, use fewer bunches of hair per stack, as the cumulative amount of hair will prevent the ability to get three stacks of hair on the body. If tying bass bugs on hooks smaller than a size 10, a much simpler color scheme is needed, perhaps a single color and fewer stacks.

When approaching the final stack for the front of the body, the amount of hair selected may have to be modified to accommodate the space left on the hook. Ideally for bodies using three stacks of hair, each stack uses one-third of the space for the body and the stacks that create the color bars or rings of hair are all the same size. In practice this often doesn't happen, so for the final stack the amount of hair must be adjusted to finish at a point that allows for an appropriate-size thread head.

If too much space is left when you finish the final stack, the thread head will be too big (the thread head should be the same size as the diameter of the hook eye). To correct this, a small amount of hair should be spun on the hook shank to adjust the space for the thread head to the proper size.

(continued on next page)

This smaller bass bug is tied on a size 10 Tiemco 8089 hook. In order to have three stacks of hair, each stack had to be composed of smaller bunches of hair.

This larger bass bug is tied on a size 2/0 Gamakatsu B10S hook. Note that there are four stacks of hair on this bug. I made the last stack smaller to adjust to the remaining space on the hook.

This deer hair bass bug has a moderately dense head. It still has excellent floating properties.

This deer hair popper has a much more densely stacked head. Density is controlled by how much hair you use in each bunch and how closely you trim the head to the hook shank.

In contrast, when tying very large deer hair heads, larger bunches of hair are selected and used. For large heads, hair bunches that are three to four pencil diameters can be selected. Normally I would use a 200-denier GSP thread for working with these larger quantities of hair. When stacking large quantities of hair, attention should be paid to balancing the amount of hair on opposing sides of the hook shank. If you only use one bunch of hair on the bottom of the fly and multiple bunches of hair on the top, the hair will migrate around to the bottom of the hook shank. If you want to maintain the belly color, additional bunches of hair should be added to the bottom to offset the hair on the top of the hook shank.

Another consideration when creating deer hair heads is how densely the head is packed. Most of the heads I tie have a moderately high density of hair. If you look at the head, especially at the front of the hair bug, you will see some space between the individual hairs. Sometimes heads will be so dense that there is no space between the individual hairs, so it looks like a solid material. Density has a function but is also a personal preference. The heads need to be dense enough to float and be durable. Stacking and packing heads to the point that no space is left between the individual hairs is not necessary for creating a fishable fly, but as long as the fly has the desired flotation, it becomes a matter of personal choice. ■

Cutting and Prepping Hair for a Collar

Here are the steps for preparing a bunch of hair for a hair collar. The hair used is a piece of general purpose hair.

STEP 1: Using your scissor tips, separate the desired amount of hair.

STEP 2: Always cut the hair right at its base next to the hide.

STEP 3: Comb out the underfur.

STEP 4: Place the hair in a stacker tips down. Grasp the stacker with your thumb and middle finger and place your index finger on the top of the stacker. Tap it against the desktop to align the tips.

STEP 5: This is a properly stacked bunch of hair. Note the alignment of the tips. With the opposite hand, pull the hair out of the stacker, keeping the tips aligned.

STEP 6: Grasp the hair so the butts are exposed while keeping the tips aligned.

STEP 7: Trim the butts. This bunch of hair is now ready to be placed on a hook shank.

Cutting and Prepping Hair for Spinning or Flaring

Here are the steps for preparing a bunch of hair for flaring or spinning. The hair used is a piece of spinning deer hair (natural).

STEP 1: Cut a bunch of hair from the hide and comb out the underfur.

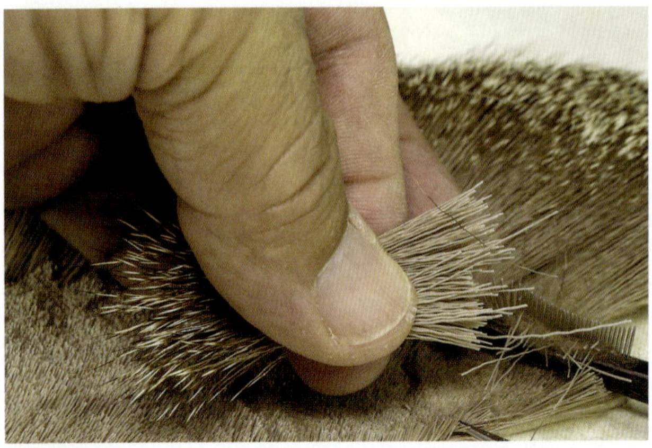

STEP 2: Using your thumb and forefinger, adjust the hair so both the tips and butts are exposed.

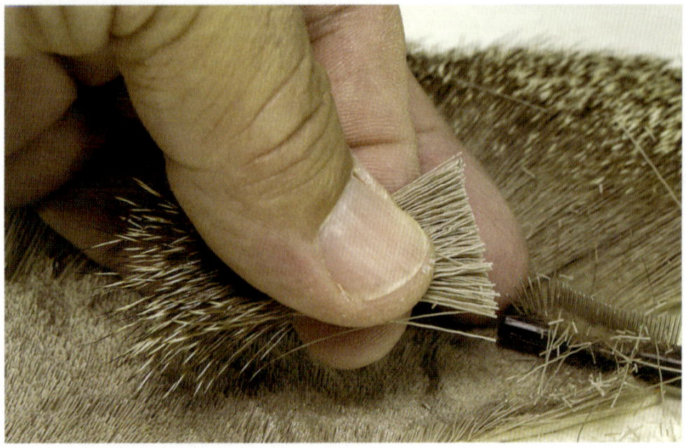

STEP 3: Trim the butts.

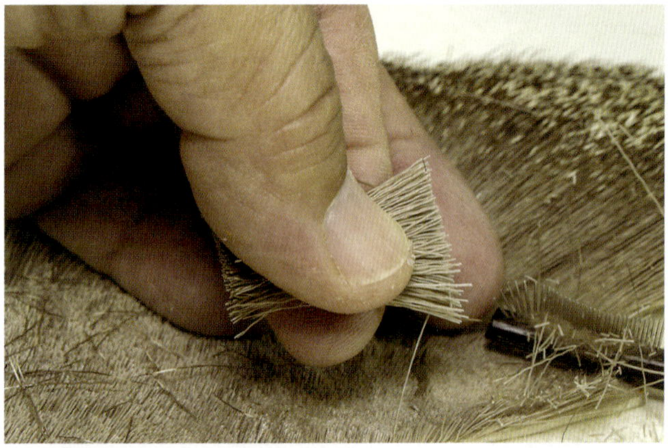

STEP 4: Trim the tips.

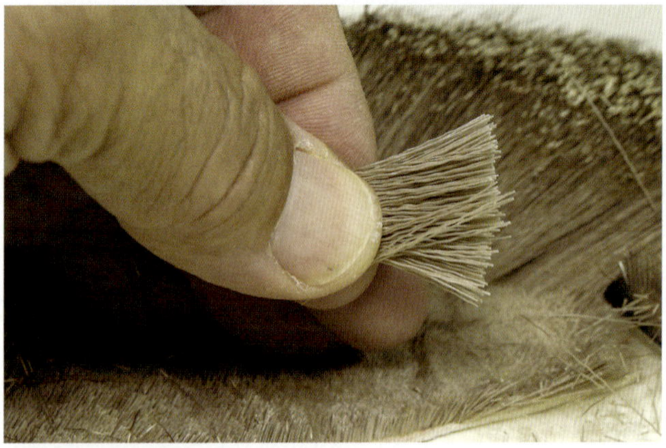

STEP 5: Adjust the hair in your fingers so the thread can be wrapped around the center of the bunch of hair. This bunch of hair is now ready to be placed on a hook shank.

Placing and Flaring a Hair Collar

This technique is most often used for spun deer hair head hoppers and Muddlers. It's the simplest of the deer hair techniques. The hair used is a piece of general purpose hair and the thread used is Wapsi GSP 75-denier.

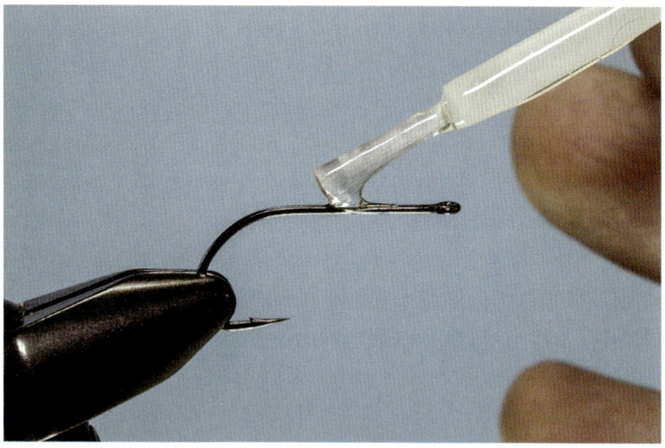

STEP 1: Apply a small amount of Zap-A-Gap glue to the hook shank.

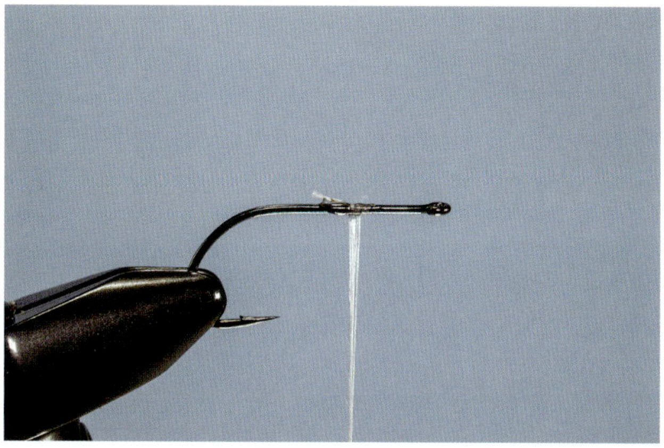

STEP 2: Use a jam knot to start the thread. Wrap the gel-spun thread through the glued section of the hook shank.

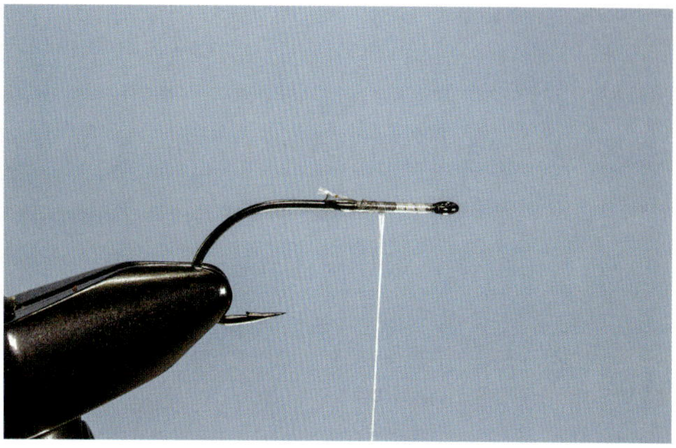

STEP 3: Continue wrapping the thread, creating a thread base for the deer hair head.

STEP 4: Place a prepared, stacked bunch of deer hair on the hook shank. Measure the hair collar to the desired length.

STEP 5: Grasp the hair with the other hand. Keep the hair collar at the desired length and push the hair down so it surrounds the hook shank.

STEP 6: Wrap the butts of hair with 3 wraps of thread.

STEP 7: Hold the tips in place and pull down on the thread, flaring the butts.

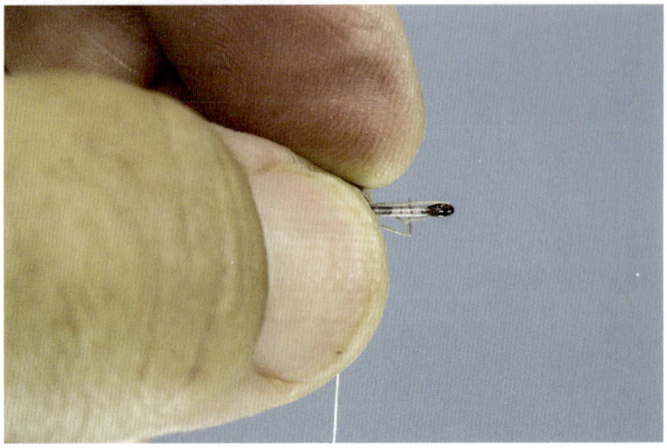

STEP 8: Pull the butts of the hair back and work the thread, under tension, through to the front of the hair bunch.

STEP 9: A flared collar and head. For smaller heads, this is all the deer hair you need. For a larger deer hair head, you would normally spin another bunch of hair in front of this bunch.

Flaring and Spinning Hair (Technique 1)

There are two techniques for flaring and spinning deer hair around a hook shank. This is the more traditional technique that most tiers think of as spinning deer hair. The hair used in the demonstration is spinning deer hair (natural) and the thread is Wapsi GSP 130-denier.

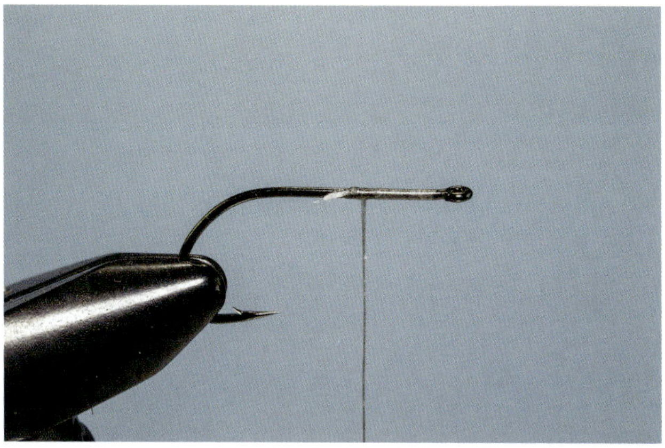

STEP 1: Apply a small amount of Zap-A-Gap glue to a hook shank. Wrap the thread through the glue and continue wrapping a thread base.

STEP 2: Cut and prepare a bunch of hair for flaring. With the butts forward, lay the hair along the far side of the hook shank at a 45-degree angle.

STEP 3: Make 3 wraps of thread around the hook shank and hair.

STEP 4: As you begin to tighten the thread, the hair will begin to flare. Allow the hair to slip out of your fingers as you continue to tighten the thread.

STEP 5: Once you have released the hair, continue wrapping the thread around the hook shank.

STEP 6: The key to having the hair evenly distributed is to maintain the same amount of thread tension all the way around the hook shank. The hair should continue moving around the hook shank for about 2 or 3 more rotations and then come to a stop. All of the thread wraps have occurred in the same plane around the hook shank. Do not wrap the thread forward through the hair!

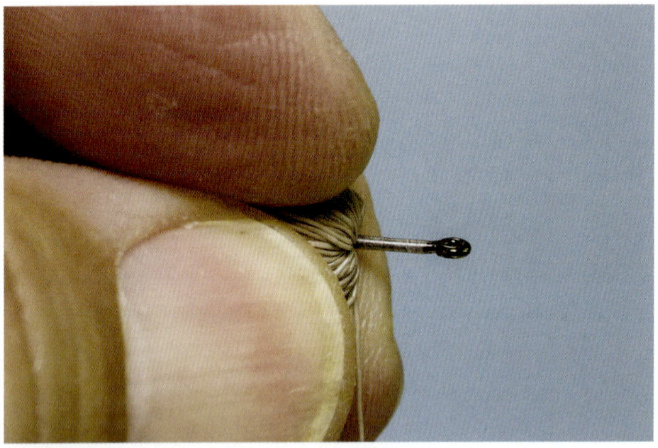

STEP 7: Pull back the butts of the hair and work the thread through the hair while keeping it under tension.

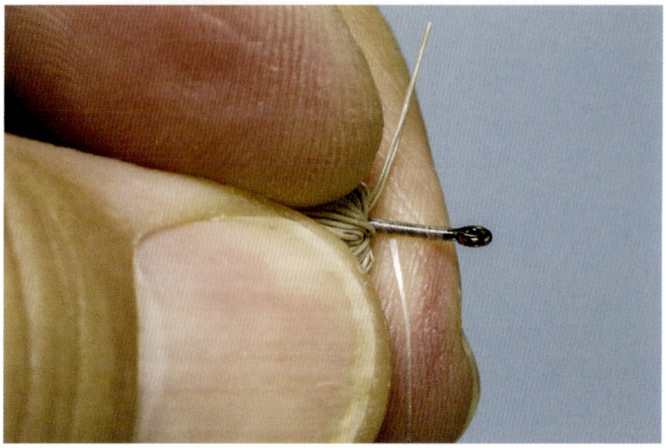

STEP 8: When you get the thread to the front of the hair, make a few wraps of thread to finish. You are now ready to add another bunch of hair if needed.

Front view.

Side view.

Flaring and Spinning Hair (Technique 2)

The second technique for flaring and spinning hair is very similar to the first with the exception of how you initially place the hair. The advantage of this technique is that it is a little easier to get the hair bunch to evenly distribute around the hook shank. It is especially useful for creating a ring of hair on larger deer hair heads. The hair used in the demonstration is spinning deer hair (natural) and the thread is Wapsi GSP 130-denier.

STEP 1: Attach the thread to the hook. Cut and prepare a bunch of hair. When placing it on the hook shank, evenly split the bunch of hair so half of it is on each side of the hook.

STEP 2: Make 3 wraps of thread around the hook shank and hair.

STEP 3: As you begin to tighten the thread, the hair will begin to flare. Allow the hair to slip out of your fingers as you continue to tighten the thread.

STEP 4: Once you have released the hair, continue wrapping the thread around the hook shank. Again, the key to having the hair evenly distributed is to maintain the same amount of thread tension all the way around the hook shank. As before, the hair should continue moving around the hook shank for about 2 or 3 more rotations and then come to a stop. All of the thread wraps have occurred in the same plane around the hook shank. Do not wrap the thread forward through the hair!

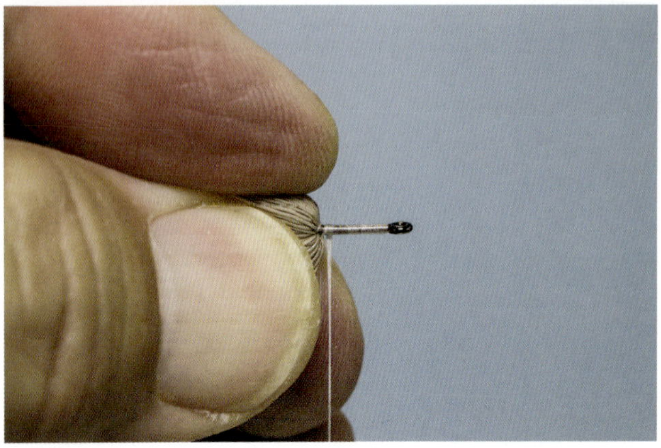

STEP 5: Pull back the butts of the hair and work the thread forward through the hair while keeping it under tension. When you get the thread to the front of the hair, make a few wraps of thread to finish. You are now ready to add another bunch of hair if needed.

Side view.

Front view.

Trimming a Small Deer Hair Head

Small heads on flies like Muddlers and hoppers can be trimmed with a good pair of scissors. These heads usually consist of a flared deer hair collar and one bunch of hair spun and flared in front of the collar.

TAPERED DEER HAIR HEAD

In this demonstration I will trim a tapered deer hair head. I used general purpose hair and Wapsi GSP 75-denier thread to create the head. I have a flared collar with an additional bunch of hair spun and flared in front of the collar. Germany Solingen Hair scissors are used to trim the head.

STEP 1: Hold the hook by the bend with the point on top. In this view the bottom of the head is on top. Note the distribution of the hair around the hook.

STEP 2: Trim the bottom of the head, leaving hair below the hook shank that is equal in length to ⅓ of the hook gape.

STEP 3: Trim the sides of the head so the hair is slightly longer than the length of the hair on the bottom.

STEP 4: Turn the hook over in your hand and trim the top of the head to equal the length of the side hair.

STEP 5: Trim around the head to create a tapered, cone-shape head.

Tapered head (side view).

CYLINDRICAL DEER HAIR HEAD

In this demonstration I will trim a cylindrical deer hair head. I used general purpose hair and Wapsi GSP 75-denier thread to create the head. I have a flared collar with an additional bunch of hair spun and flared in front of the collar. Germany Solingen Hair scissors are used to trim the head.

STEP 1: Trim the head into a rectangular shape as in the previous demo.

STEP 2: Trim the corners off, creating a cylindrical shape. Keep the scissors parallel to the hook shank

Front view.

Side view. (Note that the butts of the hair flow back into the collar. This could be considered a complete hair head. The following steps are optional depending on how you want the head to look.)

STEP 3: To create a more defined head, push the collar hairs down with the tips of the scissors.

STEP 4: Push the scissors up against the back of the head and trim the butts of the hair. Continue around the head, trimming the butts of the hair at the back of the head.

Side view.

Top view.

Front view.

MIXED HAIR

Normally when selecting and prepping a bunch of hair, only one color is selected. However, two or more colors can be selected and mixed together. Cut and prep two or more bunches of different-colored hair and set them side by side. Simply gather the different colors and shuffle them together. Once they have been mixed, put the hair into a hair stacker and even the tips. Then use the hair just as you would a bunch of single-color hair.

If the individual shafts of hair have a lot of taper to them, stacked bars and spots can become tapered into a teardrop shape. To remedy this, take half of the bunch of hair and reverse it so the tips and butts of hair are aligned. Using this bunch of hair, the stacked bar should be more symmetrical. ■

Stacked Hair Techniques

Stacking hair is the technique used to create the larger deer hair heads. Packing hair with a hair-packing tool will create some density, but to create really dense hair heads, a stacking technique must be used. In this demonstration I only stack hair on the top and bottom of the hook shank, but hair can be stacked at any point around the shank. Deer hair will tend to evenly distribute around the hook shank, so as you add stacked bunches of hair, remember that if you do a number of stacks on one side of the hook shank while leaving the other side with fewer stacks, the hair will tend to migrate to the side with less hair.

In this demonstration I use spinning deer hair (bleached, yellow, olive, and black) and the thread is Wapsi GSP 130-denier.

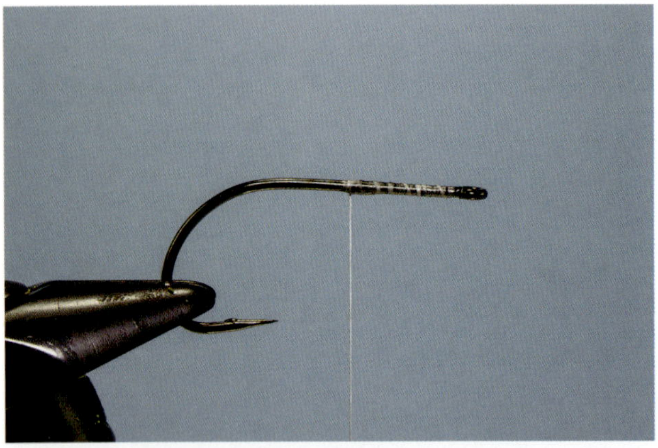

STEP 1: Attach the thread to the hook and wrap a thread base.

STEP 2: Cut and prepare a bunch of bleached hair. Lay the hair on the far side of the hook shank at a 45-degree angle.

STEP 3: Make 3 wraps of thread around the hook shank and hair. The thread tension should be enough that the hair is almost beginning to flare. If the thread tension is too tight, the hair will tend to distribute around the hook shank, and if it is not tight enough, the hair will slip out of the loops.

STEP 4: Using the thread, rotate the bunch of hair to the bottom of the hook shank. Place your thumb on top of the hook shank and pull down on the thread, flaring it on the bottom of the hook.

STEP 5: If properly done, the hair should all be on the bottom of the hook.

STEP 6: Cut and prepare a bunch of yellow hair. Place it directly on top of the hook and make 2 wraps of thread. The wraps should be in the same plane as the previous 3 wraps of thread for the bottom hair.

STEP 7: Place your finger on the far side of the hook to prevent the hair from rotating. Pull the thread down so the yellow hair flares. Put as much tension on the thread as possible without cutting through the hair. Hold the thread under tension for a moment.

STEP 8: Two bunches of hair flared on the hook shank. Note the color separation.

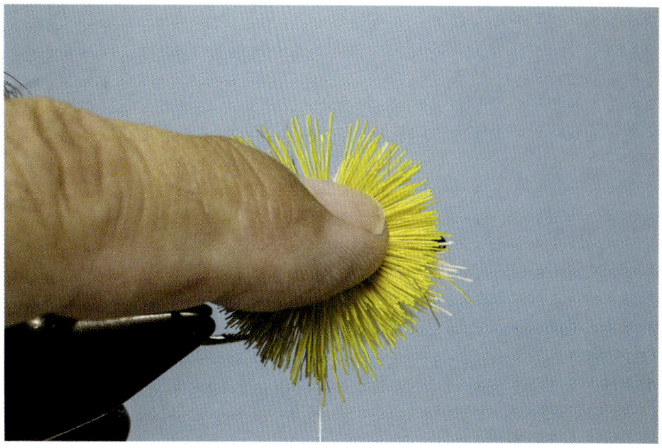

STEP 9: Use your index finger to create a space in the yellow hair. Separate the hair so there is an even amount on all sides.

STEP 10: Cut and prepare a bunch of olive hair. Place it directly on top of the hook and make 2 wraps of thread. The wraps should be in the same plane as the previous wraps!

STEP 11: Place your finger on the far side of the hook to prevent the hair from rotating. Pull the thread down so the olive hair flares. Put as much tension on the thread as possible without cutting through the hair. Hold the thread under tension for a moment.

STEP 12: Three bunches of hair flared on the hook shank. Note the color separation.

STEP 13: At this point there are two bunches of hair on the top of the hook shank and only one on the bottom. You can leave it like this, but the top hair will begin to migrate to the bottom. To prevent that, make a space on the bottom of the hook so another bunch of bleached hair can be added.

STEP 14: Cut and prepare a bunch of bleached hair and place it in the space.

STEP 15: Make 2 wraps of thread around the new bunch of hair. Keep the thread wraps in the same plane as all of the previous wraps of thread! Support the hair with your finger to keep it from rotating and pull the thread to flare the bunch of hair. Hold the thread under tension for a moment.

STEP 16: Make a space in the olive hair at the top of the body. Cut and prepare a small bunch of black hair. Place it in the space, make 2 wraps of thread, and flare it in place.

STEP 17: Five bunches of hair are currently in this stack. If stopped at this point, the black would become a bar of color on the top of the body.

STEP 18: Top view. The black hair would become a bar of color if no other hair were added.

STEP 19: To change the black from a bar to a ring, make a space in the center of the black hair.

STEP 20: Cut, prepare, and place a bunch of olive hair in the space created in the black hair. Make 2 wraps of thread and flare the hair in place. Put as much tension on the thread as possible without cutting the hair and hold it for a moment.

STEP 21: Six bunches of hair are now in this stack. There is a total of 13 wraps of thread, and they are all in the same plane!

STEP 22: Pull the hair back and while keeping the thread under tension, work it through the hair to the front of the stack. Make a couple of wraps of thread. Use a half-hitch tool and add 2 or 3 half-hitches in front of the stacked hair.

STEP 23: Using a hair-packing tool, push up against the knots and compress the hair. Support the back of the stack of hair with your other hand. The hair should compress a couple of millimeters.

STEP 24: Add a small amount of Fly-Tite tying cement to the base of the stack of hair. This is an optional step.

Side view.

Top view.

Bottom view.

Front view.

Trimming Larger Hair Heads

In this demonstration I will be trimming a stacked deer hair head. There are two stacks of hair with six bunches of hair in the back stack and five bunches of hair in the front stack. The back stack is an example of creating a ring of black around a bunch of olive hair. The front stack is an example of a black bar on top of olive hair.

Side view of untrimmed head.

Top view of untrimmed head.

Bottom view of untrimmed head.

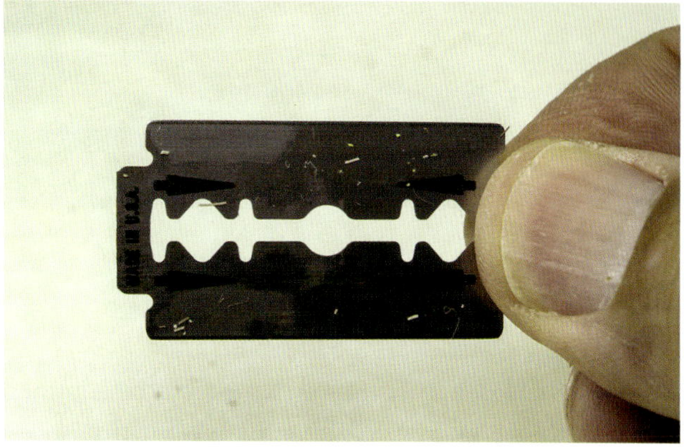

To get a smoothly trimmed head, use a double-edge razor blade. I use the razor blade to trim the fly by holding the blade on the side, being careful of the edges.

STEP 1: Most heads will be trimmed by starting on the bottom of the fly. For a deer hair head to perform properly when fished, there must be deer hair left below the hook shank. Start trimming the bottom of the head, leaving a length of hair that is equal to ⅓ of the hook gape. If the razor blade does not smoothly cut through the hair, use a slight sawing motion to create a smooth, flat bottom on the fly.

The bottom of the fly trimmed. Note that the trimmed hair length is about 1/3 of the hook gape width.

STEP 2: Make a cut along the side of the body that is perpendicular to the eye of the hook. Repeat on the opposite side of the hook. The eye of the hook should be centered between these two cuts. The total width of the body should be at least 1⅓ to 1½ the distance of the gape of the hook.

STEP 3: Turn the fly over in your hand so the bend of the hook is down, and trim the top of the fly. The total height of the body from the belly to the top of the fly should be about the same as the width.

STEP 4: Use your scissors to trim the back of the body parallel to the face of the bug. Using the initial cut along the side of the body as a reference, lay the razor blade on that cut and trim along the side of the bug. Keep the cut parallel to the hook shank. Repeat on the opposite side of the bug.

STEP 5: Use the razor blade to trim a flat face. Work with the corner of the blade. A blade can be dulled quickly if it comes in contact with the hook shank.

When the initial trim is finished, you should be left with a rectangular prism of hair on the hook shank.

STEP 6: Starting with the bottom of the fly, make a cut at a 45-degree angle, cutting off one of the edges. Repeat on the other three corners of the body.

STEP 7: Continue carefully trimming with the razor blade. Keep working the edges out of the body to create curved surfaces. Make very shallow cuts. It's almost more like sanding the body rather than cutting hair off the body. Note how small some of the cut pieces of hair are on the blade of the razor. The body can be trimmed either from the front to the back or from the back to the front as in the photo. You can also work around the bug to create a curved surface. Work slowly, as you are using a double-edge razor blade. Always be conscious of where your fingers that are holding the fly are located!

STEP 8: As you are spinning and flaring the hair, it's important to keep tension on the thread as you move it forward to begin the next stack. This will help prevent the thread from catching and folding hair in the body. However, you may still catch hair with the thread and fold it over. Work through the body with a dubbing needle and pick out any folded hair you may encounter.

STEP 9: Note the few bleached hairs that were pulled up from the folded hair. Trim them off.

This body is close to being finished. If you are only planning on tying a fly for fishing, this is an acceptably trimmed body.

STEP 10: If you want a very smoothly trimmed body, you can steam the deer hair with a teakettle. Note the difference between this photo and the previous photo. After steaming the body, the hair will expand and straighten. This makes it much easier to do a finish trim on the fly.

Side view. Note the hair on the bottom of the hook shank. The belly of hair bug bodies should not be trimmed tight against the hook shank. (See sidebar "Bass Bug Proportions.")

Top view. Note that in the stack at the back of the body, the black hair creates a ring, and in the stack at the front of the body, the black hair creates a bar.

Front view.

Bottom view.

CHAPTER 6

Spun Deer Hair Flies for Trout

"And, finally, not because I regard fishing as being so terribly important but because I suspect that so many of the other concerns of men are equally unimportant—and not nearly so much fun."

ROBERT TRAVER, *TESTAMENT OF A FISHERMAN*

The summer morning had been cool and clear as I fished along the Madison River in southwestern Montana. I was fishing downstream from the Three Dollar Bridge. The morning had provided some rising trout along the edges of the river to Pale Morning Duns, but the fishing had been slow. I did not have a lot of experience with this section of the river. I floated here with a guide out of West Yellowstone a few years before, and I had wade-fished it one other time. We were starting to consider moving to another place.

About midday the wind began to blow up the river valley. It finally got so strong and gusty that the 5-weight rod I was using became impossible to cast. While returning to the car to discuss our plans, I looked at the grassy meadows that the river flowed through and decided to grab my 7-weight rod and return to the river.

Walking downstream, I headed to a gravel bar that was on my side of the river. The bar was about 30 yards long with a slow, shallow current between it and the riverbank. The outside edge had a somewhat stronger current and a drop-off, but the really strong currents were out towards the middle of the river. I tied on a large Dave's Hopper and started along the drop-off on the downstream end of the island. Within the first few casts, I hooked an 18-inch rainbow that immediately ran out into the faster currents. I walked him downstream and eventually landed and released him in the quiet water at the end of the island. His vibrant colors and football-shaped girth made him a memorable fish. After releasing him, I returned to the place I caught him and made a cast slightly upstream and hooked another fish.

The next hour of fishing was one of those rare magical moments that happen where conditions, tactics, and fly pattern come together to create a lasting memory. I caught a number of browns and rainbows, all in that 18-to-22-inch range and all with the girth of well-fed fish. The Dave's Hopper fly pattern I was using created an immediate response from the trout, and the spun deer hair head was both durable and created a lifelike impression of the grasshoppers that abounded in the surrounding meadows.

Small spun deer hair heads and bodies have been a mainstay of many iconic trout patterns. Along with numerous variations of hopper flies like the Dave's Hopper, flies like the Muddler Minnow and the

Irresistible are early examples of patterns that take advantage of the characteristics unique to deer hair. For the angler, these flies are durable and float well. For the fish, they give realistic profiles that make them productive patterns. Few trout anglers are without some of these spun deer hair patterns in their fly boxes.

Dave's Hopper

Today it would take an entire book to chronicle all of the various grasshopper fly patterns being tied. Foam has become a popular material for hopper patterns because of its ease of use, durability, and floatability. However, the Dave's Hopper remains the iconic fly pattern for imitating grasshoppers.

Dave Whitlock first tied the Dave's Hopper in the 1950s. At that time the Joe's Hopper was one of the few commercially tied hopper patterns. Created by Art Winnie, a Traverse City, Michigan, guide and popularized by Joe Brooks, the Joe's Hopper had a large hackle collar for the head. Anglers were also using floating Muddler Minnow fly patterns as hopper imitations. The Dave's Hopper is a blending of these two patterns, retaining the original body but replacing the hackle collar with a spun deer hair head like the Muddler Minnow. The original Dave's Hopper was tied without legs; however, Jay Buchner—a Jackson Hole, Wyoming, guide and fly tier—added legs to the pattern, creating the template for most of the hopper flies tied today.

This version of a Dave's Hopper is a slight variation. I have replaced the poly yarn body with foam and used synthetic Ice Fur for the tail. Additionally, I have done a stacked deer hair head with a yellow bottom and a natural top. The head is traditionally done with all natural deer hair, which is certainly an effective way to tie it as well.

TYING THE DAVE'S HOPPER

- **Hook:** #4-10 Tiemco 5263
- **Thread:** Black UTC 70 for body; White UTC GSP 75 or 100 for deer hair head
- **Tail:** Red Hareline Ice Fur
- **Body:** 2 mm foam overwrapped with brown Whiting dry fly hackle (trimmed)
- **Wing:** Nature's Spirit turkey quill segment over natural Nature's Spirit All Purpose deer hair
- **Legs:** Pheasant tail fibers
- **Head:** Natural Nature's Spirit All Purpose deer hair over yellow Nature's Spirit spinning deer hair

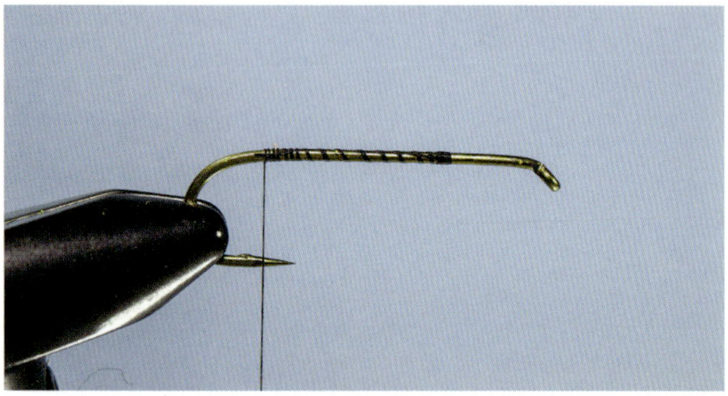

STEP 1: Attach the black UTC 70 thread at the front of the hook. Leave ¼ of the hook shank length for the deer hair head. Wrap the thread back to the tie-in point.

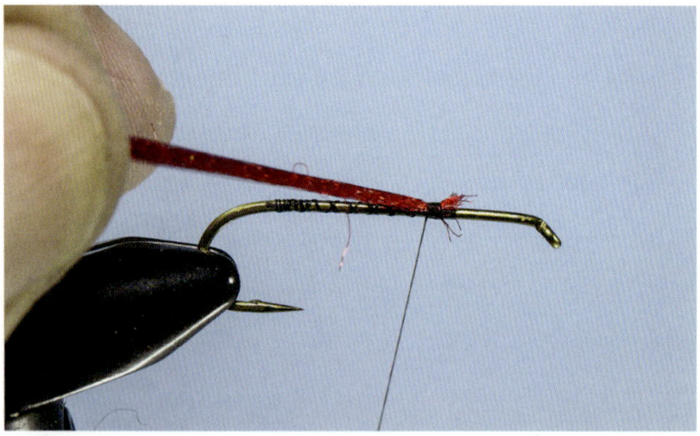

STEP 2: Wrap the thread back to the front tie-in point and attach the red Ice Fur.

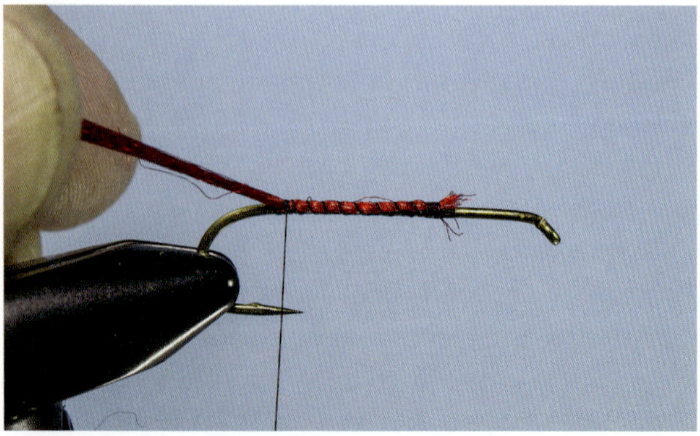

STEP 3: Keep the Ice Fur under tension and pull it slightly towards you. Wrap the thread back, attaching the Ice Fur to the top of the hook shank. Make 2 or 3 wraps of thread to secure the Ice Fur at the back tie-in point.

STEP 4: Trim the Ice Fur tail equal to the back of the bend of the hook.

STEP 5: Tie in a prepared brown hackle feather. The length of the barbules does not matter, as the hackle will be trimmed.

STEP 6: Cut a length of 2 mm yellow foam and taper the end. The width of the foam should be ⅔ the length of the hook gape.

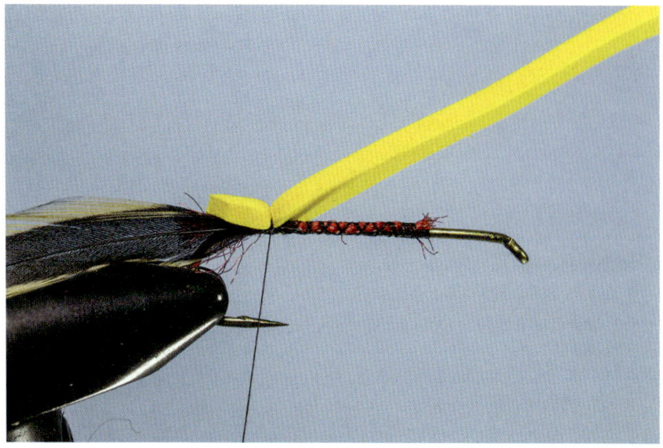

STEP 7: Attach the foam at the back tie-in point with 3 to 5 wraps of thread. Use an increasing amount of tension with each thread wrap to securely attach the foam.

STEP 8: Spiral-wrap the thread forward to the front tie-in point.

STEP 9: Spiral-wrap the foam forward to the front tie-in point and secure with 3 to 5 thread wraps.

STEP 10: Trim the foam and add a few more wraps of thread to fully secure the foam.

STEP 11: Spiral-wrap the hackle forward and secure at the front tie-in point with the thread.

STEP 12: Trim the hackle barbules to about ½ the length of the gape of the hook.

STEP 13: Cut and prepare a small bunch of the natural all-purpose deer hair. Stack the bunch to even the tips. Measure the length of the hair to equal the length of the body. Switch hands and trim the butts to the desired length.

STEP 14: Position the butts of the hair wing at the front tie-in point.

STEP 15: Tie in the trimmed butts of the underwing, allowing both the butts and tips of the hair to flare.

STEP 16: Cut a prepared section of turkey quill so the width is equal to the width of the gape of the hook.

STEP 17: Attach the section of quill at the front tie-in point.

STEP 18: Pull the quill section back, folding it equally in half. Trim the quill section with your scissors angled to the back of the fly, creating a point in the wing.

STEP 19: The length of the wing should be slightly longer than the length of the body and tail.

STEP 20: Take a prepared section of pheasant tail and measure the leg length so the knot is equal with the back tie-in point. The leg should be knotted so the tips of the feather below the knot are slightly longer than the gape of the hook.

STEP 21: Trim the leg to the correct length and place the butts of the leg at the front tie-in point.

STEP 22: Tie in the near side leg.

STEP 23: Repeat with the far side leg. Apply some Zap-A-Gap to the thread and tie off.

The finished body of the Dave's Hopper. I would normally tie a number of bodies before proceeding to the head (see "Step-Tying Large Flies" sidebar in chapter 7).

STEP 24: Apply a small amount of Zap-A-Gap to the hook shank at the front of the body and attach the GSP thread. Cut and prepare a bunch of yellow spinning deer hair. Trim the butts and tips. Using a stacking technique, rotate the bunch of hair to the bottom of the hook shank and flare.

STEP 25: Cut, prepare, and stack a small bunch of all-purpose deer hair. The tips of the hair will serve as the collar of the fly. Measure the tips to ½ the body length. Switch hands and trim the butts, leaving a length of hair equal to the length of the tips.

STEP 26: Place the hair on the top of the hook shank. Hold the tips in place and make 2 wraps of thread and flare the hair.

PREPPING QUILL WINGS

The two primary flight feathers used most often in fly tying are from ducks and turkeys. Duck primary flight feathers, or quills, are used in pairs for patterns like the No Hackle, where the quill segments serve as imitations for the wings of the mayfly. Turkey quill segments as well as tail feathers are used as wings for hopper patterns as well as the Muddler Minnow.

These feathers can be used as they come out of the package; however, the barbules can become separated in the tying process, making it difficult to complete the fly. To overcome this separation problem, prep the feather by stripping off the lower barbules, then clip the feather in an upright position and spray it with an art fixative. Companies like Grumbacher, Winsor & Newton, and Krylon market this product to finish out charcoal and pastel artwork. When sprayed on the feathers, the barbules will stay together as you tie the fly. Be sure to spray the feathers either outdoors or in a well-ventilated room. Once you start to fish with the fly, the fixative will wash off, allowing the barbules to separate. Often a frayed look to a well-fished fly is actually more attractive to the fish. ■

STEP 27: Make a space between the tips and butts of the hair directly above the thread wraps and add a small second bunch of hair using the same technique. This is an optional step. It will add density to the hair head. The amount of hair used is proportional to the size fly being tied.

STEP 28: Pull the hair back. Keep the thread under tension and work it forward through the hair. Make several wraps, then apply some Zap-A-Gap to the thread. Make a few wraps with the glued thread and finish with 2 half-hitch knots. Trim the thread.

The Dave's Hopper with the untrimmed deer hair head.

STEP 29: Using a razor blade, trim the bottom of the head flat. Leave a couple of millimeters of hair on the bottom of the head.

STEP 30: Continue using the razor blade to trim the head into a rectangular prism.

STEP 31: Continue using the razor blade to trim the head to the desired shape. Note that I trimmed the butts of hair at the back of the head to accentuate the head and collar. The butts can be left untrimmed so they flow back into the collar.

Bottom view.

Top view.

The Classic Muddler Minnow

Most anglers seem to have some knowledge of the history of certain patterns; the Muddler Minnow is one of those. First tied by Don Gapen in the early 1930s, it was used to imitate the sculpin minnows that inhabited the Nipigon River, which flows south out of Nipigon Lake in Ontario, Canada, into Lake Superior. This is the river that produced the world-record 14.5-pound brook trout caught by Dr. J. W. Cook in 1915. Due to the construction of numerous hydroelectric dams, the waters that Gapen and Cook fished in the early part of the 20th century are no longer available to modern anglers. However, the region is still known for its quality brook trout fishing.

Gapen, a descendant of an English and Scottish fly-tying family and dedicated fly fisherman, found that the bright patterns that were in common use at the time were not effective on the larger fish. Finally giving in to his guides' requests, he tried fishing with some live sculpin as bait. The results quickly showed him the wisdom of his guides, but still wanting to catch the fish on flies, he sat down to try to imitate the baitfish he had been fishing. His first attempt was essentially the fly that we consider the classic Muddler Minnow.

Today there are dozens of variations of the Muddler Minnow. Some involve the use of cones augmenting the deer hair head to help the fly sink more quickly, while others make use of variations of the tailing materials. What all these patterns have in common, however, is the use of deer hair for the head. Don Gapen used the flared deer hair for both its durability and its ability to imitate the wide head of the sculpin. Whether tied in its original form as Gapen tied it or used as a template for creative variations, the Muddler Minnow is a classic North American fly pattern.

TYING THE MUDDLER MINNOW

- **Hook:** #4-10 Tiemco 5263
- **Thread:** Black UTC 70 for body; White UTC GSP 75 or 100 for deer hair head
- **Tail:** Two Nature's Spirit turkey quill sections
- **Body:** Gold Wapsi Sparkle Braid
- **Wing:** Nature's Spirit turkey quill segment over gray squirrel tail
- **Head:** Natural Nature's Spirit All Purpose deer hair

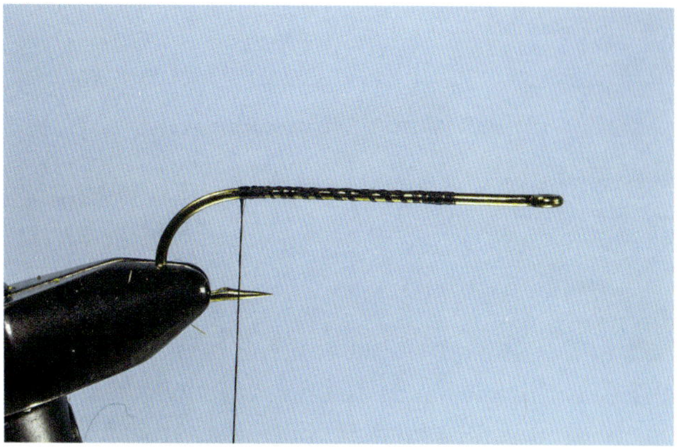

STEP 1: Attach the black UTC 70 thread at the front of the hook. Leave ¼ of the hook shank length for the deer hair head. Wrap the thread back to the tie-in point.

STEP 2: Cut a quill segment equal to the width of the gape of the hook, one each from two opposing turkey primary wing feathers (see "Prepping Quill Wings" sidebar). Match the tips of the feathers and put the two quill segments together so they curve towards each other. Measure the quill segments so they extend ⅓ of the hook shank length behind the rear tie-in point.

STEP 3: Change hands and press the two quill segments together, holding them in a vertical position on top of the hook shank. Wrap the thread forward, attaching the quill feather to the hook shank.

STEP 4: Continue wrapping the thread forward to the front tie-in point. Attach the gold braid to the top of the hook shank.

STEP 5: Continue attaching the gold braid on the top of the hook shank by wrapping the thread back to the rear tie-in point. Wrap the thread forward to the front tie-in point.

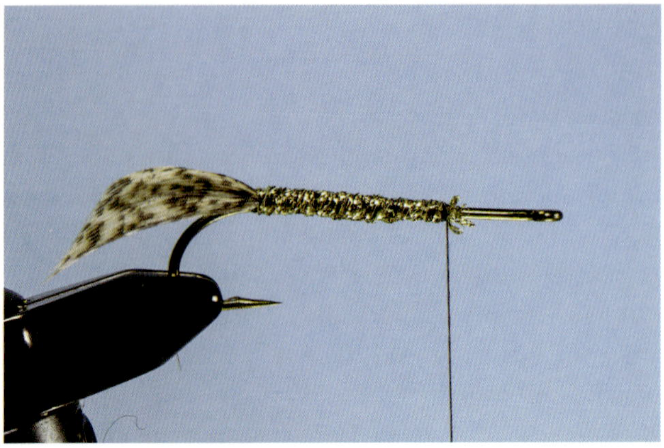

STEP 6: Wrap the gold braid forward, overlapping where necessary to create an even body. Tie it off and trim the braid.

STEP 7: Prep a small bunch of gray squirrel tail in the same way you would a bunch of deer hair. Stack the squirrel tail to even the tips. Measure the squirrel tail from the front tie-in point to a distance slightly shorter than the length of the tail.

STEP 8: Switch hands and trim the squirrel tail to the proper length. Attach the squirrel tail to the top of the hook shank.

STEP 9: Apply a small amount of Zap-A-Gap to the thread and make 3 or 4 more wraps of thread, allowing the glue to secure the squirrel tail to the hook shank.

STEP 10: Cut a quill segment equal to the width of the gape of the hook, one each from two opposing turkey primary wing feathers. Match the tips of the feathers and put the two quill segments together so they curve towards each other. Measure the quill segments so they extend ⅓ of the hook shank length behind the rear tie-in point equal to the tail length. Allow the quill segments to envelop the squirrel tail.

STEP 11: Switch hands and trim the quill segments to length. Tie the quill segments in at the front tie-in point. Apply a small amount of Zap-A-Gap to the thread and make 3 or 4 more wraps, allowing the glue to secure the quill segments to the hook. Using a whip-finish knot, tie off the thread in front of the tail. Cut the thread.

STEP 12: Apply a small amount of Zap-A-Gap to the hook shank at the front of the body and attach the GSP thread. Cut and prepare a bunch of all-purpose deer hair. Stack the hair to even the tips and measure the tips to about ½ the body length.

STEP 13: Switch hands and trim the butts, leaving a length of hair equal to the length of the tips. Push the hair down so it envelops the hook shank, make 3 wraps of thread, and flare the hair on the hook shank immediately in front of the body. Pull the hair back and work the thread, under tension, to the front of the flared bunch of hair, making 2 or 3 wraps.

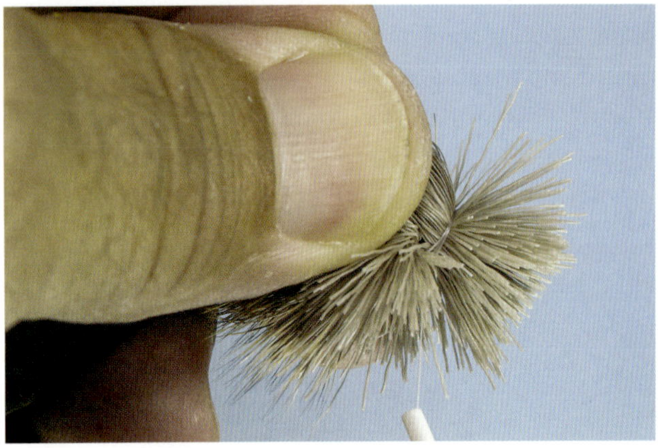

STEP 14: Cut and prepare another bunch of the all-purpose deer hair. Trim the butts and tips. Using the same technique, push the hair down so it envelops the hook shank, make 3 wraps of thread, and flare the hair on the hook shank immediately in front of the previous bunch of hair.

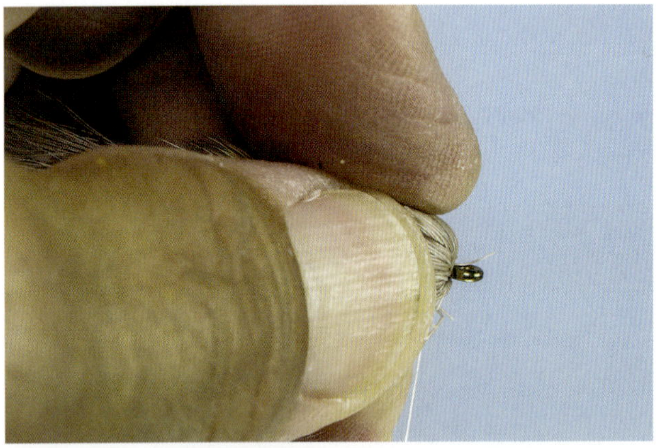

STEP 15: Pull the hair back and work the thread, under tension, to the front of the flared bunch of hair, making 2 or 3 wraps. Apply a small amount of Zap-A-Gap to the thread and use a couple of half-hitch knots to finish attaching the thread to the hook. Cut the thread.

The Muddler Minnow with the untrimmed deer hair head.

STEP 16: Start by using scissors to trim the head to its general shape. The fly can be left with just a scissor-trimmed head, but to get a smoother-shaped head, use a razor blade to finish out the final shape of the head. Note that I left the butts of the hair on this head flowing back into the collar.

Irresistible

The Irresistible fly pattern has been around for almost a century. It was created by Joe Messinger Sr. and was inspired by a bass pattern he was tying in the 1920s called the Nitehummer. The fly was originally tied to imitate the large drake mayflies that were common to eastern waters. The pattern quickly found its way to the Midwest, where it is still used today to imitate the large drake mayfly hatches as well as the renowned Hex hatch that occurs on many of these rivers (see chapter 2, "Hair Wing Duns"). This fly is also popular in the West, where it's used as a searching pattern in faster runs and the pocketwaters so common to western rivers.

Adapting it to color and size, I have also tied the Irresistible as an imitation of the Green Drake mayfly that hatches in the Roaring Fork and Frying Pan Rivers in Colorado. With the ability to modify its size and color and its trimmed deer hair body providing floatability, it's understandable that this pattern is still as popular today as when Messinger first tied it.

TYING THE IRRESISTIBLE

- **Hook:** #8-16 Tiemco 100 or #4-10 Tiemco 5212
- **Thread:** Black UTC 70 for wings and hackle collar; UTC GSP 75 or 100 for tail and deer hair body
- **Tail:** Natural Nature's Spirit moose body hair
- **Body:** Natural Nature's Spirit All Purpose deer hair
- **Wing:** Grizzly Whiting winger cape
- **Hackle:** Brown and grizzly Whiting Bronze Grade dry fly hackle

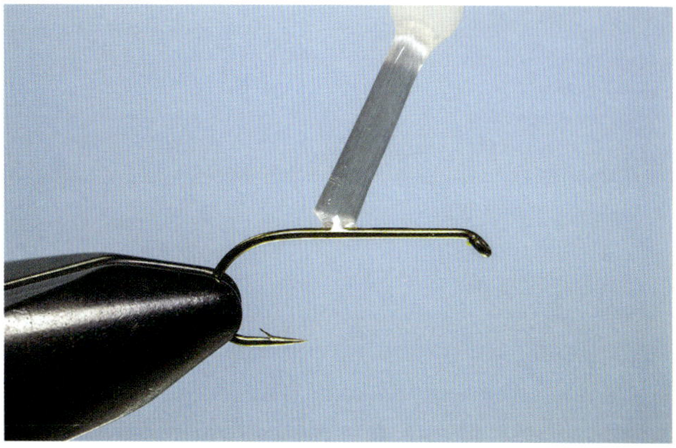

STEP 1: Wet the rear half of the hook shank with a small amount of Zap-A-Gap glue.

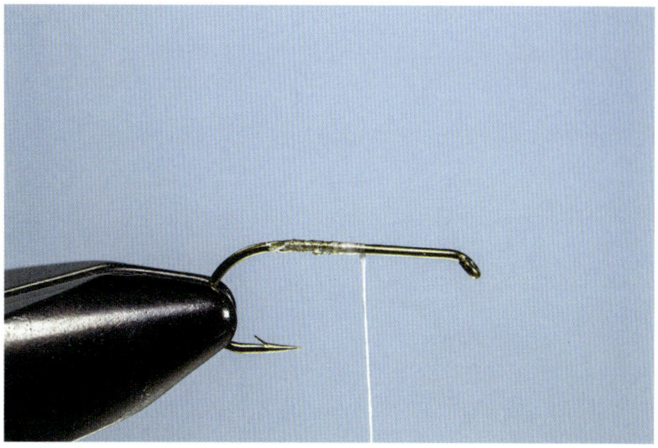

STEP 2: Using the GSP thread, wrap a thread base on the rear half of the hook. Return the thread to the center of the hook shank at the front of the thread base.

STEP 3: Cut, clean, and stack a small amount of moose body hair. Measure the hair so it extends from the front of the hook shank to the back of the bend of the hook. This measurement is also about 2 times the gape of the hook.

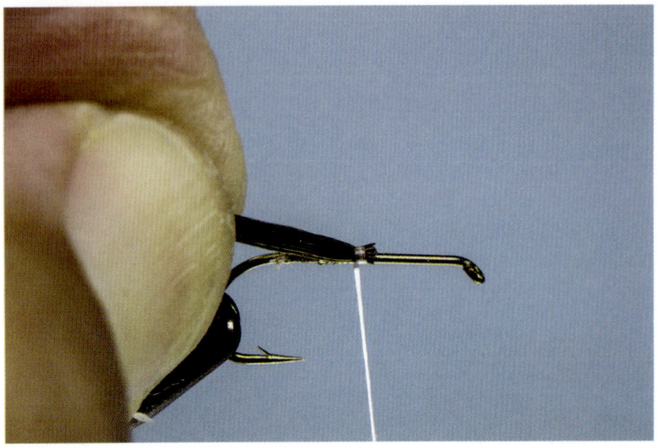

STEP 4: Cut the moose body hair to length and attach it with the thread at the halfway point on the hook shank. Holding the tail up and slightly towards you, wrap back to the rear tie-in point, keeping the tail on the top of the hook shank.

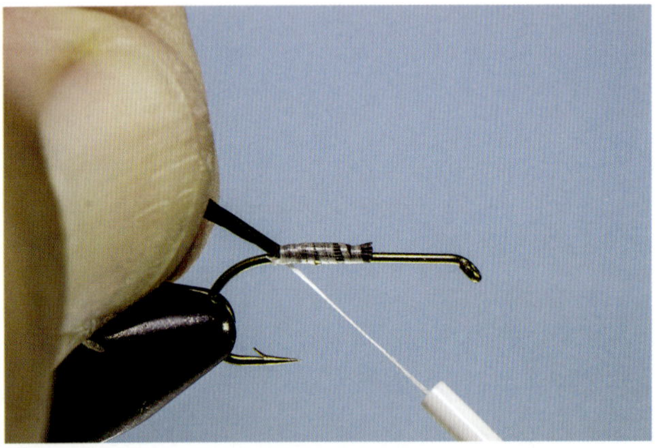

STEP 5: Make 1 wrap of thread behind the tail and pull forward on the thread to set the tail at an upward angle. Make 1 wrap of thread in front of the tie-in point for the tail.

STEP 6: Cut and prepare a bunch of the all-purpose deer hair. Trim the butts and tips. Push the hair down so it envelops the hook shank.

STEP 7: Make 3 wraps of thread and flare the hair at the rear tie-in point.

STEP 8: Pull the hair back and advance the thread forward under tension. Make 1 or 2 wraps in the front of the hair. Cut and prepare another small bunch of deer hair. Using the same technique, flare it in front of the first bunch of hair. Add some Zap-A-Gap to the thread, using a couple of half-hitch knots, then tie the thread off and trim. While holding the tail with one hand, use a hair-packing tool to compress the hair back.

STEP 9: Hold the tail, being careful not to cut any of the moose hair, and use scissors to do a rough trim of the body.

STEP 10: Using a razor blade, do a finish trim of the body. Shape the body into a tapered cylinder. Trim out the hair around the tail as well as at the front of the body.

STEP 11: Attach the UTC 70 thread in front of the body and wrap a thread base. Return the thread to the middle of the front half of the hook shank.

STEP 12: Pick 2 feathers from the grizzly winger cape. Match the tips and put them together, curving away from each other.

STEP 13: Measure the length of the wings to the back of the body or about 2 times the gape of the hook. Make 2 or 3 wraps of thread around the wings, attaching them to the hook shank.

STEP 14: Stand the wings upright and make several wraps of thread behind and in front of the wings. Trim off the butts of the feathers. Make several more wraps securing the wings to the hook. Note that the wings are attached in the center of the front half of the hook.

STEP 15: Pick 1 brown and 1 grizzly dry fly feather. Measure the barbule length to 1½ times the gape of the hook or use a hackle gage to measure to the correct barbule length for the size hook. Prep the

feathers (see "Posting a Dry Fly Wing and Wrapping a Parachute Hackle" sidebar in chapter 2). Match the butts of the feathers together with the concave sides of both feathers facing forward and attach them in front of the wing.

STEP 16: Continue attaching the butt of the feathers by wrapping the thread back to the front of the body. Return the thread to the front of the hook shank just behind the eye of the hook.

STEP 17: Wrap the first feather (here it is the brown feather, but the order makes no difference) around the hook shank. Wrap the feather forward; make sure that the feather is going away from you as it crosses the top of the hook shank. Make 3 or 4 wraps of hackle behind the wing and 3 or 4 wraps of hackle in front of the wing. Hold the feather upright and make several wraps of thread to secure it. Repeat with the second feather. After securing the second feather, trim both feather tips. Finish the fly by pulling the hackle barbules back and making a small thread head just behind the eye of the hook. Use a whip-finish knot to secure the thread and trim.

Side view.

Front view.

Deer Hair Bumblebee

When Rick Takahashi and Jerry Hubka first asked me to contribute to their book *Modern Terrestrials* (2014), I knew I wanted to tie a spun deer hair Bumblebee fly. I had tied and fished small deer hair bass bugs with a Bumblebee color scheme for many years; however, I wanted this fly to take on a more realistic look. I knew I was certainly not the first to think of a clipped deer hair body for a Bumblebee. In *This Wonderful World of Trout* (1963), Charles K. Fox mentions in one of his short stories the use of a special black-and-white hornet fly to win an annual fishing contest. While there is not a recipe describing the fly, I always imagined it as a clipped deer hair pattern.

Numerous authors over the years have included deer hair Bumblebee fly patterns in their books. *Tying and Fishing Terrestrials* (1978) by Gerald Almy, *Fly Rod Trouting* (1989) by Ed Shenk, and *Terrestrials* (1994) by Harrison R. Steeves III are just a few of the books that have recipes for spun deer hair Bumblebee fly patterns. Rusty Gates of Gates Au Sable Lodge in Michigan also had a deer hair Bumblebee that anglers used in the region.

So the pattern I submitted for Rick and Jerry's book was just a variation of the many Bumblebee fly patterns that came before mine. I did use a synthetic foam material for the wing, and that was certainly a modern material. The fly worked well when I tested it. The bluegill really loved it, as well as trout under the right circumstances. After a summer of fishing the fly, I was not entirely satisfied with the look of it and decided to change the wing material to a gray dun CDC feather. I think it was an improvement and it fished as well or better than the pattern with the foam wing. The CDC feather added more texture and movement to the fly. I have also used feathers from a grizzly Whiting winger cape with good success as well.

Most North American Bumblebees are actually just yellow and black. There are a few that have white butts, and some Bumblebees have a more orange segment than yellow. A Bumblebee common in the UK also has a white butt followed by a black strip then a yellow strip. I liked the look of the three colors so decided to tie this pattern with this color combination. Colors can certainly be varied with this pattern to either appeal to your artistic preferences or imitate specific bumblebees.

TYING THE DEER HAIR BUMBLEBEE

- **Hook:** #10-12 Tiemco 8089 or #6-10 Gamakatsu B10S
- **Thread:** Black UTC 70 for wings and front body; UTC GSP 75 or 100 for deer hair body
- **Abdomen:** White, black, and yellow Nature's Spirit spinning deer hair
- **Wings:** Natural dark dun TroutHunter CDC or grizzly Whiting winger cape
- **Thorax:** Dark gray ostrich herl
- **Legs/antenna:** Black Hareline Round Rubber Legs (small) or speckled yellow or speckled white Montana Fly Company Centipede Legs (small)

STEP 1: Wet the back half of the hook shank with Zap-A-Gap glue and wrap the GSP thread from the halfway point on the hook shank to the back tie-in point.

STEP 2: Cut and prepare a bunch of the white spinning deer hair. Trim the butts and tips. Push the hair down so it envelops the hook shank. Make 3 wraps of thread around the center of the hair and flare the hair at the rear tie-in point. Keep the thread under tension and work it to the front of the bunch of hair.

STEP 3: Repeat with a bunch of black spinning deer hair.

STEP 4: Repeat with a bunch of yellow spinning deer hair. After advancing the thread to the front of the hair, apply a small amount of Zap-A-Gap to the GSP thread and tie off and trim the thread.

STEP 5: Trim the body (abdomen) to the shape of a bumblebee. Use a razor blade to get a smooth shape. Note the front top of the body has been trimmed at a 45-degree angle. This angle is to help facilitate adding the wings. Wrap and secure the black UTC 70 thread to the front of the body.

STEP 6: Select a CDC feather and stroke the barbules back to increase the density of the wing. Measure the wing back to about ⅔ of the body length and tie the feather in at the front of the body. Angle the first wing to the back and then repeat with a second feather, angling it to the front.

Top view. Note the separation and length of the wings.

STEP 7: Tie 2 small rubber legs to the far side and near side of the hook shank.

STEP 8: Select 4 or 5 barbules from an ostrich herl feather and attach them by the butts to the front of the hook shank.

STEP 9: Twist the barbules together and then wrap them forward, creating a fuzzy thorax. The ostrich herl should be moving away from you as you cross the top of the hook shank. Tie off and trim the ostrich herl.

STEP 10: Pull the ostrich herl and legs back and wrap a small thread head. Use a whip-finish knot to tie off the thread, then trim the thread. Stretch one forward leg on each side of the body and trim, leaving just one set of forward legs. Trim the forward rubber leg materials to the length of the antenna. Trim the back set of legs. You can trim the legs to simulate the actual length of a bumblebee leg; however, I like to leave the legs longer, giving them more action in the water when fished.

Side view.

Top view.

Bottom view.

Compendium of Deer Hair Trout Fly Patterns

The following flies are variations on the Robert's Drake and Sparkle Dun fly patterns.

OLIVE MUDDLER MINNOW

- **Hook:** #4-10 Tiemco 5263 or #2/0-1 Daiichi 2461
- **Thread:** Olive UTC 70 for body and thread head; White UTC GSP 75 or 100 for deer hair head
- **Tail:** Olive Nature's Spirit Ozark select barred turkey quills
- **Body:** Gold Wapsi Sparkle Braid
- **Wing:** Olive Nature's Spirit Ozark select barred turkey quills over olive Wapsi squirrel tail
- **Head:** Olive Nature's Spirit spinning deer hair

BROWN MUDDLER MINNOW

- **Hook:** #4-10 Tiemco 5263 or #2/0-1 Daiichi 2461
- **Thread:** Black UTC 70 for body; black UTC GSP 75 or 100 for deer hair head; dark brown UTC 70 for thread head
- **Tail:** Brown Nature's Spirit Ozark select barred turkey quills
- **Body:** Bronze Wapsi Sparkle Braid
- **Wing:** Brown Nature's Spirit Ozark select barred turkey quills over natural fox Wapsi squirrel tail
- **Head:** Gold Nature's Spirit dyed Stimulator hair

LETORT HOPPER

- **Hook:** #8-16 Tiemco 5212
- **Thread:** Hopper Yellow or match body color UTC 70 for body;White UTC GSP 75 or 100 for head
- **Body:** Cream Fly-Rite Extra Fine Poly Dubbing (or color to match natural grasshopper body color)
- **Wing:** Wapsi or Nature's Spirit mottled oak turkey wing quill segment
- **Head:** Natural Nature's Spirit All Purpose deer hair for #8 and #10; Natural Nature's Spirit Comparadun deer hair for #12-16
- **Originator:** Ed Shenk

LETORT CRICKET

- **Hook:** #8-16 Tiemco 5212
- **Thread:** Black UTC 70 for body; Black UTC GSP 100 for head
- **Body:** Black Fly-Rite Extra Fine Poly Dubbing
- **Wing:** Black Wapsi or Nature's Spirit turkey wing quill segment
- **Head:** Black Nature's Spirit All Purpose deer hair
- **Originator:** Ed Shenk

DAVE'S CRICKET

- **Hook:** #4-10 Tiemco 5263
- **Thread:** Black UTC 70 for body; Black UTC GSP 75 or 100 for deer hair head
- **Tail:** Rust orangutan Hareline Ice Fur
- **Body:** 2 mm foam overwrapped with black Whiting dry fly hackle (trimmed)
- **Wing:** Black Nature's Spirit turkey quill segment over black Nature's Spirit All Purpose deer hair
- **Legs:** Black Wapsi ringneck tail feathers
- **Head:** Black Nature's Spirit All Purpose deer hair

TURK'S TARANTULA

- **Hook:** #4-16 Tiemco 5263
- **Thread:** Black UTC 70 for body; White UTC GSP 75 or 100 for deer hair head
- **Tail:** Natural Wapsi golden pheasant tippet
- **Body:** Dark tan Fly-Rite Extra Fine Poly Dubbing
- **Wing:** White Wapsi calf tail
- **Head:** Natural Nature's Spirit All Purpose deer hair for #6-10; natural Nature's Spirit Comparadun hair for #12-16
- **Legs:** Tan/brown speckled Montana Fly Company Centipede Legs
- **Originator:** Variation of a Guy Turk pattern

RUSTY'S BUMBLEBEE

- **Hook:** #10-12 Tiemco 8089 or #6-10 Gamakatsu B10S
- **Thread:** Black UTC GSP 75 or 100
- **Abdomen:** Black and yellow Nature's Spirit spinning deer hair
- **Wings:** Black and yellow Nature's Spirit spinning deer hair
- **Originator:** Rusty Gates

PARACHUTE IRRESISTIBLE

- **Hook:** #8-12 Tiemco 100
- **Thread:** White UTC GSP 75 for body; black UTC 70 for head
- **Wing:** White deer belly hair
- **Hackle:** Dark barred ginger Whiting dry fly hackle
- **Tail:** Natural Nature's Spirit moose body hair
- **Body:** Natural Nature's Spirit All Purpose deer hair

CHAPTER 7

Topwater Deer Hair Flies

"Bass bugging is a type of fly-rod fishing that was born and raised right here in America."
RAY BERGMAN, *FISHING WITH RAY BERGMAN*

Using my electric trolling motor, my boat quietly glided around to the end of the island I had been fishing. I was approaching one of my favorite locations. I had been fishing along a long bed of reeds against the shoreline, and the reeds ended against a bed of lily pads. There was a large V-shaped slot between the reeds and pads in about 2 to 3 feet of water. Casting my deer hair bass bug up into the point of the slot, I dropped my rod tip to the water and tightened up the line. Giving the bug a very short and subtle pop, I let the fly sit.

Right on cue a sizable largemouth bass slid out from under the lily pads and turned to the bass bug. He momentarily looked at the fly before tipping up and sipping it in much like a trout would an emerging mayfly. Stripping line, I set the hook with the butt of the rod and dropped the rod tip to prevent him from jumping. After working him out of the cover, he headed into the open, deeper water. Once in deep water, he made several strong head-shaking runs before I landed him. The fish was slightly larger than the average size, measuring 18 inches and weighing slightly over 3 pounds.

I was fishing Lily Lake in northern Clare County, Michigan. A surveyor from County Clare, Ireland, named the county in 1843. This 284-acre lake is somewhat unique for the area, as about half of the lakeshore is wild and undeveloped. The deepest spot in the lake is only about 14 feet. This provides a lot of shallow-water habitat for the many largemouth bass that are found here. The lake's name is also an apt description, as reeds and lily pads abound. By virtue of the abundance of natural cover and shallow water, this lake is ideal for fly fishing. As with most lakes in the area, it is lightly fished and rarely do you see any other fly fishers. With hundreds of targets to cast to and an abundance of largemouth bass, this lake is tailor-made for topwater bass bug fishing.

BASS BUG PROPORTIONS

Bass bugs need to have the proper proportions to fish correctly. A common mistake is to trim the deer hair body too close to the hook shank on the bottom of the fly. Even with floatant applied to the deer hair body, the hair will eventually soak up water. If the fly doesn't have some deer hair left under the shank, as the top of the fly soaks up water, it will eventually outweigh the bend of the hook under the body and the fly will land upside down. If you look at Joe Messinger's Bucktail Frog pattern, note the amount of hair that is under the hook shank. This was done to keep the fly landing upright when cast.

Shown below are the tie-in areas for the hook and proportions for a topwater bass bug. ■

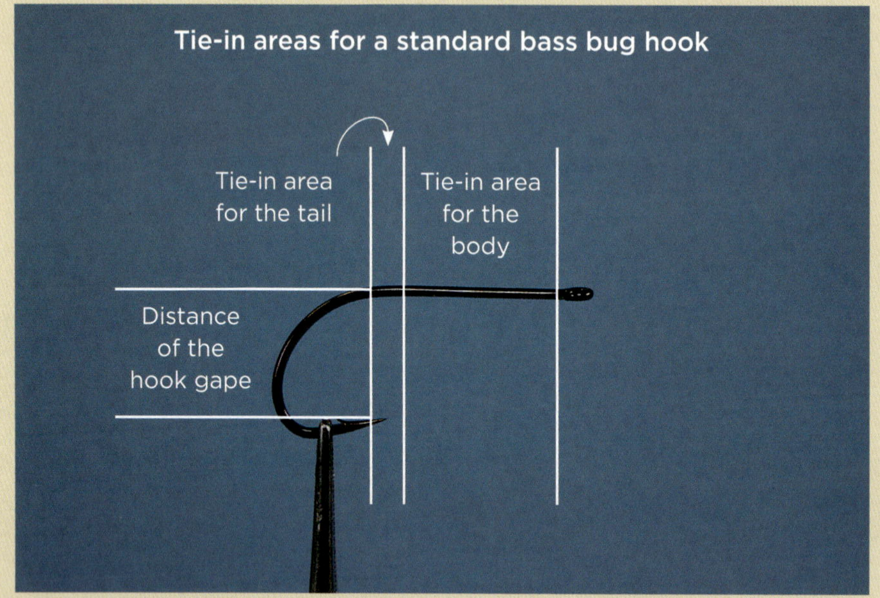

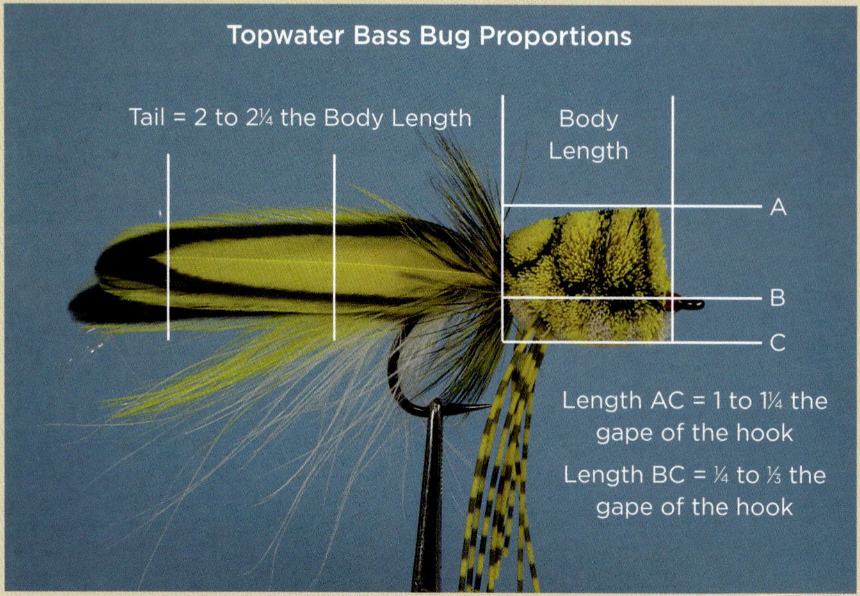

STEP-TYING LARGE FLIES

While you can tie larger or more complicated deer hair flies by completing the flies one at a time, it's often more efficient to tie these patterns in steps. Normally any time I am changing threads, I will step-tie the pattern. This includes smaller flies like hoppers as well as larger warmwater flies. Here is the typical progression when step-tying flies:

The first step is to tie the tail or body of the fly. If any glue is used in this part of the fly, step-tying will also have the advantage of allowing the glue to cure before moving on to the next part of the fly pattern.

Normally the next step would be to change to a GSP thread, then stack or spin and flare the deer hair on the fly. Here also if any glue is used, step-tying will allow it to cure before moving on to finishing the fly.

Trim the deer hair, then, if needed, add the finishing touches to the fly. Add eyes, tie a thread head, trim the legs, and complete any other finishing aspects that need to be done to the fly.

When averaged out, by step-tying the patterns you will probably decrease the time it takes to tie each fly. The flies will also probably have a more consistent look to them. Because a number of materials are usually needed for a pattern, by tying in steps you can have fewer materials on your tying bench at any given time. ■

The Topwater Deer Hair Bass Bug

The topwater deer hair bass bug is one of the most iconic patterns for fly fishing for bass. It was modeled after the cork and balsa bass bugs of the early 1900s. Ernest Peckinpaugh is credited as one of the early bass bug designers. During the 1930s his cork body and bucktail bugs were commercially available and widely used. At the same time, Joe Messinger was one of the first tiers to take advantage of the cellular nature of deer hair and began to tie flared or spun deer hair flies, with his Bucktail Frog being one of his more artful and well-known designs.

After World War II, bass bug fishing took a backseat to traditional tackle with the introduction of the spinning rod. While a number of well-known authors continued to write about bass bug fishing, it wasn't until the 1970s that Dave Whitlock began to bring fly fishing for bass and the bass bug back into the mainstream of the fly-fishing world. Whitlock designed a number of bass flies modeled on successful lures that the traditional tackle bass tournament world was using. In 1988 his *L.L. Bean Fly Fishing for Bass Handbook* appeared. While this was not a fly-tying book, its many illustrations of fly patterns inspired a number of fly tiers, including myself. Nick Lyons wrote about Whitlock's flies and tactics for bass in *Field & Stream* in an article titled "The Bass Fly Revolution" (1990). This article also included a number of photos and illustrations of innovative fly designs, with many of them utilizing spun and flared deer hair.

Today there has been a resurgence of both outstanding deer hair tiers and spun deer hair bass bugs. With a wide palette of colored deer hair and new materials for legs, eyes, and tails, tying bass bugs has entered an era of unprecedented creativity and artistry.

Deer Hair Bass Bug

I have been tying and fishing deer hair bass bugs for almost three decades. I like using natural materials for the tails, and at times the search for appropriate tailing materials has been challenging. The tail must balance with the deer hair head. By that I mean if the tailing material is too sparse, the deer hair head overwhelms the tail and the fly does not fish and behave properly in the water. Also, when the fly is just sitting in the water, it doesn't present a proper profile. At the opposite end of the spectrum, the tail of the fly can be overdressed and too bulky.

I like a split-feather tail, and having a centering material to aid in making the feather wings splay is very helpful. Additionally this centering material helps in creating a transition from the body of the fly to the tail. I have tried marabou, but it easily overdresses the fly and obscures the split-feather tail. Whiting Bird Fur works uniquely well for this purpose. The marabou-like base provides a nice transition from the head to the tail, and the natural taper in the feather allows the split tail to stand out, creating a nice balance to the fly.

TYING THE DEER HAIR BASS BUG

- **Hook:** #4-10 Tiemco 8089 or 8089N, or #6-2/0 Gamakatsu B10S
- **Thread:** Yellow or black UTC 140 for tail, red for thread head; UTC GSP 130 for deer hair head
- **Tail:** Whiting Bird Fur, olive grizzly over yellow over white; pearl Hareline Ice Wing Fiber; olive, yellow, and white Whiting black laced hen cape
- **Hackle Collar:** Olive grizzly and yellow dyed ginger Whiting American rooster cape
- **Body:** Bleached, yellow, olive, and black Nature's Spirit deer spinning hair
- **Legs:** Speckled yellow, speckled olive, and speckled white Montana Fly Company Centipede Legs (medium)
- **Eyes:** Earth Flymen Fish-Skull Living Eyes (6 mm)
- **Glues:** Zap-A-Gap for starting and finishing GSP thread; Dave's Flexament for tail thread wraps and eyes; Fly-Rite Fly-Tite Fly Tying Cement for base of deer hair stacks; GOOP for eyes; Sally Hansen Hard as Nails for thread head

STEP 1: Begin by roughing up the rear tie-in area with a file.

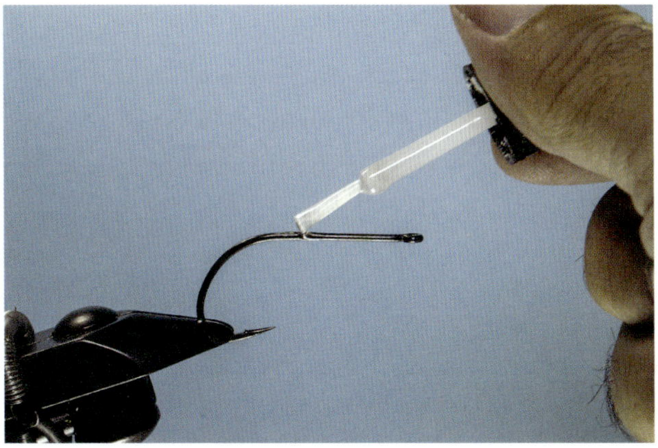

STEP 2: Apply a small amount of Zap-A-Gap to the roughed-up area.

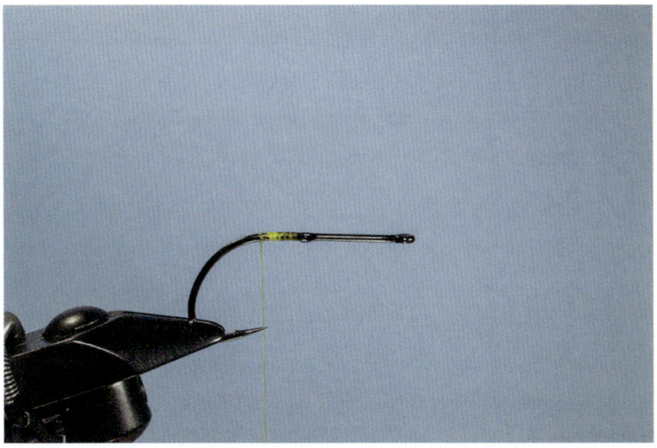

STEP 3: Attach the yellow or black UTC 140 thread at the rear tie-in point and wrap a base of thread that only covers the tailing tie-in area. By starting the thread in this manner, the tail will be more securely attached to the hook, preventing it from sliding back when the deer hair head is packed back against the tail.

STEP 4: Select 2 or 3 white Bird Fur feathers. Match the marabou-like base of the feathers together. Don't worry about the length of the barbules, as they will vary from feather to feather. Measure the marabou-like portion of the feather to be equal to the length of the hook shank. Note that the thread is placed at the back of the rear tie-in point.

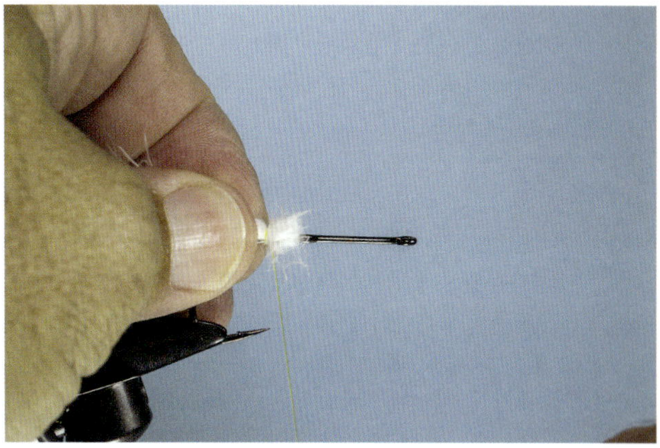

STEP 5: Trim the butt of the feather at that point and attach at the rear tie-in area. As the thread was placed at the back of the rear tie-in point, wrap forward, securing the feather to the hook.

STEP 6: Repeat with the yellow Bird Fur feathers.

STEP 7: Repeat with the olive grizzly Bird Fur feathers.

STEP 8: Center some Ice Wing Fiber on the tie-in point and make 2 wraps of thread.

STEP 9: Pull the Ice Wing Fiber back and make 2 or 3 more wraps of thread, securing the material to the hook. Pull the fibers back and around the hook shank, blending them in with the feathers.

STEP 10: Select 1 olive, 1 yellow, and 1 white black laced hen feather. Match the tips and curve of the feathers together. Place the olive as the outside feather, with the yellow next and then the white as the inside feather. Measure a length of the feathers equal to 2 to 2¼ times the shank length.

STEP 11: Place the feather with the concave side out on the far side of the hook shank. Make 3 loose wraps of thread, hold the feathers in place, and tighten the thread.

STEP 12: Slide your scissors up against the front of the tail and trim the butt of the feathers.

STEP 13: Repeat, adding the feather tails to the near side of the hook.

Top view of the split-feather tail.

STEP 14: Select 2 olive grizzly American feathers and 2 yellow dyed ginger American feathers. The barbule length can be equal to the hook gape to 1½ times the hook gape. Prep the feathers by trimming the butts and then trim a few of the barbules on each side at the base of the stem, leaving a few of them 1 to 2 millimeters long.

STEP 15: Attach the butts of the feathers to the tie-in area with the concave side away from you. (This is considered wet fly style because when the feather is wrapped, the barbules will sweep back.) After attaching the feathers, put a small amount of Dave's Flexament on the thread wraps.

STEP 16: Wrap the first feather around the hook shank as many times as the length allows, then tie off the feather.

STEP 17: Wrap the other 3 feathers, creating a full hackle collar. Tie each feather off as you wrap it.

STEP 18: Trim the tips of the feathers. Make 2 or 3 more wraps of thread to securely attach the feathers and then whip-finish the UTC 140 thread right in front of the tail. This is a side view of a completed feather wing tail.

STEP 19: Sweep the tailing materials back and wrap a band of red UTC 140 thread.

STEP 20: Use a whip-finish knot to secure the thread band and trim the thread. By doing this all of the tailing materials are swept back and out of the way as you work on the deer hair head of the fly. This thread band will be cut off, allowing the tailing material to expand when the fly is completed.

STEP 21: Use a small amount of Zap-A-Gap at the front of the tail. Wrap the UTC GSP 130 thread through the glued area and then wrap a thread base up to the eye of the hook. Wrap the thread back to the front of the tail.

STEP 22: Prep a bunch of bleached deer hair. Trim the tips and the butts. Wrap the hair with 3 wraps of thread, then rotate the hair to the bottom of the hook shank and flare.

STEP 23: Prep a bunch of yellow deer hair. Trim the butts and tips. Place the hair on the top of the hook shank with 2 wraps of thread and flare. As you flare the hair, use the index finger of your opposite hand to support the stack of hair so it doesn't rotate around the hook shank. Keep the thread wraps in the same plane; do not advance the thread forward through the hair.

STEP 24: Prep a small bunch of black deer hair. Trim the butts and tips. Separate the yellow hair evenly and place the black deer hair in the space. Make 2 wraps of thread and flare it in place; keep the thread wraps in the same plane as before.

STEP 25: Prep a bunch of olive deer hair. Trim the butts and tips. Using the same technique as with the black hair, place and flare the bunch of olive deer hair. With this final bunch, put as much tension on the thread as possible without cutting through the hair or breaking the thread. Hold the tension momentarily, allowing the thread to tighten.

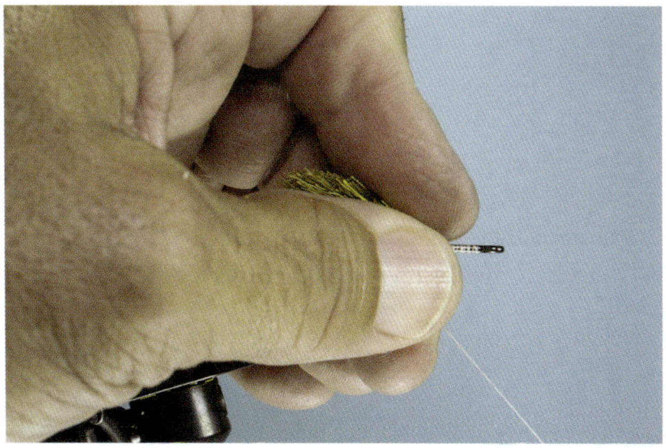

STEP 26: Pull the hair stack back; keep tension on the thread and advance it through the hair. Make 2 or 3 wraps of thread at the front of the stack.

STEP 27: Use a half-hitch tool to put a couple of half-hitches at the front of the stack of hair.

STEP 28: Find the knots with a hair-packing tool and compress the stack of hair back towards the tail.

STEP 29: Apply some Fly-Tite cement at the base of the hair stack. (This is an optional step.)

STEP 30: Put an overhand knot in the legging material. Slip the knot over the hook shank. While the knot is still loose, adjust the legs so equal lengths of leg are on each side of the hook shank. Tighten the knot.

STEP 31: Use a hair-packing tool to compress the knotted legs back into the hair stack.

STEP 32: Repeat with an identical stack of hair.

STEP 33: Pull the thread through the hair under tension and use your half-hitch tool to make a couple of knots. Use your hair-packing tool to compress the stack, then add glue to the base of the stack of hair.

STEP 34: Repeat with a third stack of hair. Note that I omitted the yellow hair on this stack.

STEP 35: Apply some Zap-A-Gap to the thread. Make a few wraps of thread and then finish with a couple of half-hitch knots. Trim the thread.

Side view of the untrimmed deer hair head.

STEP 36: Using your scissors, trim the back of the deer hair head.

STEP 37: Continue trimming until you have a relatively flat back to the head.

STEP 38: Turn the fly upside down. Hold the legs in your hands and use a razor blade to trim a flat belly. Leave 2 to 3 millimeters of hair on the bottom of the fly.

STEP 39: While still holding the legs under the fly, use your razor blade to trim the sides of the fly. Make sure to have an even length of hair on each side of the hook shank. The width of the head should be about 1 to 1¼ the width of the gape of the hook.

STEP 40: Trim the top of the body. The height of the head should be about 1 to 1¼ the width of the gape of the hook.

STEP 41: Use your razor blade to trim the front of the body flat.

The rough trimmed body of the fly should have a rectangular prism shape.

STEP 42: Using your razor blade, round the bottom edges and taper the edges toward the tail.

STEP 43: Continue trimming the body to give it a rounded shape that tapers toward the tail of the fly.

STEP 44: Here I steamed the body of the fly. Steam will expand the deer hair, making the trimming easier.

STEP 45: Continue using the razor blade to complete the trimming of the fly. As you get to the final shape, keep the razor blade very flat to the head, taking very small cuts. It's more like sanding the hair than cutting it. The body should have a smooth, rounded taper towards the tail. A cross-section of the fly should have a rounded or oval shape. Note the hair left under the hook shank; this is a critical feather allowing the fly to fish properly. (See sidebar "Bass Bug Proportions.")

STEP 46: Use the corner of the razor blade to cut the red thread band, allowing the hackle collar to expand.

Side view of the trimmed deer hair body and expanded hackle collar.

STEP 47: Attach the red UTC 140 thread in front of the body and wrap a neat thread head. Use a whip-finish knot to complete the head and trim the thread.

STEP 48: Use either a Hot Point tool or curved scissors to create an eye socket. Repeat on the opposite side of the body.

STEP 49: Put a small amount of thinned Dave's Flexament into the eye socket.

STEP 50: Put a small amount of GOOP into the eye socket. Dave's Flexament is basically thinned GOOP, so the thinner in the Dave's Flexament will interact with the GOOP and draw the glue deeper into the deer hair. As a result, the eye will be more firmly attached to the body when the glue cures.

STEP 51: Insert the eye into the socket. Rotate the eye slightly as you press it into the GOOP, ensuring a complete seal on the back of the eye with the glue. Repeat on the opposite side of the body.

STEP 52: Coat the thread head with Sally Hansen Hard as Nails.

STEP 53: Draw a feather through the eye of the hook to clear out the head cement. Trim the legs up so they are even. I prefer to keep them long, as they will provide a lot of movement to the fly when it is fished. However, leg length is a personal preference, and the fly will fish well with shorter as well as longer legs.

Side view.

Front view.

Bottom view.

Top view.

ADDING LEGS TO A SPUN DEER HAIR BODY

Adding legs to a deer hair bass bug certainly adds to its appeal to both fish and fisherman. Legs add to the overall texture and movement of the fly in the water. There are a couple of ways to add legs to a spun deer hair body.

I prefer to tie the legs around the hook shank, as I did in step 30 in the Deer Hair Bass Bug. The advantage of tying the legs to the hook shank is that you don't need any glue to hold the legs in place. This keeps the bass bug body feeling softer when a fish grabs it. The disadvantage of this method is that you have to trim the body around the legs without cutting them off.

An alternative way to attach the legs is to thread them through the completed deer hair body and glue them in place. The advantage to this method is that you can trim the body without the legs getting in the way. The disadvantage is that the body becomes harder because of the glue added to keep the legs in place. If using this technique, use the glue sparingly when applying it to the legs.

Tie a bass bug minus the legs and complete the trimming.

STEP 1: Thread some leg material through a small darning needle. Then thread the needle through the deer hair body so it passes just above the hook shank.

STEP 2: Once the darning needle passes through the body, continue pulling the leg material through the body.

STEP 3: Have about an extra body-width length of leg material on one side of the hook. Apply some Dave's Flexament to the leg material that is right next to the body on the side with the extra length.

(continued on next page)

STEP 4: Stretch the leg material and work the glued section back into the deer hair body.

The legs should exit the body at the midline just above the hook shank.

STEP 5: Work the legs back and forth slightly to distribute the glue. At the same time apply some downward pressure to the legs

Side view of the completed fly with legs. ■

Rubber Tail Deer Hair Popper

Unlike the Feather Tail Bass Bug, which has an intricate tail, this bass bug has a simple tail made out of rubber leg material. This is a simple but effective way to start a bass popper.

Most of the time when you stack hair to create bars or rings of color, the stacking is done on the top of the fly with the occasional stack on the bottom to keep the distribution of hair even around the hook shank. However, hair can be stacked anywhere around the hook shank. In this pattern I demonstrate that stacking hair on the sides of the body can create some interesting and artistic patterns.

TYING THE RUBBER TAIL DEER HAIR POPPER

- **Hook:** #4/0-6 Partridge Universal Predator
- **Thread:** Red UTC 140 for thread head; UTC GSP 130 for tail and deer hair popper head
- **Tail:** Yellow Hareline Grizzly Barred Rubber Legs (medium)
- **Body:** Yellow, black, and bleached Nature's Spirit deer spinning hair
- **Eyes:** Red/black pupil Hareline Oval Pupil 3D Eyes (5⁄16 inch)
- **Glues:** Zap-A-Gap for starting and finishing GSP thread; Dave's Flexament for eyes; Fly-Rite Fly-Tite Fly Tying Cement for base of deer hair stacks; GOOP for eyes; Sally Hansen Hard as Nails for thread head

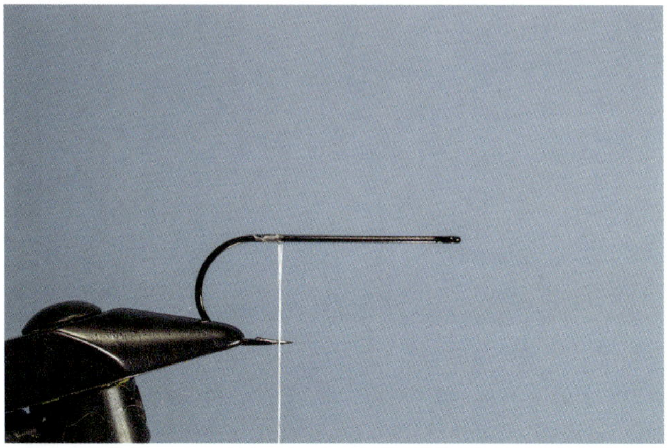

STEP 1: Rough up the rear tie-in area with a file and apply a small amount of Zap-A-Gap. Use a jam knot and wrap the GSP thread through the glued area, attaching to the rear tie-in area of the hook.

STEP 2: Evenly fold 6 to 8 rubber legs over the thread and wrap the thread around the hook shank, attaching the legs to the rear tie-in point of the hook.

STEP 3: Sweep the legs back and make 3 or 4 loose wraps of thread around the base of the legs. This will bundle the legs together instead of flaring the material.

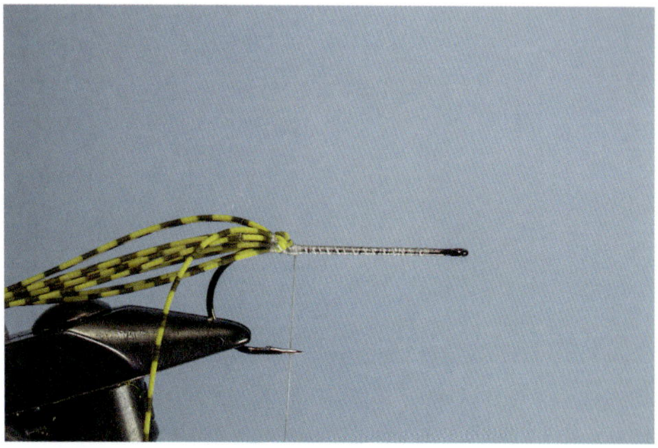

STEP 4: Wrap the thread forward, creating a thread base for the hair work. Use spiral wraps to return the thread to the rear tie-in point.

STEP 5: Prep a bunch of yellow spinning hair. Place it on the hook shank and make 3 wraps of thread, then rotate the hair to the bottom of the hook shank and flare it.

STEP 6: Prep another bunch of yellow spinning hair. Place it on top of the hook shank with 2 wraps of thread and flare it.

STEP 7: Prep a small bunch of black spinning hair. Place the hair on the opposite side of the hook shank and flare it in place.

STEP 8: Repeat with another small bunch of black spinning hair on the near side of the hook shank.

STEP 9: Make a space in the black hair on the far side of the hook shank. Place and flare a small bunch of yellow hair in the space on the black hair.

STEP 10: Repeat on the near side of the hook shank. Keep the thread under tension as you work it through the hair to advance it to the front of the stack. Tie 2 or 3 half-hitch knots in front of the stack of hair, then use a packing tool to compress the stack. Apply a small amount of Fly-Tite cement at the base of the hair stack.

Note: This is the first stack of hair. The first bunch of hair used 3 wraps of thread. Five additional bunches of hair were added using 2 wraps of thread each, for an additional 10 wraps of thread. In total there are 13 wraps of thread for the stack. All of the wraps of thread occurred in the same plane.

STEP 11: Repeat the same pattern two more times.

STEP 12: Prep a bunch of bleached spinning hair. Use 3 wraps of thread to attach it to the hook shank. Rotate and flare the hair on the bottom of the hook shank.

STEP 13: Prep a bunch of bleached spinning hair and flare it on the top of the hook shank.

STEP 14: Add another bunch of bleached hair on both the top and bottom of the stack of hair. Advance the thread under tension to the front of the hair. Apply a small amount of Zap-A-Gap to the thread and make several wraps around the hook shank with the glued thread. Tie 2 or 3 half-hitches on top of the glued thread head. Trim the thread.

STEP 15: As with the Deer Hair Bass Bug, begin by trimming the body into a rectangular prism. Then using the razor blade, continue trimming until you have a circular or oval-shaped cross-section to the body. The body should taper towards the tail. Trim the face of the popper so it is flat. Note the length of hair left under the hook shank. Add eyes and a red thread head. This is a side view of the finished fly.

Top view.

THOUGHTS ON COLOR

Unlike trout flies, there isn't really any codification of bass bug patterns, though a few fly tiers have attempted to name patterns. Dave Whitlock's Fruit Cocktail Bass Bug is one example of a recognizable fly pattern; however, very few have the same kind of recognition as that pattern. Instead of thinking of individual fly patterns, I instead think in terms of pattern templates and general color schemes for my deer hair bass bugs.

With both my topwater deer hair bass bugs and my diving bass bugs, I tend to group flies into three general categories by color. My three general groups are as follows:

BRIGHT COLORS: This group is composed primarily of white, chartreuse, orange, and yellow flies. These flies can certainly have accents of darker colors, but the overall impression is that of brighter colors.

DARK COLORS: In this group I would include black, purple, gray, and natural deer hair bass bugs. Again there could be accents of lighter colors or perhaps a white face, but the overall impression is that of darker bass bug.

FROG COLORS: This group consists of color schemes that have light-colored bellies, various colors for the midline, and darker-colored backs. My favorite color scheme is in this group: the white belly, yellow midline, and olive back frog pattern. This is the color bug that I fish most of the time.

It's difficult to tell just how much color plays into a bass's decision to take a certain bug. Where the bug is fished and how it is retrieved probably plays a bigger role than the color of the bug. However, if a bug is not working, I will usually try another one from a different color group before abandoning topwater fishing altogether.

Having said all that, color schemes are very much up to the individual fly tier. Be creative and tie the color flies that appeal to your own artistic proclivity. ■

Compendium of Topwater Deer Hair Bass Bug Patterns

The following flies are some of the more common color schemes that I have used successfully. They fall into the three categories of color schemes: bright colors, dark colors, and frog colors (see "Thoughts on Color" sidebar).

YELLOW BELLY FROG

- **Hook:** #4-10 Tiemco 8089 or 8089N, or #6-2/0 Gamakatsu B10S
- **Thread:** Black UTC 140 for tail, red for thread head; UTC GSP 130 for deer hair head
- **Tail:** Whiting Bird Fur, olive grizzly over yellow; gold Hareline Ice Wing Fiber; olive, red, and yellow Whiting black laced hen cape
- **Hackle collar:** Red grizzly and yellow dyed ginger Whiting American cape
- **Body:** Yellow, red, olive, and black Nature's Spirit spinning hair
- **Legs:** Speckled yellow/red and speckled olive Montana Fly Company Centipede Legs (medium)
- **Eyes:** Red/black pupil Hareline Oval Pupil 3D Eyes (3⁄16 inch)
- **Glues:** Zap-A-Gap for starting and finishing GSP thread; Dave's Flexament for tail thread wraps and eyes; Fly-Rite Fly-Tite Fly Tying Cement for base of deer hair stacks; GOOP for eyes; Sally Hansen Hard as Nails for thread head

ORANGE BELLY FROG

- **Hook:** #4-10 Tiemco 8089 or 8089N, or #6-2/0 Gamakatsu B10S
- **Thread:** Black UTC 140 for tail and thread head; UTC GSP 130 for deer hair head
- **Tail:** Whiting Bird Fur, chartreuse over orange; chartreuse Hareline Ice Wing Fiber; chartreuse, yellow, and orange Whiting black laced hen cape
- **Hackle collar:** Orange grizzly and yellow grizzly Whiting American cape
- **Body:** Orange, yellow, black, and chartreuse Nature's Spirit spinning hair
- **Legs:** Speckled yellow and speckled chartreuse Hareline Barred Rubber Legs (medium)
- **Eyes:** Orange/black pupil Hareline Oval Pupil 3D Eyes (3⁄16 inch)
- **Glues:** Zap-A-Gap for starting and finishing GSP thread; Dave's Flexament for tail thread wraps and eyes; Fly-Rite Fly-Tite Fly Tying Cement for base of deer hair stacks; GOOP for eyes; Sally Hansen Hard as Nails for thread head

RED FACE YELLOW

- **Hook:** #4-10 Tiemco 8089 or 8089N, or #6-2/0 Gamakatsu B10S
- **Thread:** Black UTC 140 for tail and thread head; UTC GSP 130 for deer hair head
- **Tail:** Yellow Whiting Bird Fur, red Hareline Ice Wing Fiber, yellow Whiting black laced hen cape
- **Hackle collar:** Grizzly dyed red Whiting American cape
- **Body:** Yellow, natural, and red Nature's Spirit spinning hair
- **Legs:** Speckled yellow Montana Fly Company (medium)
- **Eyes:** Red/black pupil Hareline Oval Pupil 3D Eyes (3⁄16 inch)
- **Glues:** Zap-A-Gap for starting and finishing GSP thread; Dave's Flexament for tail thread wraps and eyes; Fly-Rite Fly-Tite Fly Tying Cement for base of deer hair stacks; GOOP for eyes; Sally Hansen Hard as Nails for thread head

RED FACE WHITE

- **Hook:** #4-10 Tiemco 8089 or 8089N, or #6-2/0 Gamakatsu B10S
- **Thread:** Black UTC 140 for tail and thread head; UTC GSP 130 for deer hair head
- **Tail:** White Whiting Bird Fur, pearl Hareline Midge Flash, white Whiting black laced hen cape
- **Hackle collar:** Grizzly dyed red Whiting American cape
- **Body:** Bleached, natural, and red Nature's Spirit spinning hair
- **Legs:** Speckled white Montana Fly Company (medium)
- **Eyes:** Red/black pupil Hareline Oval Pupil 3D Eyes (3⁄16 inch)
- **Glues:** Zap-A-Gap for starting and finishing GSP thread; Dave's Flexament for tail thread wraps and eyes; Fly-Rite Fly-Tite Fly Tying Cement for base of deer hair stacks; GOOP for eyes; Sally Hansen Hard as Nails for thread head

RED FACE CHARTREUSE

- **Hook:** #4-10 Tiemco 8089 or 8089N, or #6-2/0 Gamakatsu B10S
- **Thread:** Black UTC 140 for tail and thread head; UTC GSP 130 for deer hair head
- **Tail:** Chartreuse Whiting Bird Fur, red Hareline Ice Wing Fiber, chartreuse Whiting black laced hen cape
- **Hackle collar:** Grizzly dyed red Whiting American rooster cape
- **Body:** Chartreuse, natural, and red Nature's Spirit deer spinning hair
- **Legs:** Red and chartreuse Spirit River Grizzly Legs (medium)
- **Eyes:** Red/black pupil Hareline Oval Pupil 3D Eyes (3⁄16 inch)
- **Glues:** Zap-A-Gap for starting and finishing GSP thread; Dave's Flexament for tail thread wraps and eyes; Fly-Rite Fly-Tite Fly Tying cement for base of deer hair stacks; GOOP for eyes; Sally Hansen Hard as Nails for thread head

YELLOW AND WHITE BELLY

- **Hook:** #4-10 Tiemco 8089 or 8089N, or #6-2/0 Gamakatsu B10S
- **Thread:** Yellow or black UTC 140 for tail, red for thread head; White UTC GSP 130 for deer hair head
- **Tail:** Whiting Bird Fur, yellow over white; pearl Hareline Ice Wing Fiber; yellow and white Whiting black laced hen cape
- **Hackle collar:** Grizzly dyed yellow Whiting American rooster cape
- **Body:** Bleached, yellow, and black Nature's Spirit deer spinning hair
- **Legs:** Speckled yellow and speckled white Montana Fly Company Centipede Legs (medium)
- **Eyes:** Red/black pupil Hareline Oval Pupil 3D Eyes (1⁄4 inch)
- **Glues:** Zap-A-Gap for starting and finishing GSP thread; Dave's Flexament for tail thread wraps and eyes; Fly-Rite Fly-Tite Fly Tying Cement for base of deer hair stacks; GOOP for eyes; Sally Hansen Hard as Nails for thread head

ORANGE AND YELLOW BELLY

- **Hook:** #4-10 Tiemco 8089 or 8089N, or #6-2/0 Gamakatsu B10S
- **Thread:** Black UTC 140 for tail thread head; White UTC GSP 130 for deer hair head
- **Tail:** Whiting Bird Fur, orange grizzly over yellow; pearl Hareline Ice Wing Fiber; orange and yellow Whiting black laced hen cape
- **Hackle collar:** Grizzly dyed orange and grizzly dyed yellow Whiting American rooster cape
- **Body:** Yellow, orange, and black Nature's Spirit deer spinning hair
- **Legs:** Speckled yellow Hareline Barred Rubber Legs (medium)
- **Eyes:** Orange/black pupil Hareline Oval Pupil 3D Eyes (¼ inch)
- **Glues:** Zap-A-Gap for starting and finishing GSP thread; Dave's Flexament for tail thread wraps and eyes; Fly-Rite Fly-Tite Fly Tying Cement for base of deer hair stacks; GOOP for eyes; Sally Hansen Hard as Nails for thread head

NATURAL DEER BASS BUG

- **Hook:** #4-10 Tiemco 8089 or 8089N, or #6-2/0 Gamakatsu B10S
- **Thread:** Black UTC 140 for tail, red for thread head; White UTC GSP 130 for deer hair head
- **Tail:** Natural grizzly Whiting Bird Fur, gold Hareline Ice Wing Fiber, tan Whiting black laced hen cape
- **Hackle collar:** Grizzly Whiting American rooster cape
- **Body:** Natural and black, bleached for the face Nature's Spirit deer spinning hair
- **Legs:** Natural Hareline Grizzly Barred Rubber Legs (medium)
- **Eyes:** Pearl/black pupil Hareline Oval Pupil 3D Eyes (¼ inch)
- **Glues:** Zap-A-Gap for starting and finishing GSP thread; Dave's Flexament for tail thread wraps and eyes; Fly-Rite Fly-Tite Fly Tying Cement for base of deer hair stacks; GOOP for eyes; Sally Hansen Hard as Nails for thread head

PURPLE AND BLACK

- **Hook:** #4-10 Tiemco 8089 or 8089N, or #6-2/0 Gamakatsu B10S
- **Thread:** Black UTC 140 for tail and thread head; White UTC GSP 130 for deer hair head
- **Tail:** Whiting Bird Fur, black over purple; black Hareline Ice Wing Fiber; purple Whiting black laced hen cape
- **Hackle collar:** Grizzly dyed purple Whiting American cape
- **Body:** Purple and black Nature's Spirit deer spinning hair
- **Legs:** Black Hareline Round Rubber Legs (small or medium)
- **Eyes:** Pearl/black pupil Hareline Oval Pupil 3D Eyes (¼ inch)
- **Glues:** Zap-A-Gap for starting finishing GSP thread; Dave's Flexament for tail thread wraps and eyes; Fly-Rite Fly-Tite Fly Tying Cement for base of deer hair stacks; GOOP (for eyes); Sally Hansen Hard as Nails for thread head

OLIVE

- **Hook:** #4-10 Tiemco 8089 or 8089N, or #6-2/0 Gamakatsu B10S
- **Thread:** Black UTC 140 for tail, red for thread head; White UTC GSP 130 for deer hair head
- **Tail:** Olive grizzly Whiting Bird Fur, pearl or gold Hareline Ice Wing Fiber, olive Whiting black laced hen cape
- **Hackle collar:** Grizzly dyed olive Whiting American rooster cape
- **Body:** Olive and black Nature's Spirit deer spinning hair
- **Legs:** Speckled olive Montana Fly Company Centipede Legs (medium)
- **Eyes:** Red/black pupil Hareline Oval Pupil 3D Eyes (¼ inch)
- **Glues:** Zap-A-Gap for starting and finishing GSP thread; Dave's Flexament (for tail thread wraps and eyes); Fly-Rite Fly-Tite Fly Tying Cement for base of deer hair stacks; GOOP for eyes; Sally Hansen Hard as Nails for thread head

CHAPTER 8

Waking Deer Hair Flies

"Sliders imitate calmer surface-swimming minnows, mice, water snakes, and the like. Bass are sometimes cautious because of clear water or calm surfaces; at such times sliders often outfish poppers because they make less disturbance and noise."

DAVE WHITLOCK, *L.L. BEAN FLY FISHING FOR BASS HANDBOOK*

It was late in the morning and I decided that I was tired of casting my larger bass rods. Motoring in to one of the many shoreline areas that I knew held good populations of bluegill and sunfish, I picked up my 3-weight rod that I enjoyed using for these smaller fish. Fishing with a lightly weighted nymph, I immediately began to catch panfish.

Hooking a medium-size bluegill, I began stripping line and playing the fish on the light rod. He swam around the boat and into deeper water. Reeling up my excess line, I continued to play the fish and was ready to land him. As he was struggling in the surface, there was a sudden flash from the deeper water and my rod doubled over into a deep bend. It was a largemouth bass that had taken the bluegill from the surface of the water as he was struggling.

The bass headed back for the deep water with his meal and was reluctant to give it up. I could only put a small amount of pressure with the rod I was using, so I fought the bass for almost a minute. Suddenly the pressure was released and the line and bluegill came flying back towards the boat and me. The bluegill definitely looked dazed and was missing a few scales, but other than that he was in good shape. I moved into shallower water to release him, as I figured he had seen enough for this morning.

If you fish warmwater lakes that have populations of both panfish and bass, this scenario is not unfamiliar. All bass are extremely conscious of struggling baitfish in the surface. Certainly many of our bass bugs are taken because of that trait. Striped bass are known for pushing schools of baitfish to the surface and then attacking them. Lake Powell in Arizona as well as other striped bass lakes are notable for the large schools of baitfish that will suddenly boil to the surface trying to escape the striped bass that are attacking them. While largemouth bass tend to be more solitary hunters and do not exhibit the same schooling behavior as striped bass, they will still attack a school of small panfish at the surface of the water, creating a similar experience. A waking fly that is fished as a struggling baitfish will often arouse this response in bass as well as other predatory warmwater fish.

A waking or slider fly pattern is tied in such a way as to not cause much disturbance in the water as it is being retrieved. It is a subtle presentation but often one that gets a positive response from fish. A deer hair mouse fly also falls into this waking school of fly patterns. Mouse patterns are often fished with a slow hand-twist retrieve, and whether fished across the still surface of a bass lake or out from a bank of a trout river, it is an effective combination of fly and presentation that large predatory fish have a hard time resisting.

WHITING BIRD FUR

In 2010 Richard Munoz, formerly of Whiting Farms, introduced me to Bird Fur. Seeing its potential, I began to incorporate it into my warmwater fly patterns with great results. Today it's one of the main pelts that I rely on to provide movement and texture in many of the flies I tie for bass, pike, and muskie.

The name Bird Fur was coined by onetime marketing manager Steve Schweitzer. The catchy title really captures the nature of this feather. The Bird Fur pelt is the rooster cape of the Spey line of birds. At one time "Spey cock" feathers came from a line of special roosters from the Spey River Valley of Scotland. Around the beginning of the 20th century, this line of birds began to dwindle and feathers from various heron species began to be used in its place. However, with legal protection of herons, a need arose for a suitable replacement.

Dr. Tom Whiting began working on a Spey line of birds in the mid-1990s. For about 10 years, with the help of pro team members, he developed the line. Today this line of birds provides a variety of feather pelts, including rooster capes, rooster saddles, hen capes, hen saddles, and roster breast pelts. These pelts have a variety of applications, including warmwater fly patterns.

The Bird Fur feather is unique in its appearance. I've not found another pelt that has the same properties as this one. The base of the feather has marabou-like barbules and the shaft, or rachis, is solid, providing a good tie-in point. As you move toward the tip of the feather, the rachis becomes very slender along with long, slender barbules. The feather naturally has a tapered profile. Used sparingly, this can introduce some very subtle texture to a fly. If more feathers are used it still provides

Natural-colored Bird Fur capes

Natural-colored Bird Fur feathers

White dyed Bird Fur capes

(continued on next page)

Grizzly dyed Bird Fur capes

Dyed Bird Fur feathers

Three deer hair patterns that benefit from the use of Bird Fur feathers

for a tapered profile, unlike marabou, whose feathers have a very square, blunt tip.

The Waking Shad Minnow has a great minnow silhouette and creates a muted disturbance when retrieved through the water. The grizzly Bird Fur in this pattern adds a subtle barring on the sides and provides for better movement in the water

For topwater deer hair bass bugs, I like using natural materials for the tails. I like a split-feather tail, and having a centering material to aid in making the feather wings splay is very helpful. This centering material also helps in creating a transition from the body of the fly to the tail.

Tying a diving deer hair head with a rabbit strip tail is a fly pattern that has been around for a long time, and my early efforts at this fly usually involved tying on the rabbit strip and then spinning a deer hair head. While the fly caught fish, I was never satisfied with the transition between the head and the rabbit strip tail. A few years ago when barred and multicolored rabbit strip tails began to appear, I became very motivated to create a diving fly using this material; however, the transition between the head and the tail was still an issue. I tried both Arctic fox and marabou with mixed results, but the pattern really came together when I switched to a Bird Fur collar. With different colors and types of Bird Fur, I was able to really match the color scheme of the rabbit. I especially like the grizzly, as it blends well with the barring on the rabbit strip. Since the feather has a natural taper, the fly has a great transition from the head to the tail. When fished and viewed from underneath, the fly has a fishlike profile. The Bird Fur collar on this fly really completes the pattern.

Bird Fur is truly a unique material, and these three patterns only scratch the surface of what can be done with these feathers. Streamers, swinging Spey flies, and Woolly Buggers are only a few of the other fly patterns where Bird Fur feather could be used. ■

Waking Shad Minnow

While I had been tying other waking deer hair fly patterns prior to 2000, the first time I saw the Waking Sheep Minnow was in an article that Dave Whitlock did for *Fly Fisherman Magazine* that year. He only included drawings and a photo of the Waking Sheep Minnow pattern with a deer hair head, so I had to work out the tying myself. The pattern that I tie today is, of course, heavily influenced by that article but is a slight variation of that pattern.

The Waking Shad Minnow is a great pattern for many warmwater species. This fly has a realistic minnow silhouette and creates a subtle disturbance when retrieved through the water. The addition of grizzly Bird Fur on this pattern has added a subtle barring on the sides and provided for good texture and movement in the water. Fished as a struggling baitfish in the surface provides an almost irresistible trigger to predatory fish.

TYING THE WAKING SHAD MINNOW

- **Hook:** #4-10 Tiemco 8089 or 8089N, or #6-2/0 Gamakatsu B10S
- **Thread:** Black UTC 140 for tail, red for thread head; UTC GSP 130 for deer hair head
- **Tail:** White Wapsi Supreme Hair, white and silver gray Hareline Icelandic sheep, grizzly dyed heron Whiting Bird Fur, silver Spirit River Holographic Mylar Motion
- **Gills:** Red Hareline Ice Fur, minnow gills Dave Whitlock SLF Dubbing
- **Head:** Bleached and medium dun Nature's Spirit deer spinning hair
- **Eyes:** Pearl/black pupil Hareline Oval Pupil 3D Eyes (¼ inch)

  Black spot: Winsor & Newton Black Indian Ink
- **Glues:** Zap-A-Gap for starting and finishing GSP thread; Dave's Flexament for tail thread wraps and eyes; Fly-Rite Fly-Tite Fly Tying Cement for base of deer hair stacks; GOOP for eyes; Sally Hansen Hard as Nails for thread head

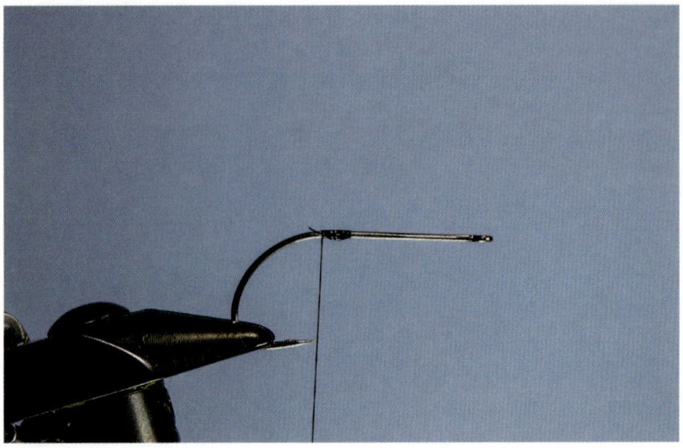

STEP 1: Prep the hook with a file, add a small amount of Zap-A-Gap to the tie-in area, and attach the black UTC 140 thread.

STEP 2: Cut a small bunch of the Wapsi Supreme Hair. Pull some of the ends to create a taper at the end of the bunch. Measure a length equal to the length from the eye to the back of the bend of the hook and trim to that length.

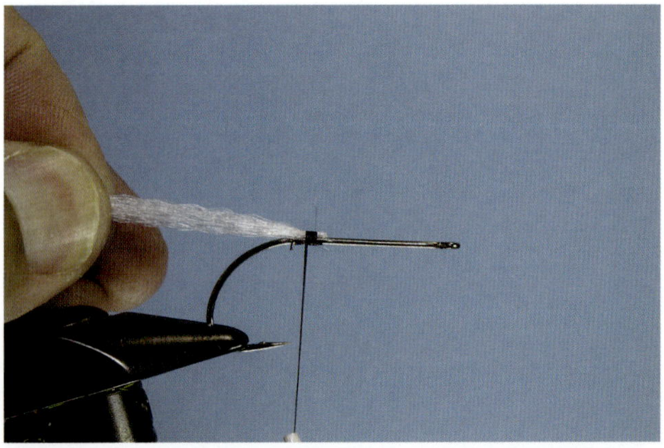

STEP 3: Attach the end of the Supreme Hair to the top of the hook shank at the tie-in area.

(continued on page 160)

WORKING WITH ICELANDIC SHEEP

Icelandic sheep is a natural streamer hair that has great movement in the water. It is readily available and comes in a variety of colors. However, if you are going to incorporate it into your flies, there are some ways of working with the material that will make your flies more durable. The first time I fished with a fly that I had tied with Icelandic sheep, it shed most of the hair within about 10 casts. I realized that I needed to work differently with the material. After rethinking how I tied the material into my patterns, I was able to create flies that fished well and were durable. Here are the steps for working with Icelandic sheep:

STEP 1: Cut a small amount of sheep from the hide. Icelandic sheep, as with most streamer hair, is more effective when it is used sparsely on a fly. It is easy to overdress a fly pattern by using too large an amount of this hair.

STEP 2: While Icelandic sheep does not have underfur the way deer hair does, it still has some shorter, more wool-like material at the base of the hair. Comb out this shorter hair, leaving only the longer hair.

STEP 3: Unlike bucktail, Icelandic sheep can't be stacked to even the tips. While holding the material in one hand, I pick out the longer hairs with my other hand. I work to create a tapered tip.

STEP 4: Measure the length required for the fly being tied and trim the butts before attaching it to the hook shank. Trimming the butts before attaching the hair to the hook shank will keep the tie-in area neater and aid in preserving the area of the hook shank for the deer hair head.

(continued on next page)

STEP 5: Place the butts of the hair at the tie-in point and attach with 2 or 3 wraps of thread.

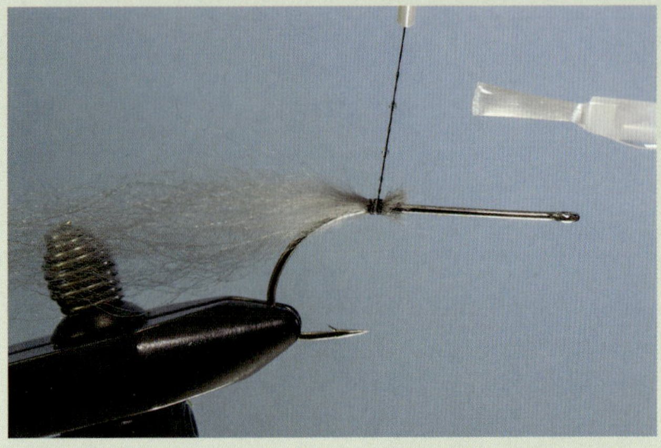

STEP 6: Apply some Zap-A-Gap glue to the thread and make 2 or 3 wraps of thread. Make sure the glue soaks down through the hair.

I usually don't glue the hair with every bunch. If attaching a bunch to the top of the hook shank and to the bottom, I will attach both bunches of hair and then apply the glue. The combination of combing the hair and then using the glue firmly attaches the hair to the fly. ■

STEP 4: Prep a small bunch of white Icelandic sheep (see "Working with Icelandic Sheep" sidebar). Measure a length equal to the length from the eye to the back of the bend of the hook. Trim the front of the hair.

STEP 5: Tie in the hair at the tie-in point.

STEP 6: Cut and prep a small bunch of white Icelandic sheep. Trim to a length equal to the first bunch.

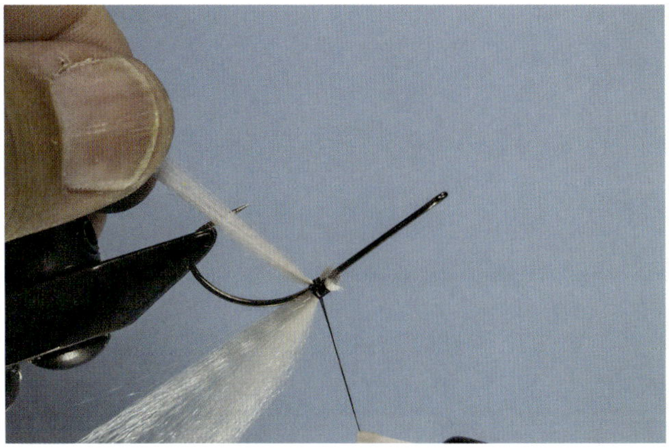

STEP 7: Rotate the vise and attach the hair to the bottom of the hook shank.

STEP 8: Rotate the vise back to upright and add 2 or 3 wraps of thread.

STEP 9: Take the hook out of the vise and sweep back the hair under the hook shank, creating the rear part of the tail. Put the hook back into the vise.

STEP 10: Add a small amount of Zap-A-Gap to the thread and make several wraps of thread, allowing the glue to penetrate the hair.

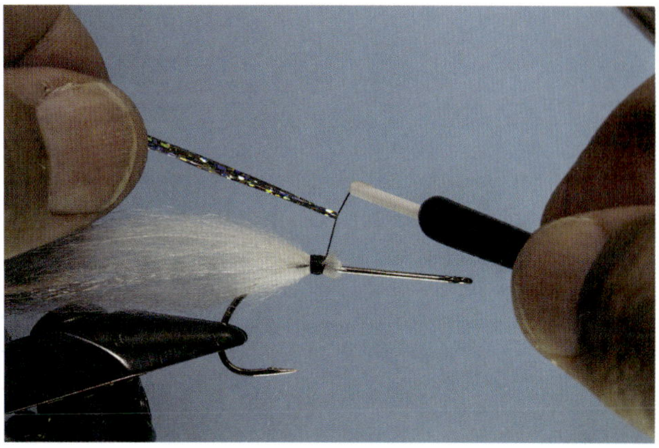

STEP 11: Attach some silver Holographic Flashabou by wrapping the flash material around the thread.

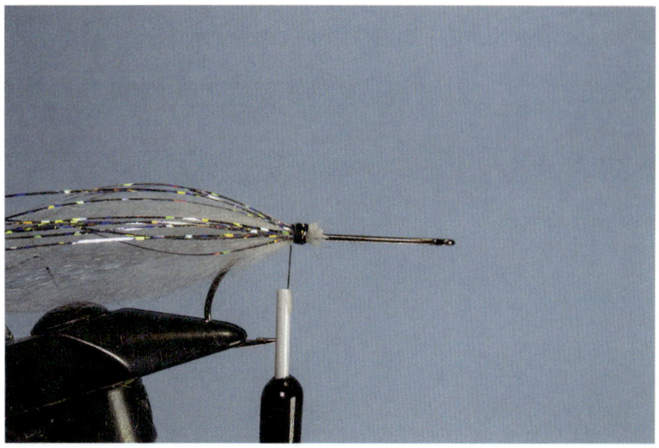

STEP 12: Make 1 wrap of thread with the flash attached. Then distribute the flash material around the hook shank and secure the material with 2 or 3 more wraps of thread.

STEP 13: Cut and prep some gray Icelandic sheep. Measure a length equal to the length of the hook shank and white Icelandic sheep tail and trim.

STEP 14: Attach the gray Icelandic sheep with 2 or 3 wraps of thread. Apply some Zap-A-Gap to the thread and make 2 more wraps, allowing the glue to secure the hair.

STEP 15: Select 2 or 3 Bird Fur feathers and measure a length equal to the length of the tail. This measurement is not critical, as some of the barbules may extend beyond the tail. (See "Whiting Bird Fur" sidebar.)

STEP 16: Attach the feathers to the tie-in point on the far side of the hook with 2 or 3 wraps of thread. Pull the butts of the feather away from the hook shank and trim.

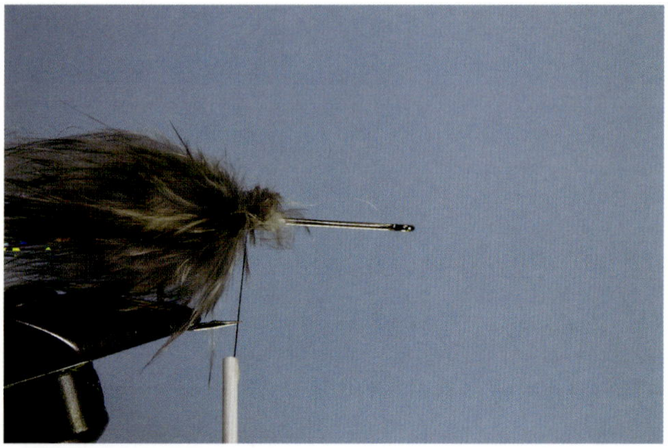

STEP 17: Repeat on the near side of the hook.

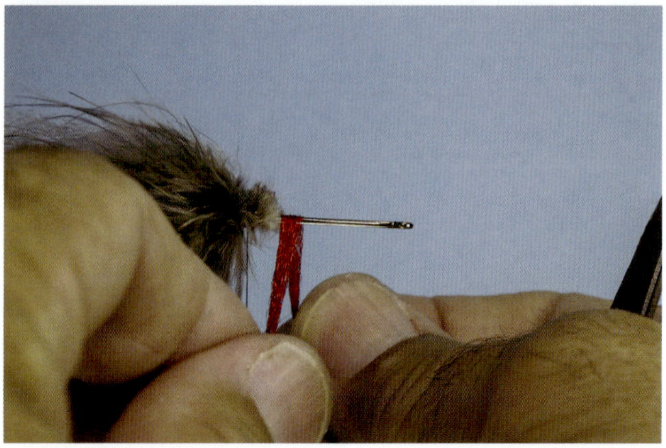

STEP 18: Cut a small amount of red Ice Fur. Wrap the Ice Fur over the top of the hook shank and pull it back against the front of the tailing materials at the tie-in point.

STEP 19: Make 2 or 3 wraps of thread around the tie-in point, securing the Ice Fur along each side of the tail. Trim the Ice Fur equal to the length of the bend of the hook.

STEP 20: Apply some minnow gills SLF Dubbing to the thread and cover the tailing thread wraps with the dubbing. Bring the thread to the front of the tail and tie off using a whip-finish knot.

Side view of the tail.

Top view of the tail.

Bottom view of the tail.

STEP 21: Apply a small amount of Zap-A-Gap in front of the tail and wrap the GSP thread through the glued area, then wrap a thread base to the front of the hook shank. Wrap the thread back to the front of the tail.

STEP 22: Clean, prep, and stack a bunch of bleached spinning hair. Align the tips with the bend of the hook shank and make 3 wraps of thread around the bunch of hair. Rotate the hair to the bottom of the hook shank and flare.

STEP 23: Clean, prep, and stack a bunch of medium dun deer hair. Align the tips with the bend of the hook.

STEP 24: Make 2 wraps of thread and flare the hair on the top of the hook shank. Make sure all the thread is wrapped in the same plane. Do not advance the thread forward through the hair.

STEP 25: Clean, prep, and stack a second bunch of medium dun deer hair. Create a space between the butts and tips of the first bunch of dun deer hair. This space should align with the wraps of thread. Align the tips with the tips of the first bunch of hair.

STEP 26: Make 2 wraps of thread around the bunch of hair and flare. Pull the hair stack back and keeping the thread under tension, advance it through the stack of hair. Make 2 or 3 wraps of thread directly in front of the hair stack and add 2 or 3 half-hitch knots directly in front of the stack. Use a hair-packing tool to compress the stack of hair. Add a small amount of Fly-Tite cement over the knots where the hair and hook shank meet.

STEP 27: Cut and prep another bunch of bleached deer hair. Trim the butts and tips of the hair. Attach the hair to the hook shank with 3 wraps of thread. Rotate it to the bottom of the hook shank and flare.

STEP 28: Cut and prep another bunch of medium dun hair. Trim the butts and tips of the hair. Use 2 wraps of thread and flare the hair on the top of the hook shank.

STEP 29: Keep the thread under tension and advance it through the stack of hair. Make 2 or 3 wraps of thread directly in front of the hair stack and add 2 or 3 half-hitch knots directly in front of the stack. Use the hair-packing tool to compress the stack of hair. Add a small amount of Fly-Tite cement over the knots where the hair and hook shank meet.

STEP 30: Repeat with a third stack of the bleached and medium dun deer hair. Keep the thread under tension and advance it through the stack of hair. Make 2 or 3 wraps of thread directly in front of the hair stack and add 2 or 3 half-hitch knots directly in front of the stack. Use the hair-packing tool to compress the stack of hair. Add a small amount of Fly-Tite cement over the knots where the hair and hook shank meet. Apply some Zap-A-Gap to the thread and make several wraps of thread. Finish with 2 or 3 half-hitch knots and cut the thread at the hook eye.

Front view. Note the distribution of hair around the hook shank.

STEP 31: Use a razor blade to make parallel cuts that are perpendicular to the eye of the hook, leaving 3 to 4 millimeters of hair on each side of the hook shank.

STEP 32: Use rounded scissors to trim the top and bottom into a fish-shaped head.

STEP 33: Use the scissors to trim the hair around the hook eye.

STEP 34: Use the razor blade to taper the front sides of the head towards the eye of the hook.

STEP 35: Continue using the razor blade to create a rounded fish-shaped head.

STEP 36: Add the eyes and a red thread head. Finish the thread head with the Sally Hansen Hard as Nails. Clean the eye of the hook with a feather to clear out any glue. Create a small, round black spot behind the eye by using a small, round wooden dowel to apply the Winsor & Newton Black Indian Ink. Side view.

Top view.

Bottom view.

Deer Hair Mouse

I bought my first deer hair mouse from Cal Gates, who owned Gates Au Sable Lodge on the Au Sable River in Michigan. It was a simple mouse with just a tail and a spun natural deer hair body. This fly was tied not to appeal to the eye of the angler, but to appeal to the predatory instinct of the brown trout that fed primarily at night on the Au Sable River system. While I don't fish with it anymore, I still have this fly in my fly box. It is a tattered reminder of the large brown trout that it fooled.

The late Chris Helm was noted for his deer hair mouse fly pattern. It was a favorite of the many fly tiers who were fortunate enough to get to see him tie it. The pattern that I tie here is similar to Chris's mouse with a few variations. I tie the whiskers at the head of the hook rather than in the deer hair. I really like Chris's technique of incorporating the moose hair for the whiskers into the spun hair at the nose of the fly; however, this does complicate the trimming of the fly. Additionally, Chris's mouse used a bare rabbit hide tail. I borrowed Colorado fly tier Jason Haddix's technique of leaving some of the rabbit fur at the tip of the tail. This gives the tail more movement, and when the rabbit hair gets wet, it tapers nicely, forming a realistic tail.

Of course, this mouse is tied for the fly tier and angler as much as it is for the trout or bass. That simple deer hair mouse that I bought from Cal still fishes as well today as it did almost four decades ago. (See "Simple Deer Hair Mouse" sidebar.)

TYING THE DEER HAIR MOUSE

- **Hook:** #4-10 Tiemco 8089, #6-2/0 Gamakatsu B10S, #2-2/0 Partridge Universal Predator or Universal Predator X, or #2-3/0 Daiichi 2461
- **Thread:** White UTC GSP 130 for tail and body; black UTC 140 for thread head
- **Tail:** Mouse gray Wapsi rabbit strip
- **Body/head:** Bleached and medium dun Nature's Spirit spinning hair
- **Ears:** Light gray, dark gray, or color to match body Wapsi Fly Foam (1 mm)
- **Eyes:** Half of a round, flat-back black plastic bead (3 to 5 mm)
- **Whiskers:** Natural Nature's Spirit moose body hair
- **Glues:** Zap-A-Gap for starting and finishing GSP thread; Dave's Flexament for eyes; Fly-Rite Fly-Tite Fly Tying Cement for base of deer hair stacks; GOOP for eyes; Sally Hansen Hard as Nails for thread head

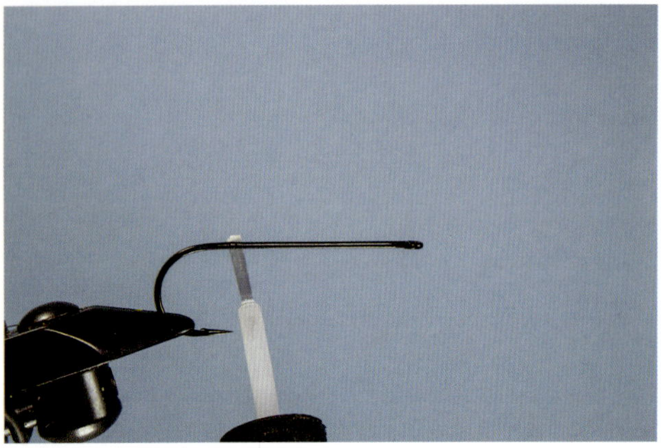

STEP 1: Rough up the tie-in area with a file and add some Zap-A-Gap.

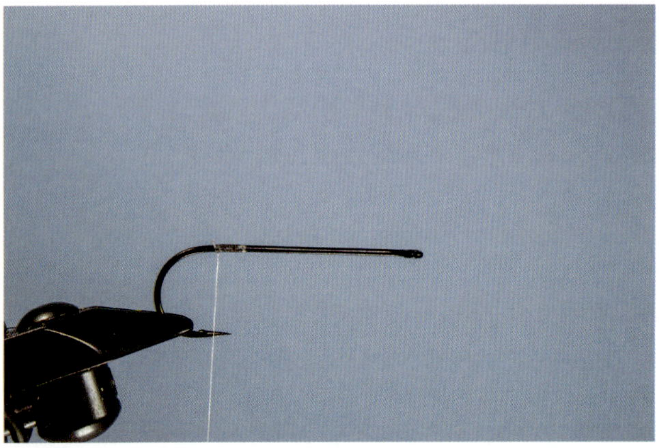

STEP 2: Wrap the GSP thread through the glued area of the hook shank.

STEP 3: Prep a strip of rabbit fur and tie in the base of the tail at the tie-in point.

STEP 4: Clean and prep a bunch of bleached deer hair. Attach the hair with 3 wraps of thread, then rotate it to the bottom of the hook shank and flare it.

STEP 5: Clean and prep a bunch of medium dun deer hair. Attach it to the hook shank with 2 wraps of thread and flare it right above the bleached hair. Keep the thread wraps in the same plane.

STEP 6: Clean and prep a second bunch of medium dun deer hair. Create a space above the thread wraps, then attach the hair with 2 wraps of thread and flare it right on top of the first bunch.

(continued on page 170)

SIMPLE DEER HAIR MOUSE

While it is fun to tie deer hair flies with eyes, color patterns, and other features that make the fly attractive, it is certainly not necessary to the process of creating flies that catch fish. This is especially true with a mouse pattern. Simple deer hair mice will fish as well as ones that have eyes, ears, and whiskers. The mouse can be tied with just natural deer hair or perhaps a bleached hair belly with a natural deer hair back. Fishing for bass or trout with mouse patterns is normally done during the low-light hours of the day, or even at night. Simple mouse patterns provide the surface disturbance and silhouette of a mouse, which is usually all that is needed to trigger a response from the fish. ■

STEP 7: Clean and prep a second bunch of bleached deer hair. Rotate either the vise or hook shank so you have access to the bottom of the stack of hair. Make a space in the bleached hair, then attach the second bunch of hair with 2 wraps of thread and flare it. Continue to keep the thread wraps in the same plane.

STEP 8: Add a third bunch of medium dun deer hair to the top of the stack of hair.

STEP 9: Keep the thread under tension and advance it to the front of the stack. Make 2 or 3 half-hitch knots right in front of the stack of hair and then use a packing tool to compress the hair stack. Add a few drops of Fly-Tite cement to the base of the hair.

STEP 10: Wind the thread forward, creating a thread base.

STEP 11: Repeat with a second stack of hair. This stack needs 1 bunch of bleached hair on the bottom and 2 bunches of medium dun hair on the top. Compress this stack of hair into the first stack. Support the first stack of hair with your fingers to prevent the stacks from sliding down the bend of the hook.

STEP 12: Apply a third stack of hair the same as the second stack. After compressing and adding cement to the stack, apply some Zap-A-Gap to the thread and make a few wraps of the glued thread around the hook shank. Finish with 2 or 3 half-hitch knots and trim the thread.

STEP 13: Use scissors to do a rough trim of the hair to a mouse-shaped body.

STEP 14: Cut 2 pieces of the 1 mm foam into a kite shape, then use scissors to round the top point of the foam. The length of each ear should be about 1¼ the gape of the hook and the width should be about the gape of the hook or slightly smaller. Reattach the GSP thread to the front of the hair body.

STEP 15: Fold one of the ears in half lengthwise and attach the long point of the foam right in front of the hair body with 2 or 3 wraps of thread. Repeat with the other ear. Pull both ears back against the body and secure with 2 or 3 more wraps of thread.

STEP 16: Apply another stack of the bleached and medium dun deer hair in front of the ears. After compressing and applying the cement to the stack, use Zap-A-Gap to tie off the GSP thread and trim.

STEP 17: Use scissors to do a rough trim on the head of the fly.

STEP 18: Use a razor blade to get the finish trim on the body.

STEP 19: Use the same technique as described in Chapter 7, "Tying the Deer Hair Bass bug," Steps 48 through 51, to add the eyes.

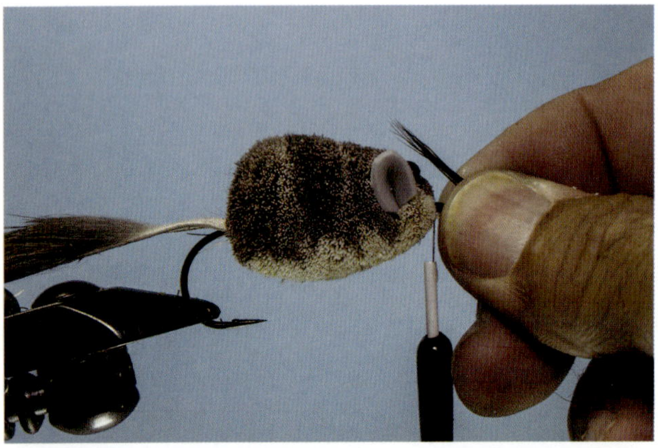

STEP 20: Attach the black UTC 140 thread to the front of the body. Cut, prep, and stack a small bunch of moose body hair. Use about 8 to 12 hairs. Measure the hair to a length just behind the ears and trim.

STEP 21: Slide the butts of the hair into the nose of the body and make 2 or 3 wraps of thread.

STEP 22: Separate the moose hair into 2 equal groups and bend each group to the side. Make several more wraps of thread, pushing the hair tips to each side. Use a whip-finish knot and trim the thread. Apply some Sally Hansen Hard as Nails to the thread wraps. Be sure to clear out the eye of the hook with a feather.

Side view.

Top view.

Compendium of Waking Deer Hair Flies

The following flies are some of the more common color schemes that I have used successfully. They fall into two categories: The first two patterns are more representative of actual baitfish, and the second two are attractor patterns.

JUVENILE BASS

- **Hook:** #4-10 Tiemco 8089 or #6-2/0 Gamakatsu B10S
- **Thread:** Black UTC 140 for tail, red for thread head; UTC GSP 130 for deer hair head
- **Tail:** White Wapsi Supreme Hair, white and olive Hareline Icelandic sheep, grizzly dyed olive Whiting Bird Fur, gold Spirit River Holographic Mylar Motion
- **Gills:** Red Hareline Ice Fur, minnow gills Dave Whitlock SLF Dubbing
- **Head:** Bleached, olive, and black Nature's Spirit spinning hair
- **Eyes:** Pearl/black pupil Hareline Oval Pupil 3D Eyes (¼ inch)
- **Glues:** Zap-A-Gap for starting and finishing GSP thread; Dave's Flexament for tail thread wraps and eyes; Fly-Rite Fly-Tite Fly Tying Cement for base of deer hair stacks; GOOP for eyes; Sally Hansen Hard as Nails for thread head

PERCH

- **Hook:** #4-10 Tiemco 8089 or #6-2/0 Gamakatsu B10S
- **Thread:** Black UTC 140 for tail, olive for thread head; UTC GSP 130 for deer hair head
- **Tail:** Yellow Wapsi Supreme Hair; orange, yellow, and olive Hareline Icelandic sheep; grizzly dyed olive Whiting Bird Fur; gold Spirit River Holographic Mylar Motion
- **Gills:** Red Hareline Ice Fur, minnow gills Dave Whitlock SLF Dubbing
- **Head:** Orange, yellow, olive, black, and bleached Nature's Spirit spinning hair
- **Eyes:** Gold Hareline 3D Holographic Eyes (¼ inch)
- **Glues:** Zap-A-Gap for starting and finishing GSP thread; Dave's Flexament for tail thread wraps and eyes; Fly-Rite Fly-Tite Fly Tying Cement for base of deer hair stacks; GOOP for eyes; Sally Hansen Hard as Nails for thread head

RED HEAD YELLOW

- **Hook:** #4-10 Tiemco 8089 or 8089N, or #6-2/0 Gamakatsu B10S
- **Thread:** Black UTC 140 for tail, red for thread head; UTC GSP 130 for deer hair head
- **Tail:** Yellow Wapsi Supreme Hair, yellow Hareline Icelandic sheep, white dyed yellow Whiting Bird Fur, gold Spirit River Holographic Mylar Motion
- **Gills:** Red Hareline Ice Fur, minnow gills Dave Whitlock SLF Dubbing
- **Head:** Yellow, black, and red Nature's Spirit spinning hair
- **Eyes:** Red/black pupil Hareline Oval Pupil 3D Eyes (¼ inch)
- **Glues:** Zap-A-Gap for starting and finishing GSP thread; Dave's Flexament for tail thread wraps and eyes; Fly-Rite Fly-Tite Fly Tying Cement for base of deer hair stacks; GOOP for eyes; Sally Hansen Hard as Nails for thread head
- **Variations:** This pattern could also be tied using either white or chartreuse as the main color.

FIRE TIGER

- **Hook:** #4-10 Tiemco 8089 or 8089N, or #6-2/0 Gamakatsu B10S
- **Thread:** Black UTC 140 for tail, red for the thread head; UTC GSP 130 for deer hair head
- **Tail:** Yellow Wapsi Supreme Hair; orange, yellow, and chartreuse Hareline Icelandic sheep; white dyed chartreuse Whiting Bird Fur; red Hareline Ice Wing Fiber
- **Gills:** Red Hareline Ice Fur, minnow gills Dave Whitlock SLF Dubbing
- **Head:** Orange, yellow, black, and chartreuse Nature's Spirit spinning hair
- **Eyes:** Chartreuse/red pupil Hareline Oval Pupil 3D Eyes (¼ inch)
- **Glues:** Zap-A-Gap for starting and finishing GSP thread; Dave's Flexament for tail thread wraps and eyes; Fly-Rite Fly-Tite Fly Tying Cement for base of deer hair stacks; GOOP for eyes; Sally Hansen Hard as Nails for thread head

CHAPTER 9

Diving Deer Hair Flies

"Today when we cast our sleek, spun-and-clipped deer-hair bass bugs onto the water for bass, we are practicing an ancient and uniquely American technique that takes advantage of the bass's aggressive surface-feeding habits, and one that predates the use of cork and wood to float the lures."

WILLIAM G. TAPPLY, *FROM BOBS TO BUGS*

It was 7:30 in the evening and as was my usual summer routine, I was out and beginning to fish a favorite shoreline on Lake George in north-central Michigan. Midweek and early in the summer meant that the evening traffic on the lake was still light. The water temperature had just crossed into the mid-70-degree range, so bass were just beginning to really tune in to feeding on the top. Shutting down the old Evinrude outboard, I stepped to the front of my boat and put the electric motor down. Using a uni knot to create a loop, I tied a white belly, frog-colored, Dalberg-style diving deer hair fly to the tippet. Being careful to only treat the collar and top of the fly with floatant, I flipped the fly into the water and gave it several pops. After a few moments the lower part of the body absorbed some water and the fly started to behave the way I wanted.

The shore was lined with docks, some with boats tied up to them, and a few emerging lily pad beds. I concentrated my casts on the shady side of this cover. Along the shady side of a dock with a pontoon boat tied up, there was a bed of lily pads. A deeply shaded slot of open water lay between the boat and lily pads. Casting into this slot, the fly landed near the shore. I began to retrieve the fly along the length of the boat with 1- to 2-foot strips of line. A satisfying chain of bubbles trailed the fly as it dived into the shaded water. As expected, a bass streaked out from under the boat and grabbed the fly as it was reaching its maximum depth. Stripping line and setting the hook, I quickly dropped the rod tip and pressured the bass out into the open water. Once in the open water, I reeled up the excess line. After several head-shaking runs, the bass was landed and released. While not a trophy fish, even for these northern waters, it still weighed in at about 4 pounds. This bass was slightly above the average for Lake George and fun to catch on a fly rod.

By most standards this would not be a location that would be on many anglers' list of fish destinations. However, even with the numerous homes and cottages along its shoreline, the lake is locally considered one of the better bass lakes in the area. The village of Lake George was founded in the late 1800s as a lumber settlement. When the Toledo, Ann Arbor and North Michigan Railway came through, passenger trains gave the first easy access to this area. The village of Lake George, located on the northwest end of the lake, had a train depot. Cabins and lodges became available to the summer tourists who began to arrive for the hunting and fishing the area offered.

For me, it is simply my home lake. My first memories of fishing here were with my grandfather. When he discovered this lake in the early 1930s, a trip from his farm in southern Midland County was a much larger undertaking than it is today. The drive was primarily on the small gravel roads of the time. He bought Lot 1 in Tompkins Resort in 1936. At the time the resort existed more on paper than as reality, as much of the lake's shoreline was wooded and wild. The few homes that were there were clustered near the train depot and village. Lot 1 stood out at the tip of a point along the southeastern shoreline about halfway down the length of the lake. For the next 14 years they camped on the lot, then in 1949 my grandfather took some lumber off of his farm and had it milled at a local lumberyard. After drying it in his barn over the winter, he built a small cottage the following summer.

My grandfather was born in 1896, so he was in his early 30s when he discovered Lake George. It was his fishing home until his death in 1968. For me, my summers have always included this place. It is a lake that I know well. It is not a large lake at about 134 acres, but it is about 3 miles long, with a somewhat winding and narrow profile. Its deepest spot is about 25 feet; however, the average depth is about 18 feet in the center of the lake. There is abundant shallow shoreline for the bass and panfish that abound here. As a fly fisherman, I am a rarity at this lake, as I almost never see anyone else with a fly rod. Additionally, while the lake is well populated today, most who spend their summers here fish it casually.

My fishing and tying ran a parallel course here during the 1980s, as this lake was my testing grounds for the deer hair flies that I was just beginning to tie and fish. I learned about and refined my deer hair bass bugs over the years by fishing here.

Diving Deer Hair Bass Bug

While the diving deer hair fly is one of the more effective deer hair bass bugs, I found it to be challenging to tie so it would fish correctly. The deer hair collar would soak up water, so the top of the fly would outweigh the bend of the hook. This would result in the fly landing upside down. It would often take several strips of line to get the fly to right itself. For the Dalberg-style diving head, the solution was to leave more hair on the bottom of the fly and let it soak up water, much like the hair left on the bottom of a topwater bass bug.

The tail on this pattern is identical to the feather tail tied for the Deer Hair Bass Bug in chapter 7. The deer hair techniques are the same as the other deer hair bodies with one exception: The hair stacking for the first stack in the fly incorporates three bunches of hair stacked at different locations on the top side of the hook shank. The first bunch is stacked directly on top, while the other two are placed on each side at a 45-degree angle to the first stack. This insures enough hair for the diving collar to be full. With this added amount of hair on the top of the hook shank, a second bunch of hair is added to the bottom of the shank; otherwise the hair on top will migrate to the bottom because the deer hair will tend to distribute itself evenly around the hook shank. (See "Stacked Hair Techniques" in chapter 5.)

TYING THE DIVING DEER HAIR BASS BUG (WHITE BELLY FROG)

- **Hook:** #4-10 Tiemco 8089 or 8089N, or #6-2/0 Gamakatsu B10S
- **Thread:** Yellow or black UTC 140 for tail, red for thread band and thread head; White UTC GSP 130 for deer hair head
- **Tail:** Whiting Bird Fur, olive grizzly over yellow over white; pearl Hareline Ice Wing Fiber; olive, yellow, and white Whiting Black laced hen cape
- **Hackle collar:** Olive grizzly and yellow dyed ginger Whiting American rooster cape
- **Body:** Bleached, yellow, olive, and black Nature's Spirit deer spinning hair
- **Legs:** Speckled yellow, speckled olive, and speckled white Montana Fly Company Centipede Legs (medium)
- **Eyes:** Red/black pupil Hareline Oval Pupil 3D Eyes (¼ inch)
- **Glues:** Zap-A-Gap for starting and finishing GSP thread; Dave's Flexament for tail thread wraps and eyes; Fly-Rite Fly-Tite Fly Tying Cement for base of deer hair stacks; GOOP for eyes; Sally Hansen Hard as Nails for thread head

WEED GUARDS

I normally don't use weed guards on my flies. If the fly is cast accurately and retrieved carefully, it can usually be fished around cover without getting hung up too often. Weed guards will keep a fly from hanging in cover (although even with a weed guard, flies can become tangled in cover), but it will also make the fish more difficult to hook. I use a lightweight foam fly with a double mono loop weed guard when I want to fish in cover that I know I will get hung up in. I find the lighter weight allows the fly to be retrieved through the cover without getting hung up as often as a deer hair fly would get caught.

That said, I still carry a few deer hair flies with weed guards. The following steps describe the process of adding a single mono weed guard to a hook. I attach all my weed guards to the hook before tying the fly.

TYING A WEED GUARD

- **Thread:** UTC 280 (any color)
- **Weed guard:** Mason Hard Mono (20-, 25-, or 30-pound test; match the diameter of the mono to the diameter of the hook wire)

STEP 1: Attach the thread to the front of the rear tie-in point and wrap a smooth thread base back along the bend of the hook. The farther down the hook the thread is wrapped, the stiffer the weed guard will be. I normally go about ⅓ of the way down the bend.

STEP 2: Spiral-wrap the thread back to the tie-in point. This will create a slightly textured surface for the mono weed guard material to be seated against.

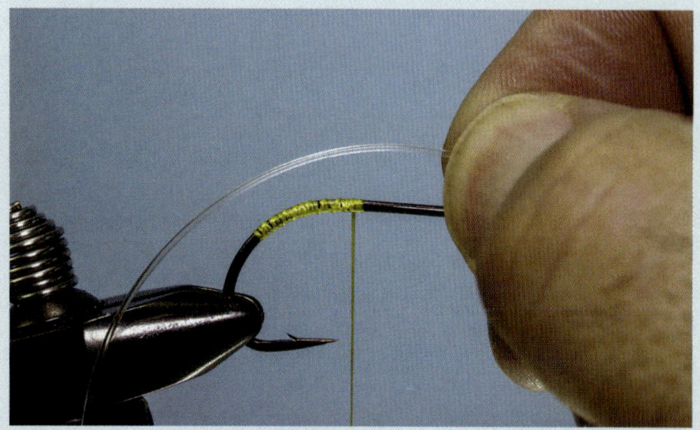

STEP 3: Use a small pair of side cutters to cut a length of Hard Mason Mono in the desired size. Use the natural curl of the material to wrap around the bend of the hook when attaching it.

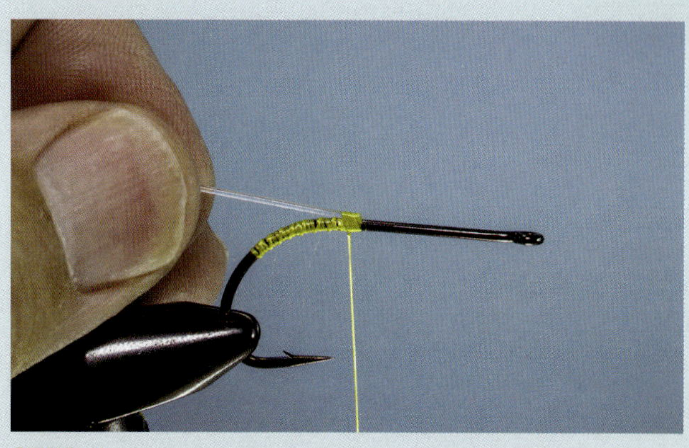

STEP 4: Attach the mono to the top of the hook shank at the front of the tie-in point.

(continued on next page)

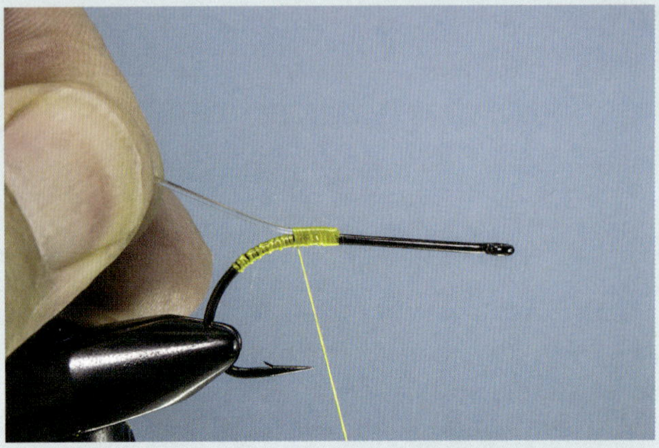

STEP 5: Pull the mono up and slightly towards you as you begin to wrap the thread back. This will keep the mono on the top of the hook shank.

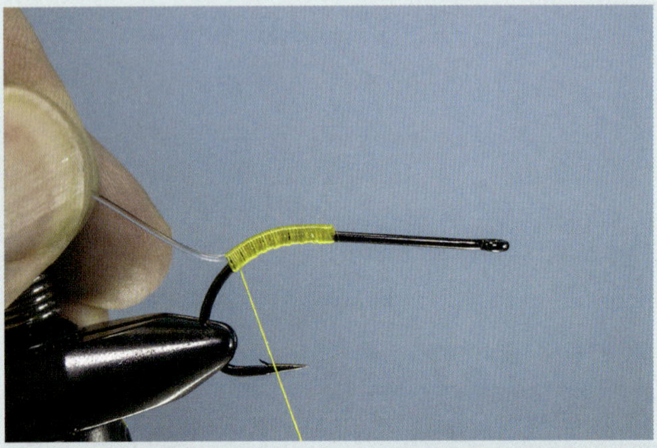

STEP 6: As you wrap the thread back, by holding the mono up, the thread wraps will slide down the mono and be seated next to the previous wrap of thread. Continue wrapping the thread back to the back of the thread base.

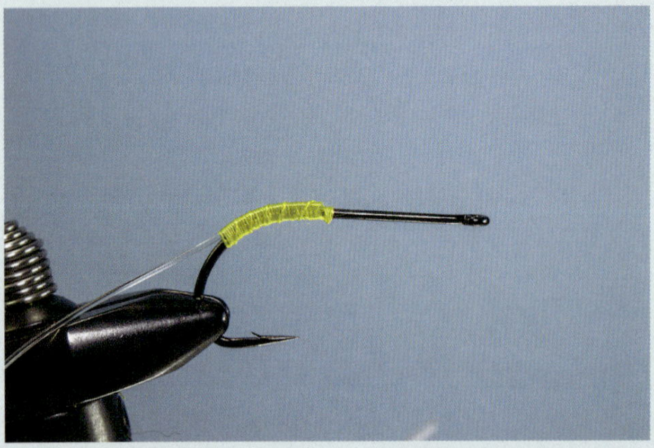

STEP 7: Spiral-wrap the thread back to the front of the tie-in point. Use a whip-finish knot to tie off the thread and trim.

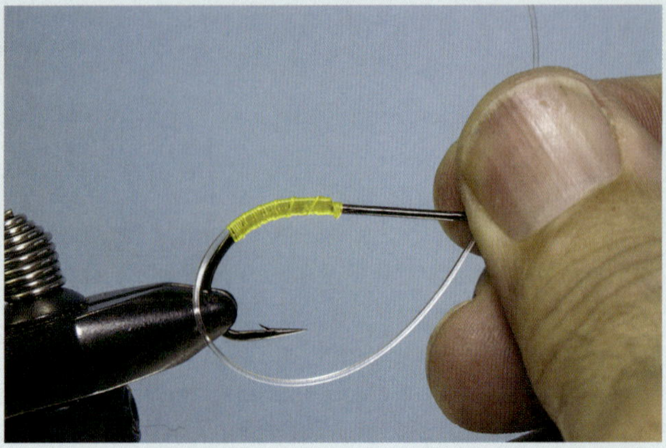

STEP 8: Measure the length of mono by passing it through the eye of the hook first and then adjusting the length. The mono weed guard should be ½ of the gape of the hook below the point of the hook.

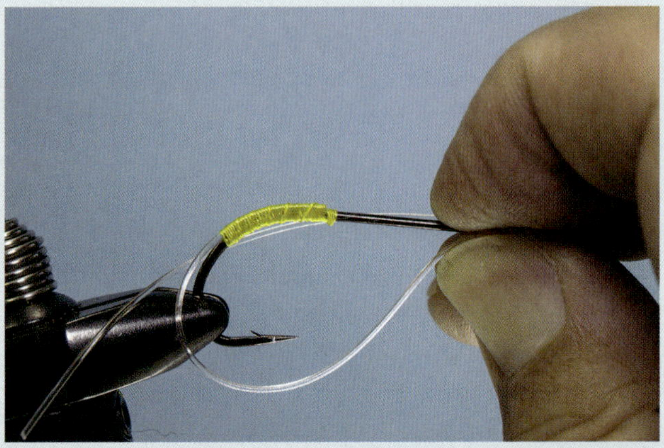

STEP 9: Holding that length, bend the mono at the eye of the hook.

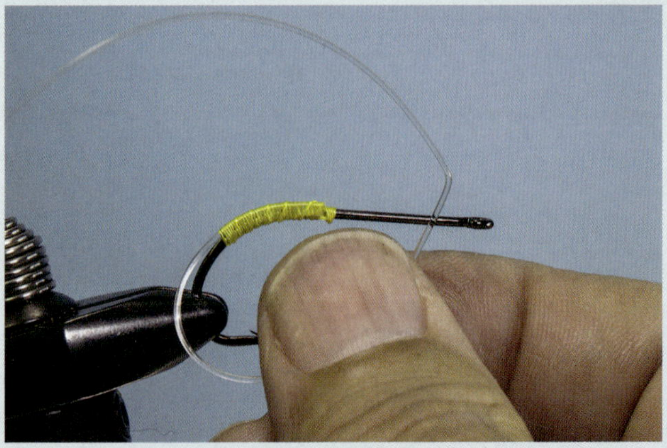

STEP 10: Pull the mono out of the eye of the hook, noting where the bend is located.

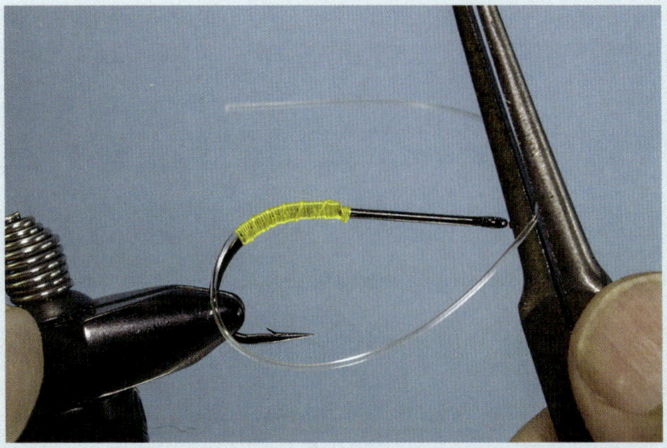

STEP 11: Use a pair of needle-nose pliers to flatten the mono right above the bend. Then use a pair of side cutters to cut the mono above the flattened area. Glue the thread wraps with Dave's Flexament and allow the glue to cure.

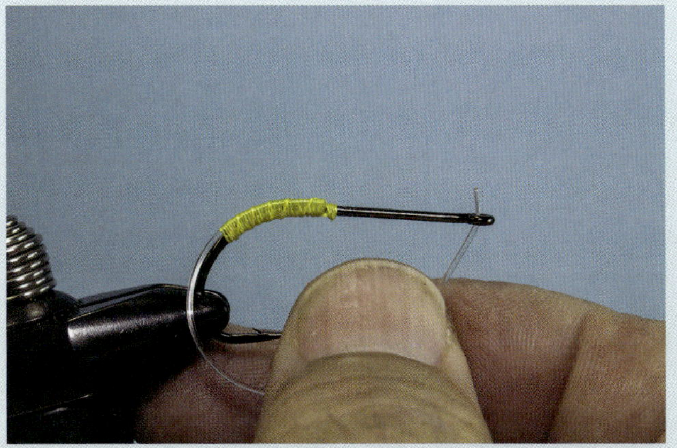

STEP 12: Once the fly has been completed, start the thread at the eye of the hook for the final thread head, then bring the weed guard forward. Pass the flattened end through the eye of the hook.

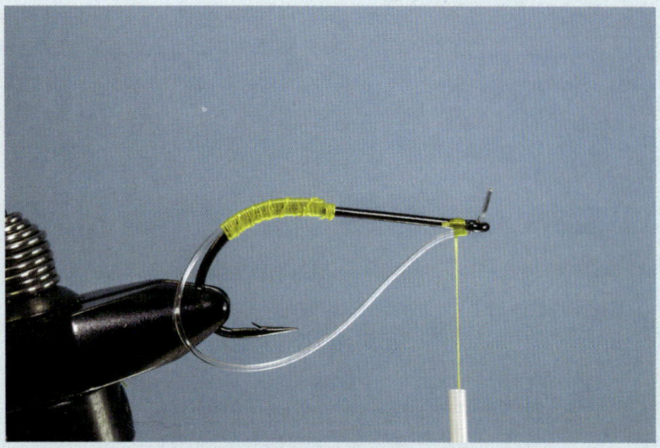

STEP 13: Catch the mono under the hook first. Some small adjustment for length can be made at this point of needed.

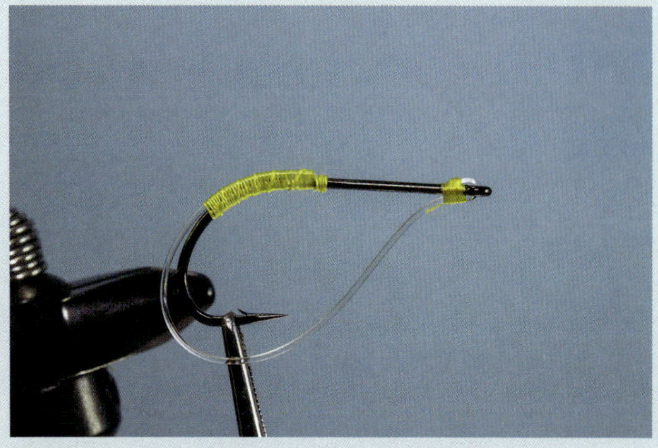

STEP 14: Fold the flattened end of the mono over the top of the hook shank and secure it with the thread. Before finishing the thread head, push a bodkin through the eye of the hook, forcing the mono material to the back. Finish the thread head and use Sally Hansen Hard as Nails to complete the head as usual. ■

STEP 1: To create the tail, repeat steps 1 through 18 of the Deer Hair Bass Bug in chapter 7.

STEP 2: Sweep the tailing materials back and wrap a band of red UTC 140 thread. Use a whip-finish knot to secure the thread band. By doing this, all of the tailing materials are swept back and out of the way as you work on the deer hair head of the fly.

STEP 3: Use a small amount of Zap-A-Gap at the front of the tail. Wrap the UTC GSP 130 thread through the glued area and then wrap a thread base up to the eye of the hook. Wrap the thread back to the front of the tail.

STEP 4: Prep a bunch of bleached deer hair; stack the hair to even the tips and then trim the butts. Place the hair on the hook shank so the tips reach the point of the barb of the hook. Wrap the hair with 3 wraps of thread, then rotate the hair to the bottom of the hook shank and flare.

STEP 5: Prep a bunch of yellow deer hair. Stack the hair to even the tips and then trim the butts. Place the hair on the hook shank so the tips are even with the bend of the hook. Wrap the hair with 2 wraps of thread and flare in place. As you flare the hair, use the index finger of your opposite hand to support the stack of hair so it doesn't rotate around the hook shank. Keep the thread wraps in the same plane; do not advance the thread forward through the hair.

STEP 6: Prep a bunch of olive deer hair. Stack the hair to even the tips and then trim the butts. Separate the yellow hair evenly and place the hair on the top of hook shank so the tips are even with the bend of the hook. Make 2 wraps of thread and flare it in place; keep the thread wraps in the same plane as before.

STEP 7: Prep a bunch of bleached deer hair. Stack the hair to even the tips and then trim the butts. Separate the bunch of bleached hair that is already on the bottom. Place this hair in that space on the bottom of the hook shank so the tips reach the point of the barb of the hook. Wrap the hair with 2 wraps of thread and flare. This bunch of hair will help to balance the hair that will be added to the top of the hook shank. Keep the thread wraps in the same plane; do not advance the thread forward through the hair.

STEP 8: Prep a bunch of olive deer hair. Stack the hair to even the tips and then trim the butts. Evenly separate the hair that is on the top of the hook shank and place this bunch of hair at a 45-degree angle from the top on the far side of the hook shank. Keep the tips of the hair even with the bend of the hook. Make 2 wraps of thread and flare it in place; keep the thread wraps in the same plane as before. Repeat with another bunch of deer hair at a 45-degree angle on the near side of the hook shank. The 3 bunches of olive hair on the top side of the hook shank will provide the hair needed to create the diving collar. There are a total of 7 bunches of hair attached with a total of 15 wraps of thread in this stack of hair.

STEP 9: Keep the thread under tension and advance it to the front of the stack of hair. Make 2 or 3 half-hitch knots and use a hair-packing tool to compress the stack. Add a few drops of Fly-Tite cement to the base of the hair. Select 5 or 6 strands of leg material. Put an overhand knot in the group and slide the knot over the hook shank. Tighten the knot while keeping the length of leg material even on both sides of the hook shank. Use the hair-packing tool to compress the leg material knot back into the stack of hair. Pull the legs back and clip them into a material keeper.

STEP 10: Prep a bunch of bleached deer hair. Trim the tips and the butts. Wrap the hair with 3 wraps of thread, then rotate the hair to the bottom of the hook shank and flare.

STEP 11: Prep a bunch of yellow deer hair. Trim the butts and tips. Secure the hair on the top of the hook shank with 2 wraps of thread and flare. As you flare the hair, use the index finger of your opposite hand to support the stack of hair so it doesn't rotate around the hook shank. Separate the yellow hair evenly and place a small bunch of black deer hair in the space. Make 2 wraps of thread and flare it in place. Keep the thread wraps in the same plane as before; do not advance the thread forward through the hair.

STEP 12: Using the same technique, place and flare a bunch of olive deer hair. With this final bunch, put as much tension on the thread as possible without cutting through the hair or breaking the thread. Hold the tension momentarily, allowing the thread to tighten. Pull the hair stack back; keep tension on the thread and advance it through the hair. Make 2 or 3 wraps of thread at the front of the stack. Use a half-hitch tool to put a couple of half-hitches at the front of the stack of hair and then use the hair-packing tool to compress the stack. Add a few drops of Fly-Tite cement to the base of the hair.

STEP 13: Repeat with a third stack of hair at the front of the hook shank. Use bleached hair for the bottom with olive, black, and then olive hair on top. Advance the thread and make a couple of half-hitch knots, then compress the stack of hair.

STEP 14: Wet the thread near the hook shank with some Zap-A-Gap and make 3 or 4 wraps of thread behind the hook shank. Finish by adding 2 or 3 half-hitch knots on top of the glued thread wraps and trim.

STEP 15: Take the fly out of the vise and begin trimming on the bottom of the fly with a razor blade. Trim a flat bottom, making sure to leave 3 to 4 millimeters of hair.

STEP 16: Use curved hair scissors to trim a cone-shaped head. Trim back to the first black ring and leave the olive hair behind that for the diving collar.

STEP 17: Continue using the curved hair scissors and trim out the hair at the front of the head and around the eye of the hook.

STEP 18: Use the curved hair scissors to do a rough trim of the hair collar. The curve of the diving collar should match the curve of the body, leaving the same length hair from side to side.

STEP 19: Use a razor blade to complete the trimming process. Note the even tips in the diving collar as well as the smooth trim in the body.

STEP 20: Use the razor blade to cut the thread band and allow the hackle collar to expand and blend into the hair collar.

STEP 21: Add eyes, trim the legs, and finish the fly with a red UTC 140 thread head. Treat the thread wraps with the Sally Hansen Hard as Nails. Be sure to clear the eye of the hook out with a feather. Side view.

Top view.

Front view.

Ty's Tantalizer

The first time I saw a Ty's Tantalizer was in Dick Stewart and Farrow Allen's book *Flies for Bass & Panfish* (1992). Without even looking at the tying credits, I knew it was a Tim England pattern. Tim is one of the premier deer hair tiers in the country, and his patterns have a signature look that is unmistakable. He utilizes his exceptional tying skills to create flies that are designed to perform in the water. With its rounded deer hair belly and sloping diving plane that runs back into the diving collar, this fly will dive as well or better than a Dalberg diving head. The deer hair belly insures that this pattern will land properly in the water every time it is cast.

This was one of the first patterns that I tied from the Stewart and Allen book, and I have tied variations of it over the years and fished it with success. A few years ago I was tying at the Fly Fishing Show in Denver, Colorado. Tim was at the show, and we had an opportunity to discuss this pattern. After learning a few of the nuances of this diving head design, the pattern has taken on a more prominent status in my fishing.

While you can add eyes and legs to this pattern, I like to keep it in the simpler form that is found in *Flies for Bass & Panfish*. The pattern is tied here using the same feather tail as described in chapter 7.

TYING THE TY'S TANTALIZER

- **Hook:** #4-10 Tiemco 8089 or 8089N, or #6-2/0 Gamakatsu B10S
- **Thread:** Yellow UTC 140 for tail, red for the thread band and thread head;White UTC GSP 130 for deer hair head
- **Tail:** Whiting Bird Fur, yellow over white; gold Hareline Ice Wing Fiber; yellow and white Whiting black laced hen cape
- **Hackle collar:** Yellow dyed ginger Whiting American rooster cape
- **Body:** Bleached and yellow Nature's Spirit deer spinning hair
- **Glues:** Zap-A-Gap for starting and finishing GSP thread; Dave's Flexament for tail thread wraps and eyes; Fly-Rite Fly-Tite Fly Tying Cement for base of deer hair stacks; GOOP for eyes; Sally Hansen Hard as Nails for thread head

STEP 1: To create the tail, repeat steps 1 through 18 of the Deer Hair Bass Bug in chapter 7.

STEP 2: Sweep the tailing materials back and wrap a band of red UTC 140 thread. Use a whip-finish knot to secure the thread band. By doing this, all of the tailing materials are swept back and out of the way as you work on the deer hair head of the fly.

STEP 3: Use a small amount of Zap-A-Gap at the front of the tail. Wrap the UTC GSP 130 thread through the glued area and then wrap a thread base up to the eye of the hook. Wrap the thread back to the front of the tail. Prep a bunch of bleached deer

hair. Stack the hair to even the tips and then trim the butts. Place the hair on the hook shank so the tips reach the point of the barb of the hook. Wrap the hair with 3 wraps of thread, then rotate the hair to the bottom of the hook shank and flare.

STEP 4: Prep a bunch of yellow deer hair; stack the hair to even the tips and then trim the butts. Place the hair on the hook shank so the tips of the hair are even with the bend of the hook. Wrap the hair with 2 wraps of thread and flare in place. As you flare the hair, use the index finger of your opposite hand to support the stack of hair so it doesn't rotate around the hook shank. Repeat with another bunch of yellow hair on top of the first bunch. Keep the thread under tension and advance it to the front of the stack of hair. Make 2 or 3 half-hitch knots and use a hair-packing tool to compress the stack. Add a few drops of Fly-Tite cement to the base of the hair.

STEP 5: Prep a bunch of bleached deer hair; trim the tips and the butts. Wrap the hair with 3 wraps of thread, then rotate the hair to the bottom of the hook shank and flare.

STEP 6: Prep a bunch of yellow deer hair; trim the butts and tips. Secure the hair on the top of the hook shank with 2 wraps of thread and flare. As you flare the hair, remember to use the index finger of your opposite hand to support the stack of hair so it doesn't rotate around the hook shank. Then while keeping the thread under tension, advance it to the front of the stack of hair. Make 2 or 3 half-hitch knots and use the hair-packing tool to compress the stack. Add a few drops of Fly-Tite cement to the base of the hair.

STEP 7: Repeat with a third stack of hair at the front of the hook. Glue, tie off, and trim the GSP thread.

STEP 8: Using curved hair scissors, trim a rounded belly that tapers toward the eye of the hook.

STEP 9: Using a razor blade, trim a flat top on the body of the fly. Leave 3 to 4 millimeters of hair above the hook shank.

STEP 10: Using the curved hair scissors, trim a rounded diving collar. Note that the collar is even with the sides of the body.

STEP 11: Continue using the razor blade to complete a smooth-finish trim on the body. Use scissors to trim out the hair around the eye of the hook.

STEP 12: Carefully use the razor blade to create a trough or channel on the top of the diving plane. If the razor blade is used as in this photo, remain conscious of the edge that is towards your hand. You may want to break the blade so you're only working with a single edge.

STEP 13: Finish the fly with a red UTC 140 thread head. Treat the thread wraps with the Sally Hansen Hard as Nails. Be sure to clear the eye of the hook out with a feather. Side view.

Top view.

Bottom view.

Front view.

Compendium of Diving Deer Hair Bass Bug Patterns

Any of the color schemes used for the topwater deer hair bass bugs will work for diving deer hair bass bugs as well.

YELLOW BELLY FROG

- **Hook:** #4-10 Tiemco 8089 or 8089N, or #6-2/0 Gamakatsu B10S
- **Thread:** Black UTC 140 for tail, red for thread head; White UTC GSP 130 for deer hair head
- **Tail:** Whiting Bird Fur, olive grizzly over yellow; pearl Hareline Ice Wing Fiber; olive, red, and yellow Whiting black laced hen cape
- **Hackle collar:** Badger dyed red Whiting Coq de Leon cape
- **Body:** Yellow, red, olive, and black Nature's Spirit deer spinning hair
- **Legs:** Red Montana Fly Company Speckled Sexi Floss and speckled olive Centipede Legs (medium)
- **Eyes:** Red/black pupil Hareline Oval Pupil 3D Eyes (3/16 inch)
- **Glues:** Zap-A-Gap for starting and finishing GSP thread; Dave's Flexament for tail thread wraps and eyes; Fly-Rite Fly-Tite Fly Tying Cement for base of deer hair stacks; GOOP for eyes; Sally Hansen Hard as Nails for thread head

ORANGE BELLY FROG

- **Hook:** #4-10 Tiemco 8089 or 8089N, or #6-2/0 Gamakatsu B10S
- **Thread:** Black UTC 140 for tail and thread head; White UTC GSP 130 for deer hair head
- **Tail:** Whiting Bird Fur, chartreuse over yellow over orange; chartreuse Hareline Ice Wing Fiber; chartreuse, yellow, and orange Whiting black laced hen cape
- **Hackle collar:** Badger dyed yellow and grizzly dyed yellow Whiting American rooster cape
- **Body:** Orange, yellow, black, and chartreuse Nature's Spirit deer spinning hair
- **Legs:** Chartreuse Spirit River Grizzly Legs and orange Montana Fly Company Centipede Legs (medium)
- **Eyes:** Orange/black pupil Hareline Oval Pupil 3D Eyes (3/16 inch)
- **Glues:** Zap-A-Gap for starting and finishing GSP thread; Dave's Flexament for tail thread wraps and eyes; Fly-Rite Fly-Tite Fly Tying Cement for base of deer hair stacks; GOOP for eyes; Sally Hansen Hard as Nails for thread head

ORANGE AND YELLOW BELLY

- **Hook:** #4-10 Tiemco 8089 or 8089N, or #6-2/0 Gamakatsu B10S
- **Thread:** Black UTC 140 for tail and thread head; White UTC GSP 130 for deer hair head
- **Tail:** Whiting Bird Fur, orange grizzly over yellow; pearl Hareline Ice Wing Fiber; orange and yellow Whiting black laced hen cape
- **Hackle collar:** Grizzly dyed orange and grizzly dyed yellow Whiting American rooster cape
- **Body:** Yellow, orange, and black Nature's Spirit deer spinning hair
- **Legs:** Orange Montana Fly Company Speckled Sexi Floss and speckled yellow Centipede Legs (medium)
- **Eyes:** Orange/black pupil Hareline Oval Pupil 3D Eyes (3⁄16 inch)
- **Glues:** Zap-A-Gap for starting and finishing GSP thread; Dave's Flexament for tail thread wraps and eyes; Fly-Rite Fly-Tite Fly Tying Cement for base of deer hair stacks; GOOP for eyes; Sally Hansen Hard as Nails for thread head

NATURAL DEER

- **Hook:** #4-10 Tiemco 8089 or 8089N, or #6-2/0 Gamakatsu B10S
- **Thread:** Black UTC 140 for tail and thread head; UTC GSP 130 for deer hair head
- **Tail:** Natural grizzly Whiting Bird Fur, gold Spirit River Holographic Motion, tan Whiting black laced hen cape
- **Hackle collar:** Pardo Whiting Coq de Leon cape
- **Body:** Natural, black, and (for the face) bleached Nature's Spirit spinning hair
- **Legs:** Speckled natural Montana Fly Company Centipede Legs (medium)
- **Eyes:** Earth Flymen Fish-Skull Living Eyes (6 mm)
- **Glues:** Zap-A-Gap for starting and finishing GSP thread; Dave's Flexament for tail thread wraps and eyes; Fly-Rite Fly-Tite Fly Tying Cement for base of deer hair stacks; GOOP for eyes; Sally Hansen Hard as Nails for thread head

CHAPTER 10

Deer Hair Flies for Pike and Muskie

"[Fly fishing] is like any other skill, whether it's the knowledge of the Ruy Lopez opening in chess, how to hit a golf ball straight, or put spin on a tennis ball, the sheer pleasure of doing something difficult well."

CONRAD VOSS BARK, *A FLY ON THE WATER* (1986)

I carefully backed my boat down the narrow gravel ramp bordered by cedar trees and into the lake. As boat ramps go, this was not a well-developed one, although not the worst either. The lake stretched out before me, reflecting the early morning sky. I motored a short way out into the lake, then tuned off the outboard and just floated for a moment to soak in the wildness and beauty of the lake. As was so often the case in past years when I fished here, I was the only boat on the lake. Other than the several loons that frequented the lake, my only companion this day was Daisy, my German shorthaired pointer. This was a lake that I often thought about while at the tying table back in western Colorado. We were here not just for the wild beauty of the lake, but for the muskellunge, or muskie, as well.

We crossed the lake to a shallow-water bay and I began to fish the shaded edge. There were a lot of fallen dead trees in the water among the numerous lily pad beds. The water suddenly swirled as I was retrieving my fly from the edge of this cover. Stripping line in, I set the hook and felt the satisfying weight of a nice fish. Rather than heading back into the woody cover along the shoreline, he ran out into the shallow bay, leaving a mud trail behind him as line was being pulled off my reel. I swung the boat out into the lake and continued to play the fish from the reel. After several runs, I used my BogaGrip to grasp his lower jaw. Using a pair of long-nose fishing pliers, I removed the fly. He measured in at about 36 inches. Not a trophy by any means, but a satisfying start to a day where I knew there would be a lot more casting than catching.

The first time I fished this lake, I was unaware that it contained muskie. We were fishing light fly rods and small bucktail streamers for the numerous panfish that were here. Working the shoreline, we cast our flies in and around the many lily pad beds that were present. On one of my retrieves, a very large elongated shape came leisurely swimming out following behind my small fly. It took me a moment to realize what I was seeing. It was a fish and later, after doing some research on this lake, I realized that it was a muskie that was probably at least 45 inches long.

That experience happened a little over 20 years ago and for many years it haunted me. At the time there was very little in print about fly fishing for muskie. Barry Reynolds and John Berryman's book *Pike on the Fly* (1993) had just been published. While it mentioned muskie, its primary focus was on pike fishing. I am sure there were people out there fly fishing for muskie, but there wasn't much written about it in the mainstream fly-fishing magazines of the day and the Internet was still in its infancy. My only real source of information came from books and magazines like *Musky Hunter* that focused on traditional tackle muskie fishing, so I had to translate what I was learning into fly-fishing ideas.

I continued to tie and fish for pike and muskie; however, it took more than a decade before I was able to return to that lake. I was fishing McKeever Lake in Hiawatha National Forest, which primarily spans two large regions on the eastern half the Upper Peninsula of Michigan. It has over 100 miles of shoreline that touches three of the Great Lakes: Lake Michigan, Lake Superior, and Lake Huron. McKeever Lake is just one of over 400 inland lakes that are in this national forest, with many of them home to the muskellunge.

Today there is a lot of information about fly fishing for muskie. Along with books, the Internet has a wealth of information on both fishing and fly tying. Tackle manufacturers are designing rods and lines specifically to target muskie as well as pike. Fly-tying materials exist today that weren't available even a decade ago. While fly fishing for muskie may not be considered mainstream even today, there is a dedicated and passionate group of anglers who are pursuing this incredible gamefish with fly rods.

Each summer when I return to McKeever Lake and the surrounding area it's always with great anticipation. Pulling out the muskie and pike rods and the large fly boxes filled with all of the fly patterns I have worked on over the winter never gets old.

Yak Hair Diver

The Yak Hair Diver is a natural progression from the waking deer hair patterns. The yak hair provides the length needed to create larger flies. In addition, yak has proven itself in streamer patterns to be an extremely effective material. Its durability is an asset along with its translucency and stiffness, making it a good choice for creating long diving patterns that will appeal to both pike and muskie. I also use Flymen's body tubing to create a disk that causes the tail materials to flare out. This creates a larger body profile while not overdressing the fly.

These flies can be tied with either elk or deer spinning hair. The elk hair is longer than whitetail. While I tie the pattern here as a diver, it could also be tied with a waking head.

TYING THE YAK HAIR DIVER (FIRE TIGER)

- **Hook:** #3/0-5/0 Daiichi 2461
- **Thread:** Black UTC 140 for tail, red for thread head; White UTC GSP 200 for deer hair head
- **Tail:** Yellow Wapsi Supreme Hair; yellow Flymen Fish-Skull Blane Chocklett's Body Tubing (¼ inch); orange, yellow, and chartreuse Spirit River yak streamer hair; fire tiger Hedron Holographic Flashabou; grizzly dyed chartreuse Whiting schlappen; white dyed chartreuse Whiting Bird Fur
- **Gills:** Red Hareline Polar Chenille
- **Head:** Orange, yellow, black, and chartreuse Nature's Spirit deer or elk spinning hair
- **Eyes:** Chartreuse/red pupil Hareline Oval Pupil 3D Eyes (⅜ inch)
- **Glues:** Zap-A-Gap for starting and finishing GSP thread and securing body tubing; Dave's Flexament for tail thread wraps and eyes; Fly-Rite Fly-Tite Fly Tying Cement for base of deer hair stacks; GOOP for eyes; Sally Hansen Hard as Nails for thread head

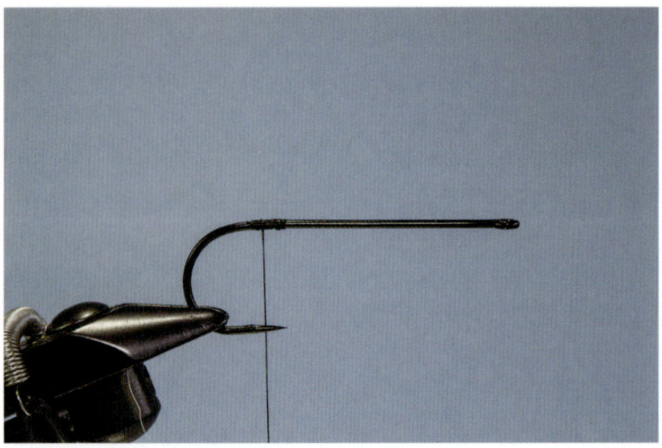

STEP 1: Rough up the surface of the hook with a file at the rear tie-in point. Note the tie area for the tail on this hook runs directly above the point of the barb to the point of the hook. Wet the hook shank with Zap-A-Gap and wrap the black UTC 140 thread through the glued area on the hook shank.

STEP 2: Attach the Supreme Hair at the tie-in point. The tail should be about 2½ to 3 times as long as the hook shank. Use a whip-finish knot to tie off the thread and trim.

STEP 3: Cut a 1-inch piece of body tubing. Seal the ends with a lighter. Slide the tubing over the hook shank and back behind the rear tie-in point. Reattach the thread and bring the tubing forward. Attach the front of the tubing to the rear tie-in area. Apply some Zap-A-Gap to the thread wraps and wrap a secure band of thread to attach the tubing to the hook shank. Use a whip-finish knot to tie off the thread and trim.

STEP 4: Push the tubing forward so it forms a forward facing cone. Reattach the thread to the hook shank, capturing the rear of the tubing. Apply some Zap-A-Gap to the thread wraps then wrap a thread band, securing the tubing to the hook shank. Use a whip-finish knot to tie off the thread and trim.

STEP 5: Push the cone tubing back towards the rear of the hook shank to create a larger disk of material. Reattach the thread to the front of the tubing.

STEP 6: Wrap 8 to 12 strands of Flashabou around the thread with one side reaching back to the end of the tail. Make 2 or 3 wraps of thread and then spread the strands of Flashabou around the tubing so it encompasses the hook shank.

STEP 7: Rotate the vise and attach a sparse bunch of orange yak hair at the tie-in point on the bottom of the hook shank. Spread the hair around the tubing so it encompasses the bottom half of the hook shank. Return the vise to the upright position, take the hook out of the vise, and pull the orange yak hair back around the bend of the hook. Apply a small amount of Zap-A-Gap to the thread and make a few wraps, allowing the glue to soak into the hair.

STEP 8: Attach a sparse bunch of yellow yak hair on each side of the hook shank.

STEP 9: Attach a sparse bunch of chartreuse yak hair at the tie-in point. Add some Zap-A-Gap to the thread and make a few wraps, allowing the glue to soak into the hair.

STEP 10: Attach two schlappen feathers, one on each side of the hook shank, with 2 or 3 wraps of thread.

STEP 11: Attach 2 or 3 Bird Fur feathers to each side of the hook shank. Pull the feather back and wrap a thread base over all the materials. Put a few drops of Dave's Flexament over the thread wraps.

STEP 12: Attach the Polar Chenille and wrap a collar, sweeping the fibers back with each wrap. Tie off the chenille and trim. Wrap a thread head and then use a whip-finish knot to tie off the thread and trim.

STEP 13: Apply a few drops of Zap-A-Gap to the thread head at the front of the tail. Wrap the GSP thread through the thread wraps, then wrap a thread base forward to the eye of the hook and spiral-wrap the thread back to the rear tie-in point.

STEP 14: To create the diving head, repeat steps 3 through 14 of the Diving Deer Hair Bass Bug in chapter 9. The Diving Deer Hair Bass Bug had 3 stacks of hair. This large deer hair head has a total of 4 stacks of hair. The first stack has 2 bunches of orange hair on the bottom and a bunch of orange hair on the top. Then a bunch of yellow hair is added to the top along with 3 bunches of chartreuse hair for a total of 7 bunches of hair. The next stack of hair follows the same pattern; however, it only has 1 bunch of chartreuse hair on the top. The following 2 stacks of hair follow the same pattern.

STEP 15: To trim the diving head, repeat steps 15 through 19 of the Diving Deer Hair Bass Bug in chapter 9. Add eyes and a red UTC 140 thread head. Apply Sally Hansen Hard as Nails to the thread wraps and clear the eye of the hook. Side view.

Top view.

Yak Hair Diver.

Deer Hair Muskie/Pike Plug Fly

Some of the first articulated fly patterns I saw were those of Florida fly tier Jim Stewart. This fly is a variation of his Jointed Popper. There are a few differences, however. Making use of some new materials like articulated shanks from the Flymen Fishing Company, the hook is at the rear of the fly rather than on the front portion. Blane Chocklett's Body Tubing is used in the tail to get a halo effect from the bucktail, giving the pattern a larger appearance. There are 9 stacks of hair using 50 bunches of hair. This is the most hair of any pattern in the book. This fly will also need a large rod, like a Sage Bass II Largemouth, which is effectively a 10-weight, to cast it.

TYING THE DEER HAIR MUSKIE/ PIKE PLUG FLY

Tail

- **Hook:** #2/0 Gamakatsu B10S
- **Thread:** Black UTC 140 for tail, red for thread head
- **Tail:** Black Nature's Spirit bucktail
- **Body:** Gold side of UTC Mylar Tinsel (large) overwrapped with gold UTC French Tinsel (large), coated with Loon UV Clear Fly Finish (flow, cured with a UV light); black Flymen Fish-Skull Blane Chocklett's Body Tubing (⅛ inch)
- **Wing:** Nature's Spirit bucktail, olive over white; gold Hedron Holographic Flashabou; Grizzly dyed Olive Whiting schlappen feathers
- **Hackle collar:** Grizzly dyed olive Whiting American rooster cape
- **Glues:** Zap-A-Gap for starting UTC 140 thread at tie-in point and securing tubing and bucktail; Dave's Flexament for thread wraps; Loon UV Clear Fly Finish (thick) for thread head

Body

- **Articulated shank:** Blane Chocklett's Articulated Big Game Shank (80 mm)
- **Thread:** White GSP 200 for deer hair work; red UTC 140 for thread head
- **Butt:** Black/olive Hareline Variegated Chenille (medium)
- **Body:** Bleached, black, and olive Nature's Spirit cow elk spinning hair
- **Eyes:** Wind Flymen Fish-Skull Living Eyes (8.5 mm)
- **Glues:** Zap-A-Gap for starting and finishing GSP thread; Fly-Rite Fly-Tite Fly Tying Cement for base of deer hair stacks; Sally Hansen Hard as Nails for thread head

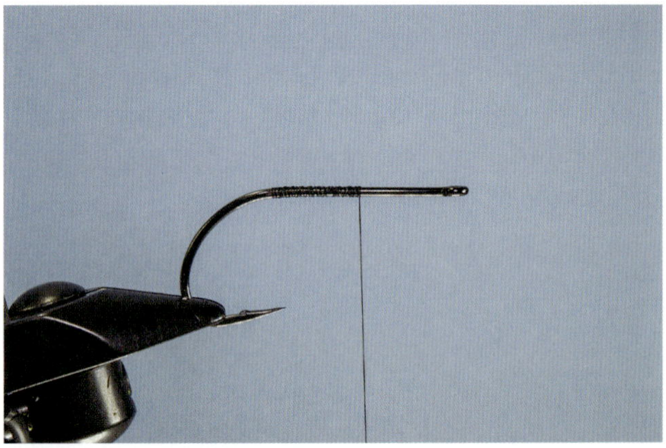

STEP 1: Put the Gamakatsu hook in the vise and use the black UTC 140 to wrap a thread base from the midpoint on the hook shank to the rear tie-in point, then return the thread to the halfway point.

STEP 2: Clean, prep, and stack a bunch of black bucktail. Measure for length (the tail should extend the length of the hook behind the rear tie-in point) and then trim the butts. Place the butts at the halfway point and with a few wraps of thread attach them to the hook. Lift up on the tail as you wrap back, keeping it on the top of the hook shank.

STEP 3: Tie a gold Mylar Tinsel and French Tinsel body on the rear half of the hook shank (see tying instructions for the Black-Nose Dace in chapter 4). Use a whip-finish knot to tie off the thread, then trim. Overcoat it with Loon UV Clear Fly Finish (flow) and cure with a UV light.

STEP 4: Cut a piece of the body tubing equal to the length of the rear half of the hook shank. Slide the tubing over the body. Reattach the black UTC 140 thread to the front of the body.

STEP 5: Push the tubing forward so the front of it aligns with the front of the tinsel body. Make several wraps of thread around the front of the tubing. Apply a small amount of Zap-A-Gap to the thread wraps. Make 3 to 4 more wraps of thread to securely attach the front of the tubing.

STEP 6: Push the rear of the tubing forward, forcing it to fold over on itself until it creates a cone shape with the wide end facing forward. Once the rear of the tubing aligns with the front of the tinsel body, make several tight wraps of thread to secure it in place.

STEP 7: Add some Zap-A-Gap to the thread wraps, then use a whip-finish knot to tie off the thread and trim.

STEP 8: Fold the tubing towards the rear of the hook shank to create a rear-facing cone shape.

STEP 9: Reattach the UTC 140 thread in the front of the tubing. Cut, prep, and stack a bunch of white bucktail. Measure the length of white bucktail to equal the length of the black bucktail. Trim the butts to that length and attach directly in front of the tubing on the bottom of the hook shank with 3 or 4 wraps of thread. Spread the bucktail so it encompasses the lower half of the tubing cone, then secure it with several more wraps of thread.

STEP 10: Cut, prep, and stack a bunch of olive bucktail. Measure the length of olive bucktail to equal the length of the black bucktail. Trim the butts to that length and attach directly in front of the tubing on the top of the hook shank with 3 or 4 wraps of thread. Spread the bucktail so it encompasses the upper half of the tubing cone, then secure it with several more wraps of thread. Apply some Zap-A-Gap to the thread and make several more wraps, allowing the glue to soak into the bucktail.

STEP 11: Fold 6 to 8 strand of Flashabou to the thread and then make 2 or 3 wraps of thread around the hook shank. Distribute the Flashabou so it spreads around the top half of the hook shank, then secure it with 3 or 4 more wraps of thread.

STEP 12: Attach 2 schlappen feathers to each side of the hook. The feathers should double the length of the tail. Wrap a secure thread head.

STEP 13: Attach 3 or 4 olive grizzly hackle feathers to the thread head and apply some Dave's Flexament to the thread wraps. Wrap a hackle collar with the feathers and tie off. Trim the tips of the feathers, then use a whip-finish knot to tie off the black thread and trim. Start the red UTC 140 thread and wrap a thread

head. Apply some Loon UV Clear Fly Finish (thick) to the red thread wraps. Rotate the fly to allow the resin to flow evenly around the thread head. Cure with a UV light.

STEP 14: Slide the larger end of the articulated shank through the eye of the hook.

STEP 15: Coat the rear half of the shank with Zap-A-Gap, then use the GSP 200 thread to wrap a thread base over the rear half of the shank. Keep the top part of the shank aligned with the bottom so they connect in a straight line.

STEP 16: Repeat with the front half of the shank.

STEP 17: Return the thread to the rear of the hook shank. Tie in a piece of the chenille and make 5 or 6 wraps each on top of the previous wrap to create a ball shape. Tie off the chenille and trim.

STEP 18: Clean and prep a bunch of bleached elk hair. Attach and rotate to the bottom of the shank and flare. Repeat with a bunch of bleached hair on the top of the shank, then add a second bunch of bleached hair to the bottom.

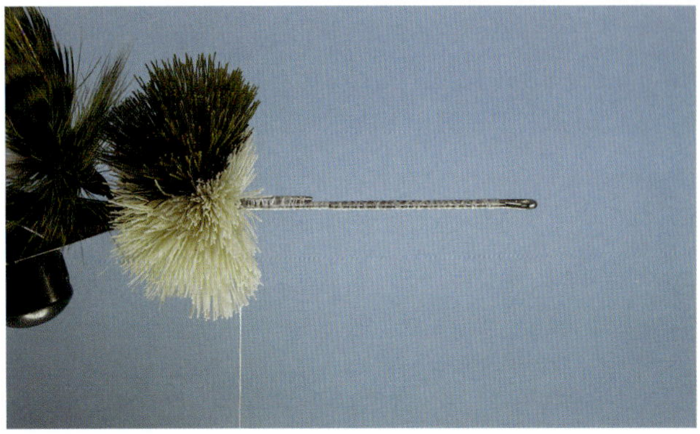

STEP 19: Clean and prep a bunch of black elk hair. Attach and flare it on the top of the hook shank. Repeat by adding a bunch of olive elk hair on top of the black hair. Work the thread to the front of the stack while keeping it under tension. Make 2 or 3 wraps of thread in front of the stack. Compress the stack and add some drops of Fly-Tite cement to the base of the stack of hair.

STEP 20: Continue adding stacks of hair to the hook shank. There should be 6 or 7 more stacks of hair with the following bunches of hair per stack: 2 bunches of bleached on the bottom; 1 bunch of bleached, 1 bunch of black, and 2 bunches of olive on the top. When you get to the front quarter of the shank, eliminate the bleached and black hair from the top and do 3 bunches of olive hair instead. Finish the hair work and tie off and trim the GSP thread.

STEP 21: Begin by using scissors to create a rough trim of the body shape. Use the tips of the scissors to trim out the hair around the chenille butt.

STEP 22: Finish the body trimming with a razor blade. Add the eyes and a red UTC 140 thread head. Finish the thread head with Sally Hansen Hard as Nails. Side view of finished fly.

Top view.

Front view.

The Deer Hair Muskie/Pike Plug Fly. This pattern can be tied in a variety of color schemes including many in this book.

Compendium of Pike and Muskie Deer Hair Flies

The following flies are color variations of the two flies in this chapter. Any of the color schemes in the previous chapters could be adapted for either of these flies.

YAK HAIR DIVER (PERCH)

- **Hook:** #3/0-5/0 Daiichi 2461
- **Thread:** Black UTC 140 for tail, red for thread head; UTC GSP 200 for deer hair head
- **Tail:** Yellow Wapsi Supreme Hair; yellow Flymen Fish-Skull Blane Chocklett's Body Tubing (¼ inch); orange, yellow, and olive Spirit River yak streamer hair; gold Hedron Holographic Flashabou; grizzly dyed olive Whiting Bird Fur; grizzly dyed olive Whiting schlappen
- **Hackle collar/gills:** Red Hareline Polar Chenille
- **Head:** Orange, yellow, black, olive, and bleached Nature's Spirit spinning hair
- **Eyes:** Yellow Spirit River 3-D Molded Eyes (5 mm)
- **Glues:** Zap-A-Gap for starting and finishing GSP thread; Dave's Flexament for tail thread wraps and eyes; Fly-Rite Fly-Tite Fly Tying Cement for base of deer hair stacks; GOOP for eyes; Sally Hansen Hard as Nails for thread head

YAK HAIR DIVER (SHAD GRAY)

- **Hook:** #3/0-5/0 Daiichi 2461
- **Thread:** Black UTC 140 for tail, red for thread head; White UTC GSP 200 for deer hair head
- **Tail:** White Wapsi Supreme Hair; clear Flymen Fish-Skull Blane Chocklett's Body Tubing (¼ inch); white and gray Spirit River yak streamer hair; moonlight Hedron Holographic Flashabou; grizzly Whiting Bird Fur; grizzly Whiting schlappen
- **Head:** Medium dun, black, and bleached Nature's Spirit deer or cow elk spinning hair
- **Hackle collar/gills:** Red Hareline Polar Chenille
- **Eyes:** Pearl/black pupil Hareline Oval Pupil 3D Eyes (⅜ inch)
- **Glues:** Zap-A-Gap for starting and finishing GSP thread; Dave's Flexament for tail thread wraps and eyes; Fly-Rite Fly-Tite Fly Tying Cement for base of deer hair stacks; GOOP for eyes; Sally Hansen Hard as Nails for thread head

DEER HAIR MUSKIE/PIKE PLUG FLY (FIRE TIGER)

Tail

- **Hook:** #2/0 Gamakatsu B10S
- **Thread:** Black UTC 140 for tail, red for thread head
- **Tail:** Yellow Nature's Spirit bucktail
- **Body:** Gold side of UTC Mylar Tinsel (large) overwrapped with gold UTC French Tinsel (large), coated with Loon UV Clear Fly Finish (flow, cured with a UV light); yellow Flymen Fish-Skull Blane Chocklett's Body Tubing (¼ inch)
- **Wing:** Fire tiger Hedron Holographic Flashabou; grizzly dyed chartreuse Whiting schlappen; chartreuse, yellow, and orange Nature's Spirit bucktail
- **Hackle collar:** Badger dyed chartreuse Whiting Coq de Leon rooster cape
- **Glues:** Zap-A-Gap for starting UTC 140 thread at tie-in point and securing tubing and bucktail; Dave's Flexament for thread wraps; Loon UV Clear Fly Finish (thick) for thread head

Body

- **Articulated shank:** Blane Chocklett's Articulated Big Game Shank (80 mm)
- **Thread:** White GSP 200 for deer hair work; red UTC 140 for thread head
- **Butt:** Yellow pearl Wapsi Tinsel Chenille (large)
- **Body:** Orange, yellow, black, and chartreuse Nature's Spirit cow elk spinning hair
- **Eyes:** Chartreuse/red pupil Hareline Oval Pupil 3D Eyes (⅜ inch)
- **Glues:** Zap-A-Gap for starting and finishing GSP thread; Fly-Rite Fly-Tite Fly Tying Cement for base of deer hair stacks; Sally Hansen Hard as Nails for thread head

DEER HAIR MUSKIE/PIKE PLUG FLY (PERCH)

Tail

- **Hook:** #2/0 Gamakatsu B10S
- **Thread:** Black UTC 140 for tail, red for thread head
- **Tail:** Yellow Nature's Spirit bucktail
- **Body:** Gold side of UTC Mylar Tinsel (large) overwrapped with gold UTC French Tinsel (large), coated with Loon UV Clear Fly Finish (flow, cured with a UV light); yellow Flymen Fish-Skull Blane Chocklett's Body Tubing (¼ inch)
- **Wing:** Gold Hedron Holographic Flashabou; grizzly dyed yellow Whiting schlappen; olive, yellow, and orange Nature's Spirit bucktail
- **Hackle collar:** Grizzly dyed olive Whiting American cape

- **Glues:** Zap-A-Gap for starting UTC 140 thread at tie-in point and securing tubing and bucktail; Dave's Flexament for thread wraps; Loon UV Clear Fly Finish (thick) for thread head

Body

- **Articulated shank:** Blane Chocklett's Articulated Big Game Shank (80 mm)
- **Thread:** GSP 200 for deer hair work; red UTC 140 for thread head
- **Butt:** Yellow/olive Hareline Variegated Chenille (medium)
- **Body:** Orange, yellow, black, olive, and bleached Nature's Spirit cow elk spinning hair
- **Eyes:** Wind Flymen Fish-Skull Living Eyes (8.5 mm)
- **Glues:** Zap-A-Gap for starting and finishing GSP thread; Fly-Rite Fly-Tite Fly Tying Cement for base of deer hair stacks; Sally Hansen Hard as Nails for thread head

BIBLIOGRAPHY

The following bibliography lists all of the books and magazine articles directly mentioned in the text. Additionally it includes the books, magazine articles, online resources, and DVDs used to research the history of anglers, flies, tying techniques, and fishing locations.

Almy, Gerald. *Tying & Fishing Terrestrials*. Harrisburg, PA: Stackpole Books, 1978.

Bates, Joseph D. Jr. *Streamer Fly Tying and Fishing*. Harrisburg, PA: Stackpole Company, 1950, 1966.

———. *Streamers and Bucktails*. New York: Alfred A. Knopf, 1979.

Bergman, Ray. *Trout*. New York: Alfred A. Knopf, 1938.

Betts, John. "Bucktails." *Fly Tyer,* Spring 1999, 27–32, 53–56.

Boyle, Robert H., and Dave Whitlock. *The Fly Tyer's Almanac*. New York: Nick Lyons Books, 1975.

Brooks, Joe. *Bass Bug Fishing*. New York: A. S. Barnes and Company, 1947.

Clouser, Bob. *Clouser's Flies*. Mechanicsburg, PA: Stackpole Books, 2006.

Colla, Sheila, Lief Richardson, and Paul Williams. *Bumble Bees of the Eastern United States,* 2011. USDA Forest Service and the Pollinator Partnership, with funding from the National Fish and Wildlife Foundation. http://www.fs.fed.us/wildflowers/pollinators/documents/BumbleBeeGuideEast2011.pdf.

Cornwall, Joe. "A Party of Blondes," 2005. Fly Fish Ohio. http://www.flyfishohio.com/a_party_of_blondes.htm.

Dennis, Jack. *Western Trout Fly Tying Manual*. Jackson Hole, WY: Snake River Press, 1974.

———. *Western Trout Fly Tying Manual*. Vol. 2. Jackson Hole, WY: Snake River Books, 1980.

England, Tim. "Banana Bug and Eel Bug." *Fly Tyer,* Summer 1983, 54–57.

———. "Gator Bug." *Fly Tyer,* Winter 1984, 48–49.

———. "Tim England." *Fly Rod & Reel,* July/October 1985, 22–25.

Flick, Art. *Art Flick's Master Fly Tying Guide*. New York: Crown Publishing, 1972.

———. *New Streamside Guide*. New York: Crown Publishing, 1969.

Fox, Charles K. *This Wonderful World of Trout*. Rockville Centre, NY: Freshet Press, 1963, 1971.

Gates, Rusty. *Seasons of the Au Sable*. Ann Arbor, MI: Sports Media Group, 2007.

Gapen, Dan D. "Muddler." *Trout: The Magazine for Trout and Salmon Anglers,* Winter 1983, 34–41.

Greenberg, Josh. *Rivers of Sand*. Guilford, CT: Lyons Press, 2014.

Helm, Chris. *All About Hair*. DVD. Bennett-Watt HD Productions, 2007.

———. "Materials Notebook: New Fly Tying Thread Standards." *Fly Tyer,* Summer 2005, 22–25.

Henshall, Dr. James A. *Book of Black Bass*. Cincinnati, OH: Robert Clarke & Co., 1881.

Joergensen, Martin. "Mickey Finn," February 9, 2013. Global FlyFisher. http://globalflyfisher.com/patterns-streamers/mickey-finn.

Krul, Jim. "The Many Faces of Mickey Finn." *Fly Tyer,* Winter 2000, 23–27.

Lyons, Nick. "The Bass Fly Revolution." Illustrated by Dave Whitlock. *Field & Stream,* May 1990, 54–58.

Marinaro, Vincent C. *In the Ring of the Rise*. New York: Crown Publishing, 1976.

———. *A Modern Dry Fly Code*. New York: Crown Publishing, 1970.

Messinger, Joe. "Simply Irresistible." *American Angler: The Magazine of Fly Fishing and Fly Tying,* May/June 1991, 54–57, 63.

Petti, Bob. "Barrel Full of Bucktails," April 13, 2011. Global FlyFisher. http://globalflyfisher.com/patterns-streamers/barrel-full-of-bucktails.

Reynolds, Barry, and John Berryman. *Pike on the Fly.* Boulder, CO: Johnson Books, 1993.

Sarudy, Barbara Wells. "Hunting, fowling, & shooting in America & Britain at both public & private gardens & grounds," July 20, 2014 (copyright 2013). Early British & American Public Gardens & Grounds. http://publicpleasuregarden.blogspot.com/2013/06/hunting-fowling-shooting-in-commercial.html.

Schullery, Paul. *American Fly Fishing: A History.* New York: Nick Lyons Books, 1987.

———. "A Dreadful Scourge." *American Angler: The Magazine of Fly Fishing and Fly Tying,* Summer 2007, 24–26.

Schwiebert, Ernest. *Matching the Hatch.* New York: Macmillan Publishing Co., 1955.

———. *Trout.* New York: E. P. Dutton, 1978.

Shenk, Ed. *Ed Shenk's Fly Rod Trouting.* Harrisburg, PA: Stackpole Books, 1989.

Steeves, Harrison R., and Ed Koch. *Terrestrials.* Mechanicsburg, PA: Stackpole Books, 1994.

Stewart, Dick, and Farrow Allen. *Flies for Bass & Panfish.* Intervale, NH: Northland Press, 1992.

Takahashi, Rick, and Jerry Hubka. *Modern Terrestrials.* Mechanicsburg, PA: Stackpole Books, 2014.

Tapply, William G. *Bass Bug Fishing.* New York: Lyons Press, 1999.

———. "From Bobs to Bugs." *Warmwater Fly Fishing,* February/March 1999, 11–13.

———. "From Bobs to Bugs, Part II." *Warmwater Fly Fishing,* April/May 1999, 6–10.

———. "From Bobs to Bugs, Part III." *Warmwater Fly Fishing,* June/July 1999: 8–11.

———. "Tap's Bug." *Warmwater Fly Fishing,* April/May 1998, 22–25.

Tomes, Robert S. *Muskie on the Fly.* Mill Creek, WA: Wild River Press, 2008.

Walton, Izaak, and Charles Cotton. *The Compleat Angler.* Oxford, UK: Oxford University Press, 2014 (originally published in 1653).

Whitlock, Dave. "Fly Tyers Notebook: The Carpenter Ant." *Trout: The Magazine for Trout and Salmon Anglers,* Summer 1987, 26–29.

———. "Fly Tyers Notebook: The Hair Wing Dun." *Trout: The Magazine for Trout and Salmon Anglers,* Winter 1987, 26–29.

———. "Fly Tyers Notebook: The Muddler Minnow." *Trout: The Magazine for Trout and Salmon Anglers,* Winter 1983, 42–43.

———. "Fly Tyers Notebook: Whit Hopper." *Trout: The Magazine for Trout and Salmon Anglers,* Summer 1987, 50–53.

———. *L.L. Bean Fly Fishing for Bass Handbook.* New York: Lyons Press, 1988, 2000.

———. "Whitlock's Sheep Minnow Series." *Fly Fisherman,* February 2000, 40–45, 59.

INDEX

ABOUT THE AUTHOR

TRACY TRULOVE PHOTO; TRACY TRULOVE PHOTOGRAPHY

Author Tim Jacobs with Daisy

Tim Jacobs, a native of Michigan, is a fly fisherman and fly tier from the Roaring Fork Valley in Colorado. He works as an instructor at the Michigan Youth Trout Camp each summer and for Project Healing Waters in Colorado. Aside from writing articles and conducting numerous clinics, Tim was a Federation of Fly Fishers–certified casting instructor who taught Sage Casting Clinics during the 1990s. He has guided in the Steamboat Springs area and the Roaring Fork Valley. Tim is also a demonstration fly tier for the Whiting Farms Pro Team and Regal Vise Pro Staff.